End-to-End Observability with Grafana

A comprehensive guide to observability and
performance visualization with Grafana

Ajay Reddy Yeruva
Vivek Basavegowda Ramu

www.bpbonline.com

First published: 2023

Published by BPB Online
WeWork
119 Marylebone Road
London NW1 5PU

UK | UAE | INDIA | SINGAPORE

ISBN 978-93-55515-483

www.bpbonline.com

Dedicated to

*From **Ajay***
My beloved Parents:
Ramakrishna Reddy Yeruva, Jayamma Yeruva
&
My Wife Sravani Thota and My Daughter Ayra Reddy Yeruva

*From **Vivek***
My Wife Thejaswini Vivek, My Son Trishan Vivek Gowda,
&
My family, friends and colleagues

About the Authors

- **Ajay Reddy Yeruva** has an IT career that spans around 10 years. He has been an Observability Subject Matter Expert using new and emerging technologies like Artificial Intelligence [AI], Machine Learning [ML], Internet of Things [IOT] and Deep Learning [DL] in Information Technology field. He is currently working as a Senior Software Engineer with the IP-DevOps team at Ritchie Bros. Auctioneers. Before his work tenure at Ritchie Bros. Auctioneers, He worked as Observability Subject Matter Expert at Fortune 500 companies. He is currently volunteering as Vice President of American Association of Information Technology Professionals (AAITP), Senior Member of Institute of Electrical and Electronics Engineers (IEEE), Advisory Board Member for notable startups and member of other reputed professional bodies. He had served as Observability Subject Matter Expert Judge in multiple Global Award Competitions. He had published multiple research papers, book chapters in international conferences and high impact factor journals as an Independent Researcher and also gained attention from global media, further validating the impact of his work. He have been awarded International Achievers' Award 2023 by Indian Achievers' Forum. He has made significant contributions as a mentor, guiding and inspiring students and professionals across 14 countries. He is a very active member of the AIOps, DevSecOps, GitOps and DataOps communities on different forums. When it comes to Observability, he tops the global list.

- **Vivek Basavegowda Ramu** is a renowned international expert in the field of Software Performance Testing, with a deep passion for optimizing software performance and ensuring exceptional user experiences. As the founder and president of the 'American Association of Information Technology Professionals', Vivek has demonstrated his commitment to advancing the industry and fostering professional growth. With a remarkable career spanning over 16 years, Vivek has amassed extensive experience across diverse domains such as Banking and Healthcare, working with Fortune 500 companies. Currently serving as an Executive QA/Performance Architect for a leading Healthcare provider in the USA, he brings invaluable expertise and insights to his role.

Vivek's exceptional contributions have earned him prestigious accolades, including the Stevie awards 'Technology Executive of the Year' and the Indian Achievers Forum's 'International Achievers Award'. These recognitions showcase his global standing as a thought leader and influencer in software performance testing and he has also been interviewed/quoted by major media over 5 times. In addition to his professional achievements, Vivek is deeply committed to sharing his knowledge and expertise with others. He has mentored and upskilled countless aspiring Performance Engineers, nurturing their growth and enabling their success. As a prolific Multiple Research Paper Author, Journal Editor, IEEE Senior Member, Technical Writer, Conference Keynote Speaker, Independent Researcher, Influencer, Udemy Instructor and International awards/hackathons Judge, Vivek actively contributes to the industry's body of knowledge.

Originally from Mysore, Karnataka, India, Vivek now resides in Connecticut, USA, with his wife and son. His expertise in various monitoring and profiling tools, including his mastery of Grafana, further solidifies his reputation as a distinguished authority in the field of software performance testing. Vivek's unwavering dedication to driving excellence and his significant contributions to the software testing community make him a sought-after expert and a trusted advisor in the industry.

About the Reviewers

- **Latha Narayanan Valli** is an accomplished professional in the field of Site Reliability Engineering (SRE) at Standard Chartered, Malaysia. With a background in computer science engineering and a Master's degree in Cyber Security and Data Science, Latha has gained expertise in Production Engineering - SRE, Observability, and AIOps. She is known for optimizing systems, enhancing observability, and driving the adoption of cutting-edge technologies. Latha's leadership roles and two decades of experience in the Information Technology sector, particularly in the BFSI domain, have made her a valuable asset to her organization. In addition to her technical prowess, she has a passion for sharing knowledge through scholarly articles and is currently writing a book on observability and AIOps.

  Outside of her professional achievements, Latha is dedicated to coaching and mentoring young girls from rural areas, supporting their personal and professional growth. She also collaborates with NGOs to provide support and education to those in need, showcasing her compassion and commitment to impact society positively.

  As a member of various organizing committees, Latha actively contributes to the technical community by coordinating seminars, reviews, and hackathons. She is also a respected judge in renowned technical competitions, recognizing and celebrating the achievements of aspiring individuals.

  Latha has been recognized with prestigious awards, including the Woman of Excellence Award, Professional Women Achiever Award, Fempreneur - Information Technology Award and the Best Woman Performer of the Year Award (Overseas) for the outstanding professional achievements and contributions to nation-building.

  Latha Narayanan Valli is a trailblazer in technology, education, and social work. She embodies qualities such as tenacity, creativity, originality, and confidence. Through her visionary leadership and transformative efforts, Latha has left a lasting impact on the world, fostering a culture centered around the Greater Good.

- **Venkata Ravi Kumar, Yenugula (YVR)** is an Oracle ACE Director and Oracle Certified Master (OCM) with 25+ years of experience in the banking, financial services, and insurance (BFSI) verticals. He has worked as a vice president (DBA), senior database architect, senior specialist production DBA, and Oracle engineered systems architect. He is an Oracle Certified Professional (OCP) from Oracle 8i/9i/10g/11g/12c/19c and also an Oracle Certified Expert (OCE) in Oracle GoldenGate, RAC, Performance Tuning, Oracle Cloud Infrastructure, Terraform, and Oracle Engineered Systems (Exadata, ZDLRA, and ODA), as well as Oracle Security and Maximum Availability Architecture (MAA) certified. He has published over 100 Oracle technology articles, including on Oracle Technology Network (OTN), OraWorld Magazine, UKOUG, OTech Magazine, and Redgate. He has spoken twice at Oracle Open/Cloud World (OOW), San Francisco, USA.

He has designed, architected, and implemented the core banking system (CBS) database for the central banks of two countries – India and Mahé, Seychelles.

Oracle Corporation, US, awarded him the title Oracle ACE Director and published his profile in their Oracle ACE Program.

https://apexapps.oracle.com/pls/apex/r/ace_program/oracle-aces/directory

They also published his profile on their OCM list and in their Spotlight on Success stories.

He has also co-authored a couple of books ("Oracle Database Upgrade and Migration Methods" and "Oracle High Availability, Disaster Recovery, and Cloud Services") and for BPB Publications, he has co-authored the book, "Oracle GoldenGate with Microservices".

https://bpbonline.com/products/oracle-goldengate-with-microservices-book-ebook?_pos=1&_sid=2c88c400c&_ss=r

Venkata Ravi Kumar Yenugula has also participated in technical review for the book for BPB Publications, "Oracle 19c AutoUpgrades Best Practices".

https://in.bpbonline.com/products/oracle-19c-autoupgrade-best-practices?_pos=1&_sid=efa54974d&_ss=r

- **Roja Boina** is an Expert and thought leader in the Field of Data Analytics. She is an Experienced Engineer focusing on solving some of the nation's most challenging problems in the healthcare Industry through Data Analytics, software applications, & IoT.

  Roja has built innovative Data Products, Data solutions from 0-to-1 for the healthcare industry. Roja enjoys presenting talks and keynotes, her thought leadership on Data Analytics, and has presented at large conferences and tech events and to global audiences online.

  Roja served as a judge for multiple global award competitions in Tech Industry. Roja has published multiple scholarly articles in international conferences and high-impact factor journals as an independent researcher and gained attention from global media, further validating the impact of her work.

  Roja has won the Mentor of the Year award in 2022. She is a chapter co-lead with women in data, an AWS Community builder, and a member of other reputed professional bodies like BCS, IET, etc.

Acknowledgements

We would like to extend our heartfelt gratitude to the individuals who have contributed to the creation of the book, "End-to-End Observability with Grafana." Their unwavering support and dedication have been pivotal in making this project a reality.

First and foremost, we would like to express our deepest appreciation to our loving wives, son/daughter and families for their constant love and support. Their understanding, patience and belief in our abilities have been the driving force behind our success. We are immensely grateful to our friends, both near and far, for their encouragement, motivation and invaluable feedback throughout this journey. Their support and uplifting words have inspired us to push the boundaries of our knowledge and expertise. We would also like to extend our gratitude to all the professional colleagues we have met along the way. Their expertise, guidance and collaboration have been instrumental in shaping the ideas and concepts presented in this book.

We are profoundly thankful to our mentor, Ranjeet Mudholkar, for his guidance, wisdom, and continuous support. We would like to acknowledge the team at BPB Publication, for their continuous assistance, guidance and professionalism throughout the publishing process. Their support has been instrumental in bringing this book to life. We also express our sincere appreciation to our technical reviewers, Mrs. Latha Narayanan Valli, Y V Ravi Kumar (Einstein Visa Recipient) and Roja Boina. Their expertise, attention to detail and valuable suggestions have greatly contributed to the quality and accuracy of the content.

To everyone who has played a part in this book's creation, your contributions are deeply appreciated. Thank you for being a part of our journey and for making "End-to-End Observability with Grafana" possible.

Preface

Welcome to the world of "End-to-End Observability with Grafana." This book represents the culmination of our deep passion for empowering individuals and organizations with the knowledge and tools needed to achieve comprehensive observability in their systems using Grafana. Observability has emerged as a critical aspect of managing modern complex systems. As digital landscapes continue to evolve and expand, the need for in-depth insights and understanding of our applications, infrastructure and user experiences becomes increasingly vital. Simply monitoring individual components is no longer sufficient, we must adopt a holistic and interconnected approach to gain a comprehensive view of our entire ecosystem.

Our journey into the realm of observability has led us to Grafana, a powerful and flexible open-source platform renowned for its data visualization and monitoring capabilities. Grafana empowers engineers and operators to gain real-time visibility into their systems, make informed decisions and proactively address any issues that may arise through its extensive features and integrations. The purpose of this book is to serve as a comprehensive guide to end-to-end observability with Grafana. Regardless of whether you are an experienced professional seeking to deepen your understanding or a beginner taking your first steps, this book provides a roadmap to help you unlock the full potential of Grafana's observability capabilities.

By combining theoretical concepts, practical examples, and hands-on tutorials, we aim to guide you on a transformative journey through Grafana's features. We will start by establishing a strong foundation of observability principles, then progress to topics such as setting up data sources, configuring dashboards, and utilizing advanced functionalities like alerting and logging. Throughout the book, we will explore real-world use cases, sharing valuable insights and strategies to enhance your observability workflows. Our intention is not only to offer a technical guide but also to inspire and spark your curiosity. We encourage you to explore, experiment and discover innovative ways to leverage Grafana's observability features within your unique environment.

We want to express our sincerest thanks to you, the reader. It is your curiosity, determination and thirst for knowledge that drive us to share our experiences and insights. Our hope is that this book will empower you to embark on an exciting and transformative observability journey with Grafana, enabling you to achieve unparalleled visibility and control over your systems. Welcome to "End-to-End Observability with Grafana." Together, let us embark on this thrilling adventure.

Chapter 1: Introduction to Data Visualization with Grafana - provides a brief introduction to the use of data visualization in general and specifically in Grafana. We will then move on to installing a Grafana server onto your machine, using either a native installer or a Docker container. Launching the server and connecting to it with a web browser will also be covered.

Chapter 2: A Tour of the Grafana Interface - explores the workings of the major interface components once you have loaded the Grafana web app.

Chapter 3: An Introduction to the Graph Panel - dives into the Graph panel for a closer look at how to work with the major components of the panel after creating a test data source. We will also identify common panel elements in preparation for looking at other panels.

Chapter 4: Connecting Grafana to a Data Source - explains different data sources available in Grafana, shows you how to install Prometheus data source and to visualize the data.

Chapter 5: Visualizing Data in the Graph Panel - show some of the more advanced features of the Graph panel.

Chapter 6: Creating Your First Dashboard - shows how to build a simple dashboard and related panels. explains the major components of a dashboard in-depth. Makes you familiar with the dashboard interface by moving and resizing panels.

Chapter 7: Visualization Panels in Grafana - takes a quick tour of the other major panels and how they're used.

Chapter 8: Organizing Dashboards - shows you how to label dashboards and organize them into folders to make them easier to find.

Chapter 9: Grafana Alerting - shows you how to create threshold alerts in the graph and connect them to notification channels. Step-by-step email notification channel setup is explained with Gmail and showcases how alerts are received.

Chapter 10: Working with Advanced Dashboard Features - explores the powerful advanced features of the dashboard, including annotations, templating with variables, and dashboard linking, as well as techniques for sharing dashboards.

Chapter 11: Exploring Logs with Grafana Loki - explains how Loki can be leveraged to answer questions about a log dataset.

Chapter 12: Managing Authorization and Authentication - discusses how Authorization can be enabled to manage User Permissions using Teams in Grafana, and how Authentication with External Services can be enabled.

Chapter 13: Blackbox Exporter - explains how Blackbox exporter can be set up and be used to monitor external data from websites.

Chapter 14: Synthetic Monitoring - This chapter discusses enabling Synthetic monitoring checks in Grafana manually and with automation.

Chapter 15: Maximizing the Grafana Plug-in - discusses types of Grafana plugins, provides recommendations to some of the widely used Grafana plugins. Also gives future direction to explore custom Grafana plugins.

Chapter 16: Kubernetes Monitoring - This chapter discusses the monitoring and alerting setup for Kubernetes cluster using Grafana and Prometheus.

Chapter 17: Grafana Cloud - explains end-to-end SAAS based Grafana Cloud monitoring setup, how to leverage cloud for monitoring and different subscription options.

Chapter 18: AIOps Monitoring - provides background information on AIOps Monitoring. The benefits of implementing AIOps monitoring, in addition to the challenges it presents. This chapter also includes information regarding well-known AIOps products that are readily accessible on the market today, as well as an illustration of how one of the most effective AIOps tools may be linked with Grafana.

Chapter 19: Dashboard Setup for Performance Testing and Engineering - explains Grafana dashboard setup strategy for an application which is focused on performance metrics and recommendation to use the best dashboard layout.

Chapter 20: Best Practices of Working with Grafana - discusses the best practices for creating and managing dashboards, how to ensure security and maintain version control.

Code Bundle and Coloured Images

Please follow the link to download the
Code Bundle and the *Coloured Images* of the book:

https://rebrand.ly/oovtee0

The code bundle for the book is also hosted on GitHub at **https://github.com/bpbpublications/End-to-End-Observability-with-Grafana**. In case there's an update to the code, it will be updated on the existing GitHub repository.

We have code bundles from our rich catalogue of books and videos available at **https://github.com/bpbpublications**. Check them out!

Errata

We take immense pride in our work at BPB Publications and follow best practices to ensure the accuracy of our content to provide with an indulging reading experience to our subscribers. Our readers are our mirrors, and we use their inputs to reflect and improve upon human errors, if any, that may have occurred during the publishing processes involved. To let us maintain the quality and help us reach out to any readers who might be having difficulties due to any unforeseen errors, please write to us at :

errata@bpbonline.com

Your support, suggestions and feedbacks are highly appreciated by the BPB Publications' Family.

Did you know that BPB offers eBook versions of every book published, with PDF and ePub files available? You can upgrade to the eBook version at www.bpbonline.com and as a print book customer, you are entitled to a discount on the eBook copy. Get in touch with us at :

business@bpbonline.com for more details.

At **www.bpbonline.com**, you can also read a collection of free technical articles, sign up for a range of free newsletters, and receive exclusive discounts and offers on BPB books and eBooks.

Piracy

If you come across any illegal copies of our works in any form on the internet, we would be grateful if you would provide us with the location address or website name. Please contact us at **business@bpbonline.com** with a link to the material.

If you are interested in becoming an author

If there is a topic that you have expertise in, and you are interested in either writing or contributing to a book, please visit **www.bpbonline.com**. We have worked with thousands of developers and tech professionals, just like you, to help them share their insights with the global tech community. You can make a general application, apply for a specific hot topic that we are recruiting an author for, or submit your own idea.

Reviews

Please leave a review. Once you have read and used this book, why not leave a review on the site that you purchased it from? Potential readers can then see and use your unbiased opinion to make purchase decisions. We at BPB can understand what you think about our products, and our authors can see your feedback on their book. Thank you!

For more information about BPB, please visit **www.bpbonline.com**.

Join our book's Discord space

Join the book's Discord Workspace for Latest updates, Offers, Tech happenings around the world, New Release and Sessions with the Authors:

https://discord.bpbonline.com

Table of Contents

1. Introduction to Data Visualization with Grafana.. 1

    Introduction... 1

    Structure.. 1

    Objectives.. 2

    1.1 Technical requirements.. 2

        1.1.1 Supported operating systems.. 3

        1.1.2 Hardware recommendations 3

        1.1.3 Supported databases for Grafana configuration storage 3

        1.1.4 Supported web browsers... 3

    1.2 Data storage and visualization.. 4

    1.3 What is the appeal of Grafana? 6

    1.4 Grafana installation 10

        1.4.1 Grafana for Linux 10

            Debian Linux... 10

        1.4.2 Grafana for Windows... 11

        1.4.3 Grafana for Mac 11

            Homebrew 11

            Command line... 11

        1.4.4 Grafana in a Docker container.. 12

        1.4.5 Managed Grafana on the cloud... 12

    1.5 Grafana server connection... 12

    Conclusion 14

    Multiple choice questions.. 14

        Answers... 14

2. A Tour of the Grafana Interface..15

    Introduction... 15

    Structure.. 15

    Objectives.. 16

    2.1 Technical requirements.. 16

    2.2 Exploring Grafana – The home dashboard 16

2.2.1 Glancing at the sidebar menu..17

2.2.2 Dashboard settings..18

2.2.3 View modes..18

2.2.4 Learning to use the icons on Grafana's left sidebar..........................19

2.2.5 Create dropdown menu 19

2.2.6 Folder...22

2.2.7 Import...22

2.2.8 Dashboards..23

2.2.9 Manage...24

2.2.10 Playlists..24

2.2.11 Snapshots...25

2.2.12 Library panels...26

2.2.13 Explore...26

2.2.14 Alerting..27

    Alert Rules..28

    Contact points 29

    Alert Manager 30

2.2.15 Data sources 30

    Users 32

2.2.16 Teams..33

2.2.17 Plugins 34

2.2.18 Organization preferences 34

2.2.19 User preferences..36

2.2.20 API keys..37

2.2.21 Server admin 38

2.2.22 Users 38

2.2.23 Orgs...39

2.2.24 Settings..39

2.2.25 Stats 40

Conclusion 41

Multiple choice questions...41

    Answers..41

3. An Introduction to the Graph Panel **43**

    Introduction...43

Structure..43

Objectives...44

3.1 Technical requirements..44

3.2 Touring the Graph Panel...44

   3.2.1 Creating a simple Data Source 45

   3.2.2 Creating a Graph Panel 46

3.3 Generating data series in the Query tab 47

   3.3.1 What is a query? 48

   3.3.2 Query tab features...49

3.4 Editing the Graph in the Panel tab 51

   3.4.1 Panel options 51

   3.4.2 Tooltip...51

   3.4.3 Legend...52

   3.4.5 Graph styles 53

   3.4.6 Axis..53

   3.4.7 Standard options 54

   3.4.8 Data links 55

   3.4.9 Value mappings 56

   3.4.10 Thresholds..56

3.5 Monitoring with the Alert tab 57

   3.5.1 Rule..57

   3.5.2 Conditions 57

   3.5.3 No data and error handling..58

   3.5.4 Notifications 58

Conclusion 58

Multiple choice questions...59

   Answers..59

4. Connecting Grafana to a Data Source **61**

Introduction...61

Structure..61

Objectives...62

4.1 Technical requirements..62

4.2 Installing the Prometheus server 62

   4.2.1 Installing Prometheus from Docker......................................62

4.2.2 Configuring the Prometheus data source 65

4.3 Exploring Prometheus 66

4.3.1 Using Explore for investigation 67

4.3.2 Configuring Grafana metrics 69

4.4 Querying the Prometheus data source 70

4.4.1 Typing in a metrics query 71

4.4.2 Querying for process metrics 72

4.5 Detecting trends with aggregations 73

4.5.1 Applying aggregations to our query data 74

4.6 Limitations of data source 78

4.6.1 Querying for series aggregations 78

4.6.2 Querying for time aggregations 79

Conclusion 80

Multiple choice questions 81

Answers 81

5. Visualizing Data in the Graph Panel **83**

Introduction 83

Structure 83

Objectives 84

5.1 Technical requirements 84

5.2 Executing advanced queries 84

5.2.1 Probing Prometheus 84

5.2.1.1 Dashboards' query editor 84

5.2.1.2 Query editor in explore 86

5.2.1.3 Templating 86

5.2.1.4 Query variable 86

5.2.1.5 Using interval and range variables 87

5.2.1.6 Using the $__rate_interval variable 87

5.2.1.7 Using variables in queries 88

5.2.1.8 Annotations 88

5.2.2 Sample queries 88

5.2.3 Advanced queries 89

5.3 Understanding time series data display 91

5.3.1 Aggregating time series 92

5.3.2 Time series and monitoring...*93*

5.3.3 Time series databases..*93*

5.3.4 Collecting time series data..*94*

5.4 Setting vertical axes 95

5.4.1 Right Y-axis..*95*

5.4.2 Log scale...*95*

5.4.3 Setting up a dual axis graph..*96*

5.4.4 Finding correlation..*97*

5.4.5 Resource utilization..*97*

5.4.6 Dangers of using dual axis graphs...*98*

5.4.7 Increase contrast between series *98*

5.4.8 Align baselines...*99*

Conclusion 99

Multiple choice questions..99

Answers..*99*

6. Creating Your First Dashboard **101**

Introduction...101

Structure 101

Objectives 102

6.1 Technical requirements 102

6.2 Designing a dashboard...102

6.2.1 Target audience for your dashboard...*102*

6.2.2 Installing TestData DB..*103*

6.2.3 Creating a dashboard..*105*

6.2.3.1 Select data source *106*

6.2.3.2 Visualization *107*

6.2.3.3 Title change *109*

6.2.3.4 Panel standard options *109*

6.2.3.5 Panel link for external website...*111*

6.2.3.6 Threshold *112*

6.2.3.7 Query inspector...*113*

6.2.3.8 Saving panel and dashboard *115*

6.2.3.9 Time range on dashboard *116*

6.2.3.10 Dashboard refresh frequency..*117*

6.3 Information-heavy Grafana dashboard 117

    6.3.1 Multiple panels *117*

    6.3.2 Graphs placement *118*

Conclusion 119

Multiple choice questions 120

    Answers *120*

7. Visualization Panels in Grafana **121**

Introduction 121

Structure 121

Objectives 122

7.1 Technical requirements 122

7.2 Introducing the Stat panel 122

    7.2.1 Value options *124*

    7.2.2 Stat styles *125*

7.3 Introducing the Gauge panel 126

    7.3.1 Value options *128*

7.4 Introducing the World Map panel 129

    7.4.1 Data sources format *130*

7.5 Introducing the Table panel 130

Conclusion 133

Multiple choice questions 133

    Answers *134*

8. Organizing Dashboards **135**

Introduction 135

Structure 135

Objectives 136

8.1 Technical requirements 136

8.2 Dashboard naming 136

    8.2.1 Naming a dashboard *136*

    8.2.2 Dashboard naming best practices *137*

8.3 Dashboard folders 138

    8.3.1 Creating a dashboard folder *138*

    8.3.2 Adding dashboards to a folder *139*

8.3.3 *Deleting folders*...140

8.3.4 *Folder management best practices*...............................141

8.4 Dashboard starring and tagging 142

8.4.1 *Marking dashboards as favorites*................................142

8.4.2 *Tagging dashboards*...143

8.4.2.1 *Adding tags*...143

8.4.2.2 *Deleting tags*...144

8.5 List panel in dashboard 144

Conclusion 145

Multiple choice questions...145

Answers...146

9. Grafana Alerting...**147**

Introduction..147

Structure..147

Objectives..148

9.1 Technical requirements 148

9.2 Threshold setup 148

9.3 Alerts configuration...149

9.3.1 *Accessing alerts*...149

9.3.2 *Setting up alerts*...150

9.4 Alerts to notification channel...152

9.4.1 *Setting up notification*...153

9.4.2 *Alert triggers*..154

9.5 Alert state history and management 155

9.5.1 *Viewing alert state history*..156

9.5.2 *Alerts silences* 157

Conclusion 157

Multiple choice questions...158

Answers...158

10. Working with Advanced Dashboard Features............................**159**

Introduction..159

Structure..159

Objectives..160

10.1 Technical requirements 160

10.2 Templating dashboards using Grafana variables 160

10.3 Linking dashboards 161

    10.3.1 Grafana dashboard hierarchy *162*

        Panel links *162*

        Dashboard links *163*

10.4 Annotations 166

    10.4.1 Use annotations in dashboards *167*

        Creating an annotation *167*

10.5 Exporting dashboards 168

    10.5.1 Sharing a dashboard *169*

    10.5.2 Sharing a direct link *169*

    10.5.3 Publishing a snapshot *170*

    10.5.4 Exporting a dashboard *171*

Conclusion 171

Multiple choice questions 171

    Answers *172*

11. Exploring Logs with Grafana Loki **173**

Introduction 173

Structure 173

Objectives 174

11.1 Technical requirements 174

11.2 Loki architecture 174

11.3 Installing Loki and Promtail 175

11.4 Setting-up config files for Loki and Promtail 176

    11.4.1 Updating .yaml files *176*

    11.4.2 Run Loki and Promtail locally *180*

11.5 Loki log visualization in Grafana 181

    11.5.1 Adding Loki as data source *181*

    11.5.2 Visualizing logs in Grafana *183*

Conclusion 184

Multiple choice questions 185

    Answers *185*

12. Managing Authorization and Authentication............................**187**

Introduction... 187

Structure.. 187

Objectives.. 188

12.1 Technical requirements... 188

12.2 Understanding key permissions concepts 188

12.3 Managing users in Grafana organization........................... 190

12.4 Establishing teams in Grafana.. 190

12.5 Administering users and organizations in Grafana 191

12.6 Configuring Google OAuth2 authentication 193

12.7 Testing the Google OAuth2 authentication configuration.... 194

Conclusion 195

Multiple choice questions.. 195

    Answers.. *195*

13. Blackbox Exporter...**197**

Introduction... 197

Structure.. 197

Objectives.. 198

13.1 Technical requirements... 198

13.2 What is Blackbox Exporter? 198

13.3 Installing Blackbox Exporter... 199

13.4 Setting-up Blackbox and .yml files 200

    13.4.1 Updating .yml files *200*

    13.4.2 Run Prometheus and Blackbox Exporter locally *202*

13.5 Monitoring websites performance in Grafana.................... 204

    13.5.1 Prerequisites *204*

    13.5.2 Visualizing in Grafana.. *205*

Conclusion 208

Multiple choice questions.. 208

    Answers.. *209*

14. Synthetic Monitoring **211**

Introduction... 211

Structure.. 211

Objectives 212

14.1 Technical requirements..212

14.2 Introduction of synthetic monitoring 212

14.3 Initialization of synthetic monitoring 214

14.4 Configuring synthetic monitoring check..214

    14.4.1 Recommended practices for synthetic monitoring alerts.................217

        Recording rules...218

        Alert expressions..218

        Alerting on probes 219

        Testing alert expressions...219

Conclusion 219

Multiple choice questions..219

    Answers..220

15. Maximizing the Grafana Plug-in **221**

Introduction..221

Structure 222

Objectives 222

15.1 Technical requirements..222

15.2 What is the Grafana plugin? 222

15.3 Types of Grafana plugins 223

    15.3.1 Data source plugins..223

    15.3.2 Apps plugins 225

    15.3.3 Panels plugins...226

15.4 Best Grafana plugins to download..227

    15.4.1 Boom table...227

    15.4.2 FlowCharting 227

    15.4.3 Status panel 228

    15.4.4 Discrete..228

    15.4.5 Polystat 229

15.5 Building your own plugin 230

Conclusion 231

Multiple choice questions..231

    Answers..232

16. Kubernetes Monitoring..**233**

Introduction..233

Structure..234

Objectives..234

16.1 Technical requirements..234

16.2 Reasons to monitor Kubernetes...234

16.3 Set up and access Prometheus and Grafana dashboards.....................236

    16.3.1 Prerequisites for exploring Prometheus on macOS.........................*237*

    16.3.2 Accessing the dashboards..*238*

    16.3.3 Visualizing Prometheus Data with Grafana................................*241*

16.4 Monitor Kubernetes resources and workloads 241

    16.4.1 Kubernetes cluster level compute resources dashboard...................*242*

    16.4.2 Kubernetes node exporter dashboard..*242*

    16.4.3 Kubernetes CoreDNS dashboard...*243*

    16.4.4 Kubernetes namespace level compute resources dashboard *244*

    16.4.5 Kubernetes API server dashboard..*245*

    16.4.6 Kubernetes node exporter utilization dashboard *246*

    16.4.7 Prometheus overview dashboard..*247*

16.5 Alerting for Kubernetes cluster with alert manager............................248

Conclusion 251

Multiple choice questions...251

    Answers...*252*

17. Grafana Cloud...**253**

Introduction..253

Structure..253

Objectives..254

17.1 Technical requirements..254

17.2 What is Grafana cloud...254

17.3 Grafana cloud subscription 255

17.4 Setting up data source 257

17.5 Monitoring a Windows machine from Grafana cloud 258

Conclusion 261

Multiple choice questions...262

Answers..262

18. AIOps Monitoring **263**

Introduction..263

Structure...263

Objectives...264

18.1 Technical requirements...264

18.2 Pros and cons of AIOps monitoring setup..................................264

    18.2.1 Pros of AIOps monitoring setup 265

    18.2.2 Cons of AIOps monitoring setup 265

18.3 Popular AIOps monitoring tools available in market..................266

18.4 Moogsoft AIOps Plugin Integration with Grafana.....................269

    18.4.1 Plugin installation for Moogsoft AIOps 269

    18.4.2 Enable the Moogsoft AIOps Application: 269

Conclusion 270

Multiple choice questions..271

    Answers...271

19. Dashboard Setup for Performance Testing and Engineering **273**

Introduction..273

Structure...274

Objectives...274

19.1 Technical requirements...274

19.2 Performance testing and engineering 274

19.3 Role of Grafana in performance testing and engineering 275

19.4 Grafana dashboards for performance analysis.............................276

    19.4.1 JMeter load test 277

    19.4.2 OracleDB monitoring...279

    19.4.3 Zabbix for server monitoring...281

Conclusion 282

Multiple choice questions..283

    Answers...283

20. Best Practices of Working with Grafana **285**

Introduction..285

Structure...286

Objectives..286

20.1 Technical requirements...286

20.2 Significance of using Grafana best practices 286

20.3 Designing effective dashboards..287

20.4 Optimizing performance 290

20.5 Ensuring security 292

20.6 Collaboration and version control....................................293

Conclusion 294

Multiple choice questions..295

    Answers...295

Index **297-303**

CHAPTER 1
Introduction to Data Visualization with Grafana

Introduction

In this chapter, you'll learn the basics of data visualization and how to use Grafana. Grafana is one of the most popular data visualization tools available today. It is simple to use, open source, and adaptable. Additionally, Grafana offers a huge selection of plugins that let you increase its capability. Grafana is a great tool for expressing your data, regardless of your experience level with data visualization.

You can learn how to install Grafana on your computer in this chapter, which includes instructions for doing so via a native installer, a Docker container, or even with Helm charts. When the server is started, you'll learn how to use a web browser to connect to it.

Structure

In this chapter, we will learn the following:

- Technical requirements
- Data and visualization
- What is the appeal of Grafana?
- Grafana installation

- Grafana for Linux
- Grafana for Windows
- Grafana for Mac
- Grafana in a Docker container
- Managed Grafana on the cloud
- Grafana server connection
- Conclusion
- Questions

Objectives

This chapter aims to give you a basic introduction to data visualization with Grafana. We will touch upon the details of Grafana installation requirements on different operating systems, what makes Grafana appealing as a monitoring tool and how to connect to Grafana from a local browser.

1.1 Technical requirements

Since Grafana is a web-based application, you'll need to run a few commands to get it up and running. The following are the technical requirements and prerequisites for installing and running Grafana v9.0:

- Knowledge of the command shell
- Installation of Grafana on the machine of your choice using a terminal application or an SSH
- Java 8 or higher
- Python 3.5 or later
- Git CLI tool
- Docker
- Kubernetes cluster
- Optionally, you'll be able to login as an administrator to use the command line to set up and run Grafana
- Dashboards, chapter details, and other helpful resources of this chapter can be found at **https://github.com/bpbpublications/End-to-End-Observability-With-Grafana/tree/main/Chapter-01**.

1.1.1 Supported operating systems

Grafana installation is compatible with the following OSes:

- MacOS
- Ubuntu/Debian
- Windows
- RPM-based Linux (OpenSUSE, RedHat, Centos, Fedora)

1.1.2 Hardware recommendations

Grafana consumes few resources and is very light on memory and CPU. Following are the minimum recommendations:

- 2 GB of memory
- 10 GB of disk space
- 4 CPUs

1.1.3 Supported databases for Grafana configuration storage

A database is required for Grafana to store its configuration data, which includes things like users, data sources, and dashboards. The precise requirements are determined by the size of the Grafana installation and the features that are being utilized. Grafana is compatible with the following database types:

- SQLite (default)
- MySQL
- PostgreSQL

1.1.4 Supported web browsers

The most recent version of each of the following browsers includes support for Grafana. It's possible that older versions of these browsers won't be supported, so if you want to use Grafana, you should always use the most recent version available.

- Internet Explorer 11 (Grafana versions < v6.0)
- Chrome/Chromium
- Safari

- FireFox
- Microsoft Edge

Note: JavaScript needs to be enabled in the browser.

In the next section, more details of data storage and visualization will be provided.

1.2 Data storage and visualization

Researchers, scientists, NGOs, and ordinary citizens all over the world are creating, storing, and using their own sets of data. Each of them faces the same challenge: how to aggregate, collate, or distill the vast amounts of information into a form that is easy for humans to comprehend and act on in a matter of seconds or less. To solve this problem, we need a better way to store and display our data, as shown in the following figure:

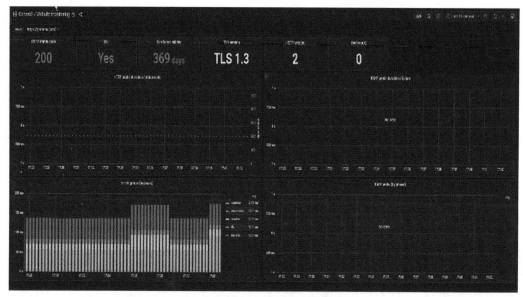

Figure 1.1: Website Monitoring Dashboard

Data is everywhere. It's in our phone, car, and everything else around us. This means businesses will need more data storage and visualization capabilities than ever before to make sense of the information they collect.

Data storage and visualization is also commonly known as data science, and they are two sides of the same coin. Data storage and visualization is the process of organizing, storing, and displaying information in a way that is easy for humans to understand. Both are critical components of any data science project. If you can't store or visualize data, there's no point in analyzing it.

Data storage has evolved from simple text files to complex relational databases and NoSQL data stores like MongoDB. This evolution has allowed us to store more information than ever before in an accessible format. Data storage is one of the most important factors in determining the effectiveness of a computer system. It is often measured (along with response time) in IOPS. The two terms are related, as the number of IOPS depends on how fast data can be written to or read from storage devices.

The term *data visualization* is used to describe techniques for representing information so that it can be perceived quickly and accurately by users. The goal is to present complex information so that it will be easy for people to understand and allow them to make sound decisions based on that information.

Effective visualizations make heavy use of color, size, and shape to convey meaning more efficiently than text or numbers could do it alone. Data visualization is one of the most important aspects of data analysis and data science. Data visualization tools have also evolved from simple charts to interactive dashboards that allow users to explore large data sets interactively using gestures like panning, zooming or filtering by information like date or location. Data visualization tools allow you to see your data in a new way, which can often reveal patterns that were previously hidden.

Data visualization tools include charts like line graphs, scatter plots, bar charts, pie charts, and many others; maps showing geographical information; and network diagrams showing relationships between different pieces of information. For example, if we want to compare two countries in terms of population size and birth rate, we can do so by simply dragging-and-dropping countries onto a scatter plot! In a world where everything is becoming *smarter* and more connected, it is important to be able to visualize data to make sense out of it.

For example, let's say you have a large amount of information about traffic patterns on a city street over time. Using simple bar charts or line graphs will not give you an accurate picture of how traffic flows through this street at different times of the day or on different days. However, using advanced visualization tools like heat maps (which are graphics that represent data values as colors) or 3D representations (which show three dimensions) can help you gain much more insight into this problem than just looking at simple bar charts or line graphs. A good example of this concept can be seen in an article written by *Coby Kennedy* for *InfoWorld* entitled *Visualizing Data for Better Decisions*.

1.3 What is the appeal of Grafana?

The data visualization market is crowded, but Grafana is one of the most promising data visualization tool, showing rapid expansion in scope and features, a wide range of options for deployment and support, and a dedicated community that is actively contributing to its development. For the purpose of this discussion, let's take a look at the criteria that might be used to identify a useful data visualization application.

This book's focus is on software that performs exploration, analysis, presentation, and notification, which are all major functions of software. Drilling-down is a term used to describe the process of quickly loading and displaying a data set to identify the most interesting features for further analysis. Next, we may want to analyze our data further. It's possible that we'll want to analyze the data statistically or compare it to other information. We might, for example, be interested in determining the data's average or maximum value over a particular period.

Alternatively, we may want to examine multiple data sets at the same time to identify time-correlated events.

To effectively tell a story with data, we need to first identify the data we're looking for and then present it in a visually appealing way that makes it clear to the viewer what the data means. Without this specific domain knowledge, it would be difficult to do so.

Finally, if the data is critical, we may have to keep an eye on it overtime or even in real time. We may need to be alerted immediately if the data crosses a certain threshold. Many powerful data analytics tools are available, but Grafana has a few features that make it an attractive option:

- **Fast**: Querying data sources or feeding thousands of data points to multiple dashboard panels is no problem for Grafana's back end, which is written in Google's brand new Go programming language.

- **Open**: Grafana's capacity to readily extend and personalize its functionality using plugins is one of its most potent advantages. Users can add new data sources, panel types, dashboards, and other features using plugins. Grafana Labs' official plugins and plugins created by the community make up the two different categories of plugins. Community-developed plugins are made and maintained by Grafana users, while official plugins are published and updated by Grafana Labs.

- **Beautiful**: Grafana uses the D3 library, which is both beautiful and powerful. DataDog and Zabbix are two of the most popular dashboard tools, but they offer only a limited amount of control over the design of the graphs they generate. Annotations, fills, axes, lines, points, and legends can all be customized to a fine degree in Grafana. Even the much-desired dark mode is available.

- **Versatile**: Grafana is a database-independent visualization tool. In Elasticsearch, Logstash, and Kibana stack, Kibana is a powerful and well-known member, but it can only visualize Elasticsearch data sources. Elasticsearch's analysis tools can now be better integrated into its graphing panels, giving it an advantage over Grafana. But Grafana's plugin architecture allows it to support an ever-growing number of databases, from traditional relational databases like MySQL and PostgreSQL to more modern transactional databases like Influx DB and Prometheus. An array of data can be displayed in a single graph and a synthesis of different data sets in a single visual representation.

- **Free**: Both DataDog and Splunk are commercial products, and as such, despite their impressive power, they charge for the management of all but the smallest data sets. Open-source Grafana can be used without charge under the Apache license, but if you want to use it in your business, you can buy tiers of support that unlock additional features. It's possible to compare Grafana with other products using these criteria. If you're in the market for visualization tools, now is a great time to explore Grafana. Apart from some minor differences in usability, all the applications that compete with Grafana have a lot going for them.

Grafana is a powerful and popular open-source data visualization platform that provides visualization of time series data for developers, analysts, and operations teams to monitor their applications and systems. Grafana was originally created by the people at InfluxData to visualize their own metrics, but it's now used by various companies and organizations. It can be used to monitor any kind of metrics, from CPU load on a server to the number of sales per month in a retail store. It allows you to graphically display and explore your monitoring data in real time. You can create dashboards to provide a high-level summary or dive deep into the details of what happened (or is happening) on your systems. It can collect data from a wide range of sources, including Influx DB, Graphite, Prometheus, and Elasticsearch. Grafana is completely customizable and has a powerful query language.

Grafana is available in three versions:

- Open-Source Edition (free to use)
- Enterprise Edition (paid subscription)
- Grafana Cloud Edition (Free Forever Cloud, Pro accounts available)

Free Forever Cloud accounts have the following restrictions:

- 3 users
- 10,000 active series for metrics
- 50 GB of logs
- 50 GB of traces
- 30 notifications for On Call
- 14-day retention

Grafana has been designed with extensibility in mind. Plugins allow users to connect Grafana to any data source or back-end system you can imagine. Following is the Grafana Plugins page where you can see a few examples of available Grafana plugins:

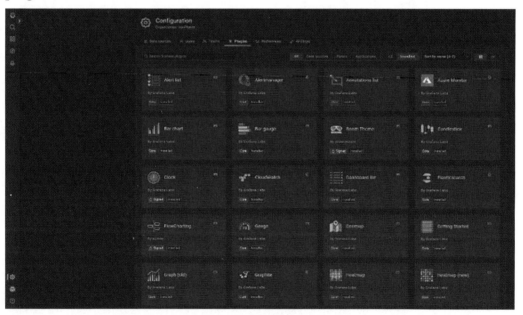

Figure 1.2: Grafana Plugins Page

There are currently hundreds of plugins available through the official plugin repo. For instance, the World Map Panel plugin extends Grafana with an interactive map, enabling users to view data globally. A rapid summary of the status of all your servers, services, and applications is provided by the Status Panel plugin. Additionally, you can display your data by creating stunning pie charts using the Pie Chart plugin. Grafana is a very flexible platform that can be used to create almost any type of data visualization because it has so many different plugins available.

The first step in setting up Grafana is importing an existing dashboard or creating a new one from scratch. The Dashboard Editor is where you create your visualizations, add panels and make them interactive. It's also where you can import an existing dashboard from another project or create a new one from scratch. For example, if you want to monitor your infrastructure, you can use the Hosts panel in the Data sources section to display metrics about CPU usage, memory usage, or disk space usage on your servers. You can also use the Graph panel for displaying metrics over time, such as CPU utilization or the number of requests per second.

Monitoring is an integral part of DevOps and Site Reliability Engineering. It is the process of gathering, analyzing, and reporting information about your systems, applications, and services. Monitoring helps business to know how their applications are performing, what the bottlenecks are and where they should focus. Monitoring data can help you understand how your systems are performing and help you to identify when issues arise.

Grafana has many different panels that can be used to create dashboards for monitoring. There are several different types of dashboards:

- **Infrastructure**: This type of dashboard displays performance information about the hardware (CPU usage, disk usage, memory usage, and so on) and software applications running on the server.

- **Application performance**: This type of dashboard displays information about the performance of your application (latency, request throughput, errors, and so on). It's important to know what metrics are being monitored so that you can spot any anomalies as they occur.

- **Endpoint**: This type of dashboard displays information about the health status of an endpoint (HTTP requests per second, and so on).

- **Synthetic**: This type of dashboard displays synthetic metrics that are usually generated by an external system or process (like provisioning new instances or creating new user accounts). The aim of synthetic transactions is to see how an application would respond under load conditions when there are no real users yet (for example, during off-peak hours). It allows us to test our systems under load conditions before going into production.

- **Alerting**: This type of dashboard displays recent sent and recovered alerts.

In the next section, installation details of Grafana on different OS are provided.

1.4 Grafana installation

Grafana is not a typical **DoubleClick** application because it functions as a web server at its core. In order to install Grafana on a computer, you'll need command-line skills and administrative privileges. If you're running Windows or macOS X, you can use the Grafana application server, which can be installed locally on a laptop or workstation, or remotely on a server.

To install the latest version of Grafana on different operating systems and options including Docker and Kubernetes, visit **https://github.com/bpbpublications/End-to-End-Observability-With-Grafana/blob/main/Chapter-01/README.md**.

1.4.1 Grafana for Linux

Following are the methods to install Grafana for Linux.

Debian Linux

The **dpkg** is the installer for Debian-based distributions (Debian and Ubuntu). To download and install (**$GRAFANA VERSION** should be replaced with the current version), follow these steps:

```
|$  wget  https://dl.grafana.com/oss/release/grafana_$GRAFANA_VERSION_
amd64.deb
```

```
|$ sudo apt-get install -y adduser libfontconfig1
```

```
|$ sudo dpkg -i grafana_$GRAFANA_VERSION_amd64.deb
```

To start up Grafana, use the following:

```
|$ systemctl daemon-reload
```

```
|$ systemctl start grafana-server
```

```
|$ systemctl status grafana-server
```

To keep Grafana running even after a reboot, use the following:

```
|$ sudo systemctl enable grafana-server.service
```

RedHat Linux

Yum is the RedHat distribution installer (CentOS, RedHat, and Fedora). To download and install, use the following (replace **$GRAFANA VERSION** with the current version):

```
|$  wget  https://dl.grafana.com/oss/release/grafana-$GRAFANA_VERSION.
```

```
x86_64.rpm
```

```
|$ sudo yum install initscripts urw-fonts
```

```
|$ sudo yum localinstall grafana-$GRAFANA_VERSION.x86_64.rpm
```

```
Use systemd to launch Grafana.
```

```
|$ systemctl daemon-reload
```

```
|$ systemctl start grafana-server
```

```
|$ systemctl status grafana-server
```

You can use the following to keep Grafana functioning after a reboot:

```
|$ sudo systemctl enable grafana-server.service
```

1.4.2 Grafana for Windows

For Windows, the installation process is simple, follow these steps:

1. Go to **https://grafana.com/grafana/download?platform=windows**.
2. Click on the download link to get the most recent version of the MSI installer.
3. To complete the installation, run the **.msi** file.

1.4.3 Grafana for Mac

Grafana can be installed on a Mac using either of the following two methods.

Homebrew

Following are commands to install Grafana on a Mac using Homebrew:

```
|$ brew install Grafana
```

```
|$ brew tap homebrew/services
```

```
|$ brew services start grafana
```

Command line

Following are commands to install Grafana on a Mac using a TAR file:

```
|$ wget https://dl.grafana.com/oss/release/grafana-$GRAFANA_VERSION.
darwin-amd64.tar.gz
```

```
|$ tar -zxvf grafana-$GRAFANA_VERSION.darwin-amd64.tar.gz
```

Once the file has been extracted, cd to the directory and launch Grafana with binary:

```
|$ . /bin/grafana-server web
```

1.4.4 Grafana in a Docker container

The simplest and least complex installation approach involves running Grafana inside a Docker container. Visit **https://www.docker.com/** to get Docker for all main platforms.

Open a terminal window after installing Docker and enter the following command:

```
|$ docker run -d --name=grafana -p 3000:3000 grafana/Grafana
```

Docker will automatically download and run the most recent version of Grafana for the architecture of your computer. Considering that this basic container lacks persistent storage, nothing will be retained if the container is deleted. We recommend running the container with a temporary volume so that Grafana's internal database will persist even if the container is deleted:

```
|$ docker volume create grafana-storage
```

```
|$ docker run -d --name=grafana -p 3000:3000 \
```

```
-v grafana-storage:/var/lib/grafana grafana/Grafana
```

1.4.5 Managed Grafana on the cloud

This option is available if you don't have access to an operating system capable of running Grafana or if you don't want to install Grafana on any computer. Hosting Grafana may be an option for those who are only interested in following along with the book until we use data sources, but there are some limitations, such as the fact that a paid subscription is required to access a specific data source. Visit **https:// grafana.com/get** and sign up for a free account.

1.5 Grafana server connection

Once you have installed and launched Grafana, open a browser page to access the Grafana application. It can be found at `http://localhost:3000`. If everything goes well, you should see a login page, as follows:

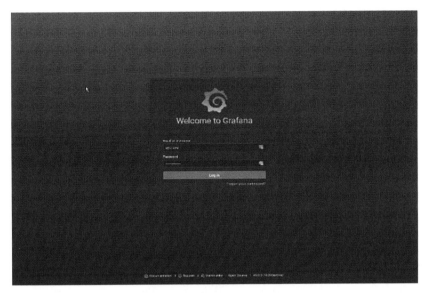

Figure 1.3: *Grafana Login Page*

Use the administrator username and password to log in. After that, you'll be prompted to switch to a more secure password. Grafana's default user interface should appear once you log in to Grafana, as shown in the next figure:

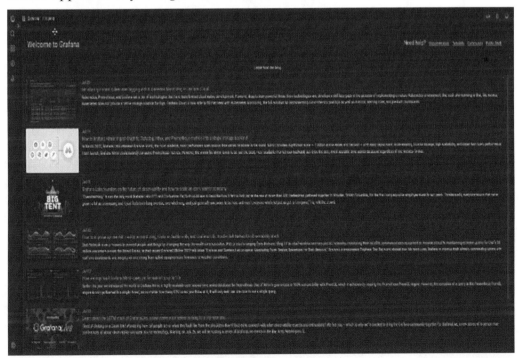

Figure 1.4: *Grafana Home Dashboard*

Great job! You've successfully installed and connected your Grafana application.

Conclusion

Greetings! Now that you have a running Grafana server, you are ready to explore the many powerful features of Grafana. We'll explore the interface, examine data sources, and learn about Grafana administration's advanced management practices in the upcoming chapters.

Multiple choice questions

1. Which of the following OSes are supported for Grafana installation?

    a. Linux   b. Windows   c. Mac   d. All the above

2. Are plugins supported in the Enterprise Edition of Grafana?

    a. Yes   b. No

3. Which browsers are not supported to load Grafana v9.0?

    a. Safari   b. Google Chrome

    c. Firefox   d. None of the above

4. This chapter covered the installation details of which Grafana version?

    a. v7.0   b. v8.0   c. v9.0   d. None of the above

Answers

1. d
2. a
3. d
4. c

Join our book's Discord space

Join the book's Discord Workspace for Latest updates, Offers, Tech happenings around the world, New Release and Sessions with the Authors:

https://discord.bpbonline.com

CHAPTER 2

A Tour of the Grafana Interface

Introduction

This chapter will provide an overview of the default home dashboard, focusing primarily on the icons on the sidebar menu. You will find the side menu to be a useful navigation hub, providing quick access to Explorer, Dashboard Search filter, Dashboards List, Alert Management, User Settings, Admin Settings, and Help.

Structure

In this chapter, we will learn the following:

- Dashboard's menu
- Plugin's menu
- Alert's menu
- Admin settings menu
- Personal settings menu

Objectives

This chapter will provide a tour of the user interface for the Grafana application. It will give you an overview of the Grafana dashboards and panels, and it will also provide insights into how to browse, how to modify the Grafana dashboard, and how to customize the user and organization settings.

2.1 Technical requirements

Since Grafana is a web-based application, you'll need to run a few commands in order to get it up and running. The following are the technical requirements and prerequisites for installing and running Grafana v9.0:

- Knowledge of the command shell
- Install Grafana on the machine of your choice using a terminal application or an SSH
- Java 8 or higher
- Python 3.5 or later
- Git CLI tool
- Docker
- Docker-Compose

Optionally, you'll be able to log in as an administrator using the command line to set up and run Grafana.

2.2 Exploring Grafana – The home dashboard

The following Grafana home dashboard is the first thing you see when you connect to Grafana. It's a great place to explore your data and get an overview of what's happening in your environment. The Grafana home dashboard is a collection of panels that are built from the same set of metrics and displayed in different ways. It is also a web page, so you can bookmark it or share it using a simple URL. Even the entire dashboard can be imported and exported as a JSON text file, making it simple to share, store, or transfer to a different version of Grafana. Although the dashboard looks simple at first glance, there's a lot going on behind the scenes to make it work. The panels are the fundamental building blocks of the dashboard's functionality. Panels serve various purposes, ranging from generating graphs to organizing data into tables. The Grafana logo button returns the user to the Grafana dashboard's home page:

Figure 2.1: Home Dashboard

The following UI elements are displayed on the default home dashboard:

- Panel for **Recently viewed** dashboards list
- Panel for **Grafana blog** posts
- Panel for **Help** links like documentation, community discussions, and tutorials

2.2.1 Glancing at the sidebar menu

The Grafana sidebar menu is located on the left of the screen and contains various options for configuring and managing your Grafana instance. Below are the most important menu items:

- **Dashboards**: This is where you can create, view, and edit your Grafana dashboards. You can also add new data sources and plugins here.

- **Data Sources**: This is where you can manage your Grafana data sources. You can add, edit, and delete data sources here.

- **Plugins**: This is where you can install Grafana plugins. Grafana has many plugins available, which can be used to extend the functionality of your Grafana instance.

- **Admin**: This is where you can manage Grafana users and configure Grafana settings. Only users with admin privileges will have access to this menu item.

- **Help**: This is where you can find Grafana documentation and support resources. Grafana has excellent documentation, which can be very helpful if you run into any problems.

2.2.2 Dashboard settings

At the upper right of the home dashboard is a small gear icon that represents the dashboard settings button. Clicking on this button gives you access to a wide array of settings for the dashboard. The following are some of the main functions in settings page:

- General settings
- Annotations
- Variables
- Links
- JSON model

2.2.3 View modes

View mode icon is to the right of the dashboard settings icon. This button toggles between the following three visual modes for the Grafana application:

- Normal mode
- Kiosk mode
- Kiosk mode (with auto fit panels)
- TV (Television) mode
- TV (Television) mode (with auto fit panels)

2.2.4 Learning to use the icons on Grafana's left sidebar

The left sidebar is located to the left of the actual dashboard, and the icons on it lead to some of Grafana's most potent and impressive features. For instance, you can do the following:

- Explore and configure data sources
- Manage alert rules and notification channels
- Configure users and teams
- Download plugins
- Generate API keys
- Manage Grafana users and organizations
- Set individual preferences
- Get help

2.2.5 Create dropdown menu

The plus sign designates the **Create** dropdown menu. It serves as a link for rapidly creating or importing dashboards and folders of dashboards. The **New Dashboard** option within the **Create** menu generates a brand new dashboard with a single panel to help you get started, as shown in *Figure 2.2*:

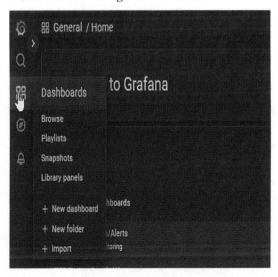

Figure 2.2*: Dashboards dropdown*

The **Add a new** panel button creates a **Graph** panel and opens the query pane, while converting to row converts the placeholder panel into a dashboard row. Rows are an effective structure for dynamically constructing dashboard pages. Assigning a special template variable to a row causes Grafana to duplicate appropriately configured panels on that row, with each panel reflecting the value of the assigned template variable. To create a new graph panel, click the **Add new panel** button, as shown in *Figure 2.3*:

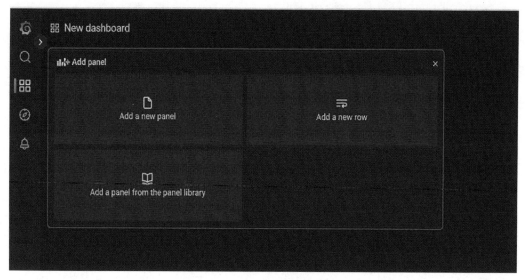

Figure 2.3: *Panel Creation*

Click on the **Save** button to save dashboard with the panels created, as shown in *Figure 2.4*:

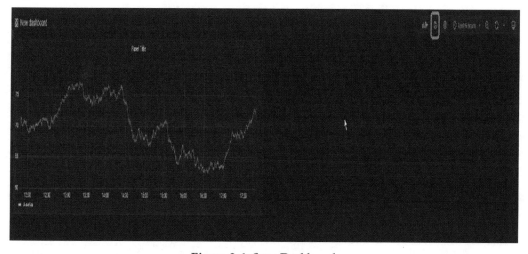

Figure 2.4: *Save Dashboard*

We can rename the dashboard in the dashboard settings, which we can access by clicking the gear icon:

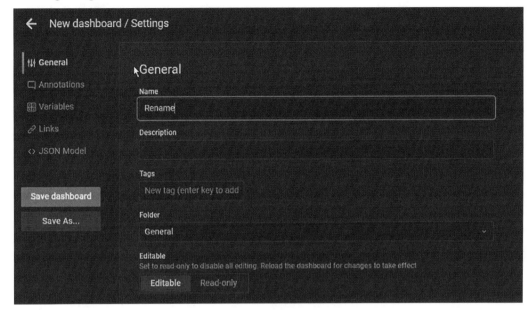

Figure 2.5: Rename Dashboard

The dashboard icons are shown in *Figure 2.6*:

Figure 2.6: Dashboard Buttons

Dashboard icons serve the following purposes:

- Adds new dashboard panel
- Saves the changes of dashboard
- Displays settings of dashboard
- Changes view mode
- Applies time range of data to be displayed of configured time zone in dashboard
- Time range zoom out
- Refreshes dashboard

2.2.6 Folder

The **Create | Folder** option is located at the top of the **Dashboards** tab. To create a new folder, click the button, give it a name, and then hit the **OK** button. The new folder will appear in the list under **Browse**. You can drag any dashboard into this folder to move it there permanently, as shown in *Figure 2.7*:

Figure 2.7: *New Folder Creation*

2.2.7 Import

To import dashboards into Grafana, navigate to Dashboard's page | **Import Dashboard**, and click on the **Import** button, as shown in *Figure 2.8*:

Figure 2.8: *Import Dashboard Button*

We can import a dashboard using the dashboard's ID or a JSON file, as shown in *Figure 2.9*:

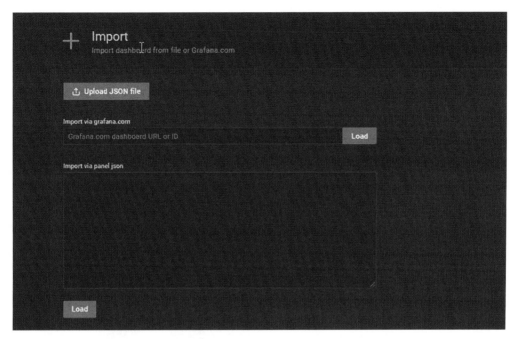

Figure 2.9: *Import Dashboard using JSON or Grafana URL*

2.2.8 Dashboards

The **Dashboards** dropdown is denoted by a square with panels. Each option serves as a link to a tab on the Dashboards administration page, as shown in *Figure 2.10*:

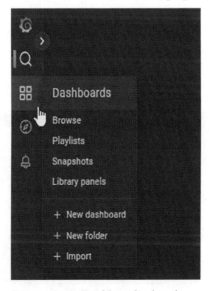

Figure 2.10: *Dashboard's dropdown*

2.2.9 Manage

The **Dashboards** | **Browse** option navigates to the **Manage** tab of Dashboards, where dashboards can be rapidly created and organized as shown in *Figure 2.11*:

Figure 2.11: *Manage Dashboards*

The **Browse** tab enables the creation or import of dashboards and the creation of dashboard folders. The search box in the dashboards page can be used to locate dashboards by name. The **New Dashboard**, **New Folder**, and **Import** buttons have nearly identical functionality to their **Create** counterparts. New Dashboard will create a new dashboard using a panel wizard, while **New Folder** and **Import** will execute their respective functions on the **Manage** tab.

2.2.10 Playlists

Dashboards | **Playlist** navigates to the **Playlists** tab, where you can create groups of dashboards that are orchestrated to run in a specific order and timing, as shown in *Figure 2.12*:

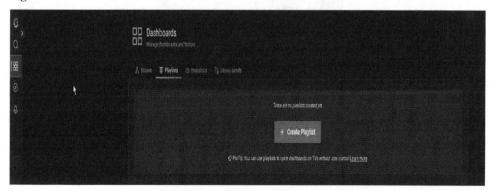

Figure 2.12: *Playlists Creation*

Create a playlist to show your team or visitors your metrics or to help them get a feel for the current situation. Using Grafana, dashboards can be automatically scaled to fit any resolution, making them ideal for large displays. The setup of a Grafana-powered kiosk-style display typically involves the use of playlists. Here are the measures to take when making a playlist:

1. Click the **Create Playlist** button.

2. Give your playlist a name.

3. Set the time interval between playlists.

4. Incorporate dashboards into the list.

5. Select **Create**.

2.2.11 Snapshots

The **Snapshots** tab, which can also be accessed via the **Dashboards | Snapshots** menu, allows you to capture the current state of a dashboard in the form of snapshots, as shown in *Figure 2.13*. This shows your data sets but does not allow you to access the original data sources or queries. Snapshots are a great way to share a live dashboard when you need to demo your dashboards offline or cannot share access to your data sources:

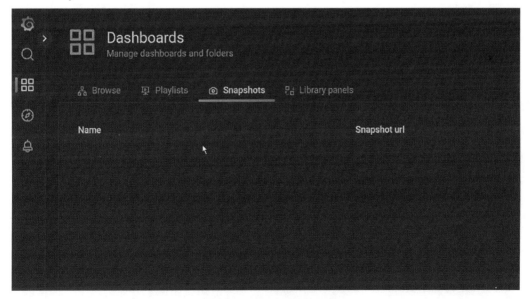

Figure 2.13: Snapshot Creation

2.2.12 Library panels

A library panel is a reusable panel that can be added to any dashboard. When you change a library panel, the change is applied to all instances where the panel is used. Library panels make it easier to reuse panels across multiple dashboards. A library panel can be saved in the same folder as saved dashboards. Library panels list is displayed in *Figure 2.14*:

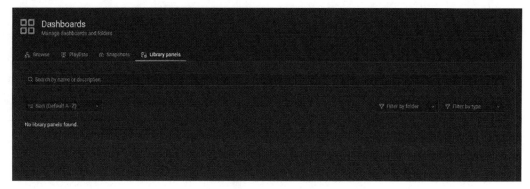

Figure 2.14: *Library Panels List*

2.2.13 Explore

Explore is one of the most exciting features of Grafana; it functions as a data-driven scratchpad for exploring a data source before implementing it on a dashboard graph. It can be used for **Query Management, Exploratory Log analysis, Tracing and Inspection**. A sample view of the **Explore** page is displayed in *Figure 2.15*:

Figure 2.15: *Explore Feature*

- **Query Management in Explore**: To aid with query debugging, you can examine query requests, response bodies, and query statistics with Explore's Query inspector. The inspect query performance and inspect query request, and response data panel inspector tasks both accomplish comparable functions.

- **Logs in Explore**: Explore not only provides access to metrics but also to the following log data sources for in-depth analysis:

  o Loki

  o InfluxDB

  o ElasticSearch

  During infrastructure monitoring and incident response, detailed metric and log analysis is possible to identify the root cause of the issue. Measurements and logs can be compared side by side in Explore. This leads to the new debugging process described below:

  o Be notified of a problem using Alert.

  o Analyze metrics at a finer level of detail.

  o Explore further to find logs that pertain to the metric and time frame (and in the future, distributed traces).

- **Tracing in Explore**: You can use Explore to visualize traces from tracing data sources. This is available in Grafana v7.0+.

  Supported data sources are as follows:

  o Jaeger

  o Tempo

  o X-Ray

  o Zipkin

- **Inspector in Explore**: The inspector assists you in understanding and troubleshooting your problems. You can examine raw data, export it to a **comma-separated values (CSV)** file, export log results to TXT, and view query requests.

2.2.14 Alerting

Using Grafana Alerting, you can identify system issues as soon as they arise, and you can improve your team's capacity to swiftly detect and handle issues by creating, managing, and acting on alerts in a centralized manner. The **Alerting** dropdown is denoted by a bell icon. Each option serves as a link to a tab on the **Alerting** administration page, as shown in *Figure 2.16*:

Figure 2.16: Alerting Dropdown

Any Grafana deployment, whether **Open-Source Software (OSS)**, Commercial, or in the Cloud, can take advantage of Grafana Alerting. Use the familiar Grafana UI to manage Mimir and Loki alert rules to run alert expressions nearer to your data and on a gigantic scale. Similar to the Dashboards dropdown, the Alerting dropdown contains links to the page's tabs.

Alert Rules

Grafana managed alerts' most powerful feature is their alert rules. Complex alert rules can be created, which fire when multiple series or expressions are combined in a single rule. Indicate the standards to be used in deciding whether or not to activate an alert. Alert rules can be created and managed in the page displayed in the following figure:

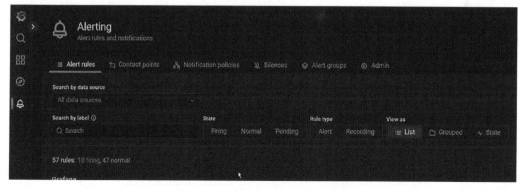

Figure 2.17: Alerting Rules

One or more queries and expressions, a condition, the number of occurrences and optionally, the amount of time that the condition is met for make up an alert rule. Multi-dimensional alerting is supported by Grafana managed alerts, meaning that a single alert rule can trigger many alert instances. When monitoring many series in a single expression, this is the most efficient method. During the process of making an alert rule, it passes through several phases. The alert rules' health and state provide context for a number of important metrics.

Contact points

A contact point can be as simple as an email address or as complicated as PagerDuty's integration plugin. Currently, nearly 18 notification integrations are supported by Grafana, and this number is growing rapidly. A sample list of contact points can be checked in *Figure 2.18*:

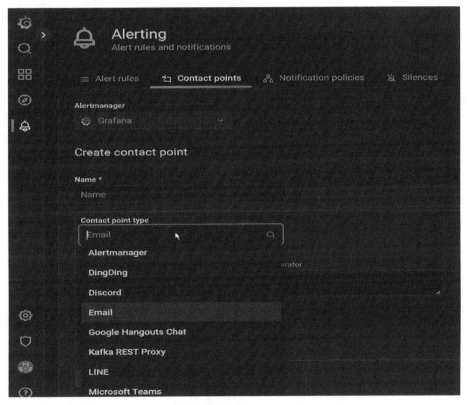

Figure 2.18: *Contact Points*

Alert Manager

The Alert Manager adds a layer of orchestration on top of the alerting engines by assisting in the grouping and management of alert rules. Grafana includes Prometheus Alert Manager integration. By default, Grafana managed alert notifications are handled by the embedded Alert Manager that is part of core Grafana. By selecting the Grafana option from the **Alert Manager** dropdown, you can configure the Alert Manager's contact points, notification policies, silences, and templates from the alerting UI, as shown in *Figure 2.19*:

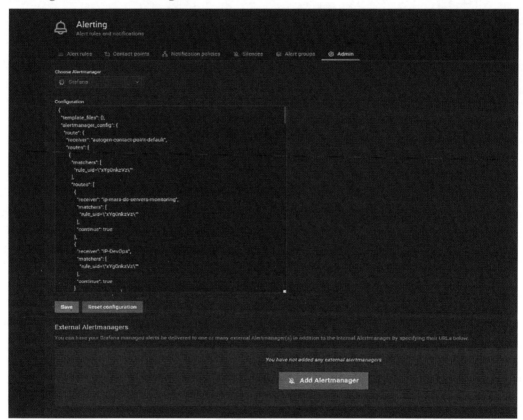

Figure 2.19: Alert Manager

2.2.15 Data sources

A data source is a collection of related metrics. It's possible to have multiple data sources in one instance of Grafana, but it's also possible to have only one. The **Data Sources** page can be accessed by clicking **Configuration | Data Sources**, as displayed in *Figure 2.20*:

Figure 2.20: Data Sources

Real power comes from the ability to build custom data sources, **time series databases** (**TSDB**), panels and graphs. A TSDB is a database that holds time series data. Each row in TSDB represents a single metric value at a point in time (example: CPU load during a specific hour). Each column represents some metadata about this value (example: hostname). Grafana supports many different types of TSDBs out-of-the-box, including Graphite, InfluxDB and Prometheus; but you can also write custom ones if needed!

The following figure contains a list of sample data sources available to be configured in Grafana:

Figure 2.21: Add Data Source

Users

When you select **Configuration** I **Users**, the **Users** tab appears, where you can invite new users, set access levels for existing users, or delete users entirely, as shown in *Figure 2.22*:

Figure 2.22: Users Page Selection

In the following figure, clicking the **Submit** button opens a page where you can enter the email address and optional name of a new user:

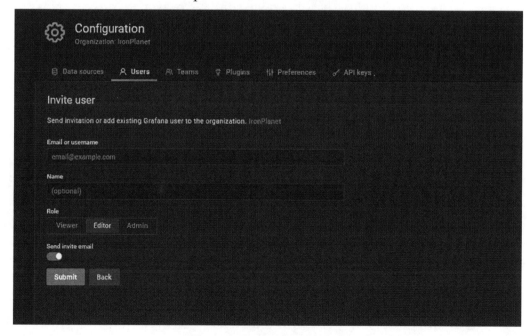

Figure 2.23: Invite New User

Click the **Invite** button to invite a new user with the role selected from **Viewer**, **Editor**, or **Admin**. If the **Send Invite Email** switch is activated, an invitation will be sent to the user's email address. Once you've completed this page, click on **Submit**. This will take you back to the list of users and indicate that your new user has been created successfully!

2.2.16 Teams

The **Teams** tab is adjacent to the **Users** tab and can be accessed via **Configuration** > **Teams**, as shown in *Figure 2.24*:

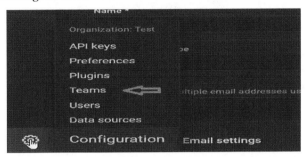

Figure 2.24: *Teams*

Teams is a relatively new concept in Grafana and is primarily used to configure UI settings for an entire group of users. Simply create a new team, and then add users to the team. Then, default UI settings can be established for all team members. A team can have its own home dashboard, user interface (UI) theme, and **Time Zone** settings. A team can share dashboards and data sources. This feature is useful if you manage Grafana for multiple groups within an organization, each of which desires a customized experience for its users. A team can be created by providing name and email ID details, as shown in *Figure 2.25*:

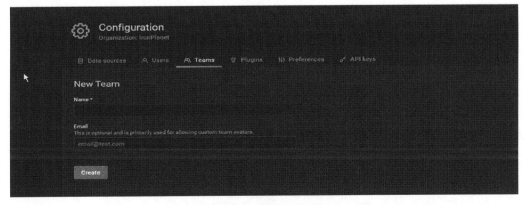

Figure 2.25: *Team Creation*

2.2.17 Plugins

The Grafana plugins page can be accessed from **Configuration | Plugins**, as shown in *Figure 2.26*:

Figure 2.26: *Configuration*

The Grafana plugin ecosystem has grown to include hundreds of plugins that add new functionality to the application. Some of these plugins have been developed by the Grafana team, while others are community-created. Grafana plugins are the best way to extend the capabilities of Grafana. With a growing number of plugins, you can add new features, customizations, and integrations to Grafana instances. The Plugins page is a resource page that lists all installed data sources and panel plugins.

2.2.18 Organization preferences

Preferences in Grafana are the foundational settings. They determine the time zone, default dashboard, and other aspects of the Grafana user interface. Organization preferences can be configured by clicking the button shown in *Figure 2.27*:

Figure 2.27: *Organization Preferences Selection*

Organization name, **UI Theme**, **Home** dashboard, **Timezone**, and **Week** start preferences can be configured as shown in *Figure 2.28*:

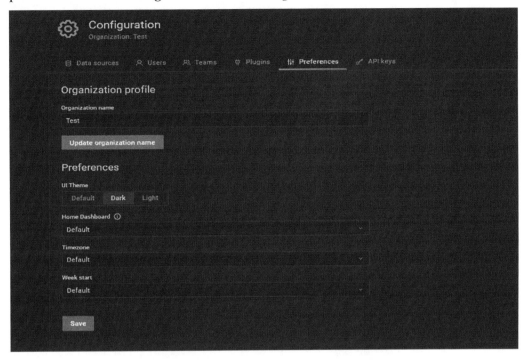

Figure 2.28: *Organization Profile Details*

There are four tiers of preferences that may be specified, which can be a bit of a muddle:

- **Server**: This affects all users on the Grafana server; a Grafana server administrator configures this.

- **Organization**: All users in an organization are affected; it is set by an administrator of the organization.

- **Team**: This affects all team members; it is set by an organization or team administrator; refer to teams and permissions for more information on these roles.

- **User account**: This affects the specific user; the user configures their own account.

The lowest level is always given priority. For example, if a user sets their theme to Light, their Grafana visualization will reflect that theme. Nothing on a higher level can change that. If the user is aware of the change and intends to make it, that's fantastic! However, if the user is a Server Admin who changed their user preferences a long time ago, they may have forgotten that they did so. If that Server Admin tries to change the theme at the server level, they will become frustrated because none of their changes have any visible effect.

2.2.19 User preferences

You are given the ability to manage certain parts of your user account using Grafana. These components include your username, email address, and password. You also have the ability to access key information on your account, such as the organizations and roles to which you have been assigned and the Grafana sessions that are associated with your account. User preferences can be set in Grafana by clicking the button shown in *Figure 2.29*:

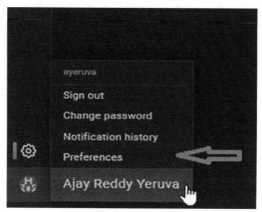

Figure 2.29: User Preferences

Profile details of a user, such as name, username and email; and user preferences like UI theme, home dashboard, time zone, and week start can be configured as shown in *Figure 2.30*:

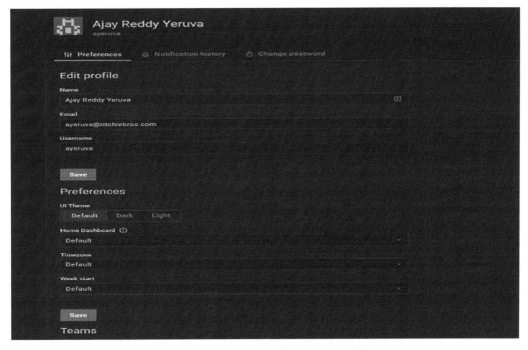

Figure 2.30: User Preferences Details

2.2.20 API keys

Grafana uses an API key for authentication. Administrators use API Keys on behalf of developers who create software applications that interact with Grafana through its REST API. An application with an API key will have access to all Grafana, so you must create API keys with the least privileged access possible and distribute them only to trusted developers. The API Keys page can be accessed by clicking the button shown in *Figure 2.31*:

Figure 2.31: API Keys Selection

2.2.21 Server admin

The creation of users and organizations, and the management of permissions falls under the purview of the Grafana server administrators. The **Server Admin** page can be accessed by clicking the button shown in *Figure 2.32*:

Figure 2.32: Server Admin Dropdown

2.2.22 Users

The **Users** tab under **Server Admin** is similar to the **Users** tab under **Configuration**; however, you have significantly more control in the **Server Admin** context. We can navigate to the **Users** tab by clicking the button shown in *Figure 2.33*:

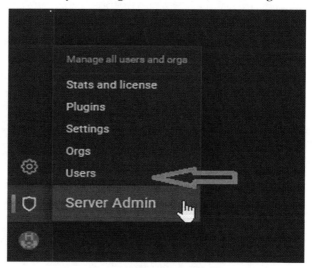

Figure 2.33: Users Selection

In addition to creating a new user, you can change their password, add them to different organizations, and log them out of Grafana entirely. Here is a brief overview of the various sections under the **Users** tab:

- **User Information**: Update a user's name, email, username, and password; buttons to delete/disable user
- **Permissions**: enable/disable admin permissions
- **Organizations**: Add users with specific roles to organizations
- **Sessions**: Review user login information, button to force log out of all devices

2.2.23 Orgs

Organizations can be used to create separate Grafana sites on a single server. To add or remove an organization, click the **Orgs** tab. The following figure contains the details of all organizations created:

Figure 2.34: Organizations Page

The steps to create, delete and use new organization are follows:

1. The **New org** button leads to a page where you can set the name of a new organization.
2. To delete an organization, click the cross button in red.
3. Organization must be populated with users before it can be accessed.

2.2.24 Settings

Server Admin | **Settings** displays the current server configuration settings as stored in the grafana.ini file. For more details of configuration settings in the grafana.ini file, visit **https://grafana.com/docs/installation/configuration**. The following figure contains sample details of the **Server Admin Settings** page:

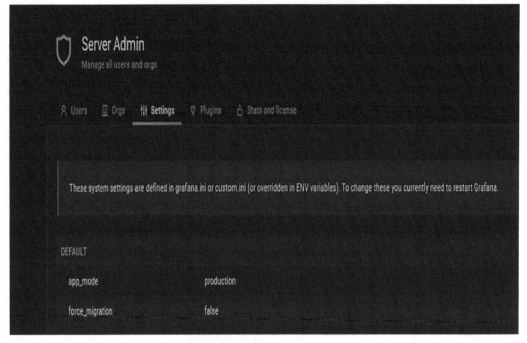

Figure 2.35: Settings Dropdown

2.2.25 Stats

If you would like to determine how many users, dashboards, and alerts have been created on your server, select the **Stats** tab on the **Server Admin** page to view a list of potentially interesting statistics, as displayed in *Figure 2.36*:

Figure 2.36: Stats and License

Conclusion

Our journey through the core components of the Grafana interface has come to an end. Evidently, we haven't even begun to scratch the surface, and we haven't made a dashboard or a panel yet! It is recommended that we conduct research on the dashboard's interface before beginning work on the actual dashboard panels.

Multiple choice questions

1. Which of the following view modes are supported in the Grafana dashboard?

    a. Normal

    b. Tv

    c. Kiosk

    d. All of the above

2. Is Snapshots creation possible for Grafana dashboards?

    a. Yes

    b. No

3. Explore lets you investigate logs of which of the following data sources?

    a. Elasticsearch

    b. InfluxDB

    c. Loki

    d. All of the above

Answers

1. d

2. a

3. d

Join our book's Discord space

Join the book's Discord Workspace for Latest updates, Offers, Tech happenings around the world, New Release and Sessions with the Authors:

https://discord.bpbonline.com

CHAPTER 3
An Introduction to the Graph Panel

Introduction

This chapter will provide an overview of the Grafana native plugin panel, known simply as the Time Series Graph panel. The Grafana Graph Panel is a powerful and flexible way to display and interact with your monitoring data. You can use it standalone or combine it with the other Grafana panels to build dashboards for your needs. It comes with several out-of-the-box features. It is designed to allow easily accessible at-a-glance summaries of time series data.

Structure

This chapter will cover the following topics:

- Exploring the data display window
- Inputting query to produce a data set
- Modifying the chart under the Panel menu
- Monitoring with the Alert tab

Objectives

This chapter will provide a tour of Time Series Graph panel of the Grafana application. It will give you an overview of the Graph panel, and it will also provide insights into how to create and connect a data source with Graph panel and customize the Grafana panel settings.

3.1 Technical requirements

Since Grafana is a web-based application, you'll need to run a few commands to get it up and running. The following are the technical requirements and prerequisites for installing and running Grafana v9.0:

- Knowledge of the command shell
- Install Grafana on the machine of your choice using a terminal application or an SSH
- Java 8 or higher
- Python 3.5 or later
- Git CLI tool
- Docker
- Docker-Compose

Optionally, you'll be able to log in as an administrator using the command line to set up and run Grafana.

3.2 Touring the Graph Panel

The user interface of the Graph panel can be loosely divided into three primary functional areas:

- **Panel display**: Time-selection widget and preview window
- **Data configuration**: Information retrieval, data wrangling, and notification
- **Display settings**: Panel options, legend, tooltip, axis, graph styles, standard options, value mappings, data links, and thresholds

Time series graph panel is shown in *Figure 3.1*:

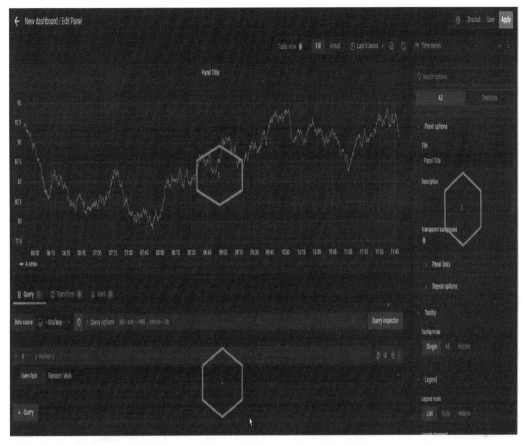

Figure 3.1: *Timeseries Graph Panel Modify View*

In the upcoming sections, we'll examine these characteristics in greater detail. Let's start with the **Query** tab and understand how to use it to generate graphed data. Next, we'll look at how a panel's title and other common display aspects can be adjusted, and how different display settings affect the appearance of the graph. Finally, we'll look at how the **Alert** tab may be used to set up threshold monitoring rules that, if exceeded, will result in notifications being sent to the user.

3.2.1 Creating a simple Data Source

Data sources refer to the Grafana add-ons that feed information into the visualization tools. Having such a data source is a given if you plan on creating a graph panel.

1. Start **Page Dashboard** | **Choose Settings** | **Data Sources**.

2. Choose the option + **Data Source**.

3. Select **Test Data DB** from the **Other** options.

4. Verify that on is selected as the default setting.

5. Make sure the data source is active by clicking **Save & Test**.

As can be seen in *Figure 3.2*, you have just finished creating your first data source:

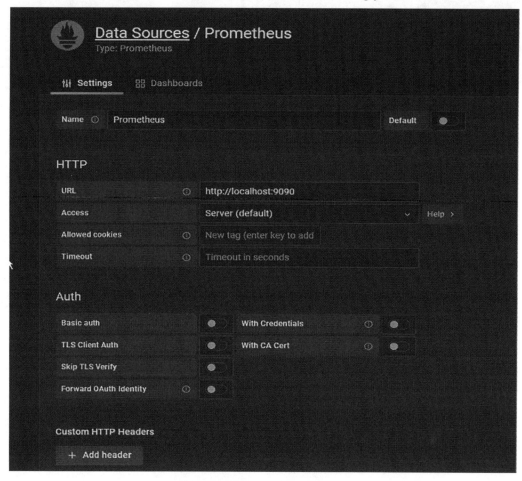

Figure 3.2: *Data Source Creation*

3.2.2 Creating a Graph Panel

A Graph panel can be made with the help of the following steps:

1. **Home Dashboard | New Dashboard**.

2. To add a new panel, simply click the plus sign next to the new panel.

3. To store the current dashboard for later use, click the **Save Dashboard** button in the top right. Save your dashboards on a regular basis.

4. To store the panel modifications, click the **Apply** button.

5. To make changes to a panel, click the **Panel Title** dropdown, and then click **Edit**.

Following this quick exercise, you should have something resembling what is depicted in *Figure 3.3*:

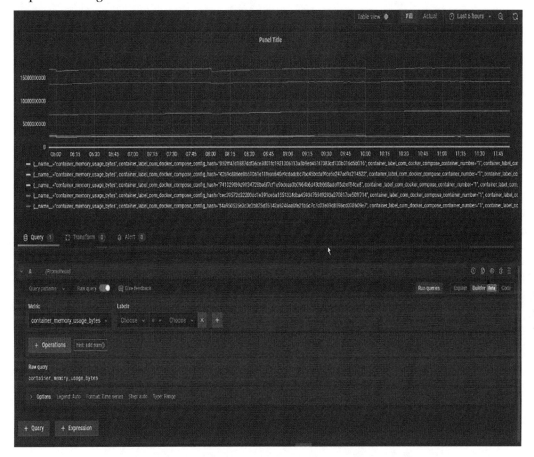

Figure 3.3: Query Data from Data Source

3.3 Generating data series in the Query tab

In the **Query** menu, we will choose a data source for the queries used by the panel. In addition to providing a streamlined query interface for Grafana users, data source plugins are also responsible for feeding the returned data into the Grafana 9 unified data model, which is used by many panels. Most Grafana users will discover that even with a simplified query UI, they are still capable of making rather intricate searches. The data source query interface will not protect you against malicious queries, so if you insist on using native queries, talk to your database administrator about creating a limited user account just for your Grafana data sources.

Five key features of the **Query** tab are shown in *Figure 3.4*:

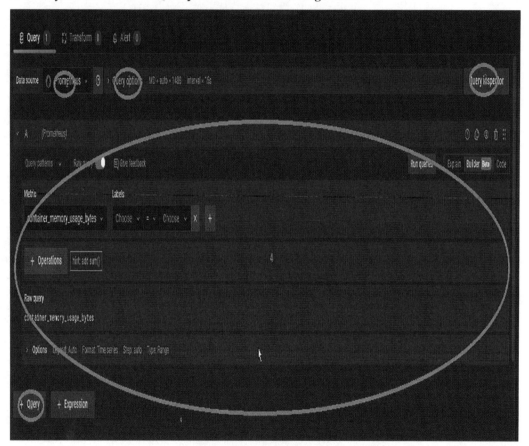

Figure 3.4: Query Tab Parts

3.3.1 What is a query?

A query is a means for retrieving a data series for the purpose of visual display on the panel. Multiple searches can be extracted from a single data source or a combination of data sources using the **Query** tab. There's the possibility of citing information from other panels as well. Grafana will translate the tab's searches into API calls to the data source server, retrieve the data in an internal structure called a data frame, and then show some or all of it based on the current time period; all of this is controlled by the data source plugin. To focus on the various components of the graph panel interface, we will initially only use the existing Prometheus DB as our data source.

3.3.2 Query tab features

Key elements identified in **Query** tabs parts are listed as follows:

- **Data source menu**: Panel data sources are chosen from the Data source menu. Select **Mixed** if you'd like to plot information from more than one source on the same graph. When you add queries, you'll be able to designate their data source.

- **Query options**: The panel's choices for manipulating the presentation of time series data are located here. Setting the max data points option limits the number of data points shown, even if the time range is quite large. By specifying a minimum interval, you can tell Grafana how often it should sample the information in the query to figure out how small a time range to display using a single data point. When working with large time ranges, Grafana's time series panels benefit greatly from having their values set to the frequency of each data point.

- **Query inspector button**: By clicking the Query inspector button, you can see the whole query that Grafana is sending to the API in a text terminal. Having a more efficient query can greatly enhance the responsiveness of a Grafana dashboard, especially one with multiple panels.

- **Query**: A data set is created primarily based on the query. The information utilized to construct it may allow more than one component. You can produce test data in several ways with the Prometheus DB data source, by choosing a scenario from a drop-down menu.

- **Query controls**: By dragging the query up or down with the mouse, you can rearrange the shown data sets in a new order.

- **Duplicate query**: Since we already have a question from when we made the panel, let's make another one and see how it looks:

  o To access information from Prometheus DB, choose it from the list of available sources.

  o To create a duplicate query, as shown in *Figure 3.5*, click on the corresponding icon. Two queries using container memory usage bytes metrics should appear.

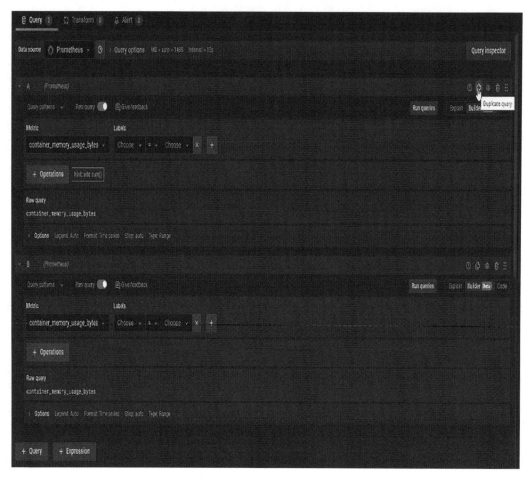

Figure 3.5: Duplicate Query

- **Query visibility toggle**: You can quickly toggle query visibility for your entire company with the new Grafana Query Visibility Toggle. This is helpful in situations where some questions may contain confidential information that isn't relevant to all employees.

- **Delete Query**: If you want to get rid of a panel from your dashboard in Grafana, you can do so with the panel delete query.

- **+ Query button**: After activating this functionality, you can run additional queries in the Grafana panel from the same or alternative data sources. See *Figure 3.4* for an explanation of how these components collaborate to give you control over a data source query and the resulting data series.

3.4 Editing the Graph in the Panel tab

Panel options, tooltip, legend, graph styles, axis, standard options, data links, value mappings, and thresholds are useful settings that can be customized in the edit panel view.

3.4.1 Panel options

Panel Options allows the creation of a graph panel with a specific layout, as shown in *Figure 3.6*. The panel **Title** and **Description** details can be provided in the **Panel** options. Transport background feature is another panel option that can be enabled or disabled:

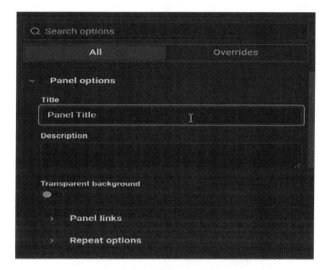

Figure 3.6: *Panel Options*

3.4.2 Tooltip

Grafana has tooltips that appear when you move the mouse over the visualization:

- Single: Only the selected series in the visualization will be displayed in the hover tooltip.
- All: Whenever you hover over a series in the visualization, a tooltip will appear with further information about it. Grafana makes the series you are now viewing in the tooltip stand out in bold.
- Hidden: Don't show the help text whenever you hover over a visualization element.

Figure 3.7 demonstrates the tooltip choices that govern the information overlay that shows when you hover over data points in the graph:

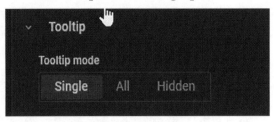

Figure 3.7: *Tooltip*

3.4.3 Legend

To conceal the legend, deselect the **Show** option. If it is displayed, you have the option of seeing it as a table of values by selecting the **Table** option. Using the **Hide empty** option, you can hide series that have no values from the legend. *Figure 3.8* displays the options for the legend:

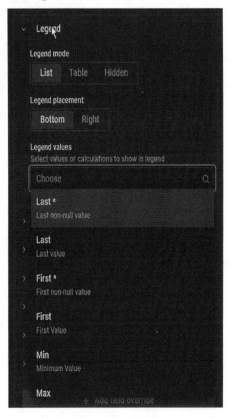

Figure 3.8: *Legend*

3.4.5 Graph styles

The graph's attributes can be adjusted via the display style:

- **Bar**: Show data in a bar graph format
- **Lines**: Show data as a line chart
- **Points**: Represent numerical values with points

Figure 3.9 demonstrates how the graph's attributes can be adjusted via the display style:

Figure 3.9: *Graph Styles*

3.4.6 Axis

You can also hide the axis by deselecting the axis from **Show Axis**. You can use thresholds to make it more obvious when a graph reaches a certain point by drawing in arbitrary lines or sections. *Figure 3.10* demonstrates how axis settings can be seen and altered:

Figure 3.10: Axis

3.4.7 Standard options

You can modify your data visualizations using the standard options available to you. Customizations you make to Grafana's presentation settings (through options and overrides) have no effect on the underlying data. Any series or columns affected by a setting's modification are updated automatically. If you set the unit to %, for instance, all numerical fields will show their values in that format. *Figure 3.11* demonstrates how standard options settings may be seen and altered:

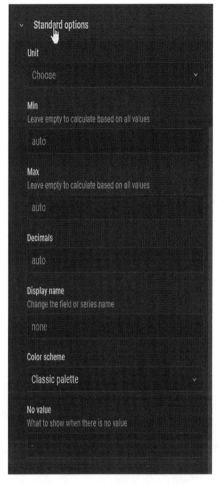

Figure 3.11*: Standard Options*

3.4.8 Data links

Panel data links allow you to create a graph panel for a query that returns structured data, as shown in *Figure 3.12*:

Figure 3.12*: Data Links*

3.4.9 Value mappings

Panel value mappings control how Grafana maps a particular data source onto a graph panel. For example, we can map the average response time of a group of servers to the data points on a graph. Mapping values like this makes it easy to spot anomalies and patterns in the data, as shown in *Figure 3.13*:

Figure 3.13: *Value Mappings*

3.4.10 Thresholds

Depending on the circumstances you choose, thresholds will change the value of text color or the backdrop color. *Figure 3.14* depicts the two possible approaches to define thresholds:

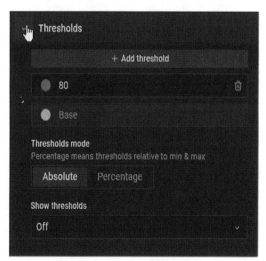

Figure 3.14: *Thresholds*

Two possible approaches to define thresholds are as follows.

- The definition of an absolute threshold is a number, such as 80 on a scale of 1 to 150.

- Values of a certain percentage, such as 80%, are typically expressed in relation to a minimum or maximum.

3.5 Monitoring with the Alert tab

Click on the **Create Alert** button in the **Graph** panel to take a look inside an alert. *Figure 3.15* shows a newly created alert:

Figure 3.15: *Configuring Alerts*

3.5.1 Rule

An alert rule can be broken down into two basic settings: the rule name and an evaluation period. The rule **name** is used by Grafana to keep track of each rule so that it can continuously check each alert that's spread over every dashboard for a triggering event. As you understood in the previous chapter, Alerts are managed in the **Alert Rules** tab, which can be found on the Alerting page. Once you have configured the **Alerts**, you'll find it much easier to manage them from Alerting page, rather than clicking through many dashboards and panels.

3.5.2 Conditions

Thresholds are set in the Conditions group. Rather than simply triggering it on a single value, aggregation is done over a time window, for examples, 2m, 5m. So an alert condition can represent a more qualitative measure than the simple quantitative measure of a threshold. The alert enters the Pending state after a condition is broken. If the specified condition persists for the specified period, the alert changes to the Firing state; otherwise, it reverts to the Normal state.

3.5.3 No data and error handling

In this section, you'll learn to determine whether data loss or an error should trigger an alert or whether the system should wait it out.

Take the following steps to configure an alert for situations where there is no data:

1. Select the panel you want to monitor for data.
2. Click on the **Alert** tab in the panel.
3. Configure the alert rule and set the **No Data** option to the desired value (for example, **5m**).
4. Choose the notification channel(s) for the alert.

Take the following steps to configure an alert for situations where there are errors:

1. Create an alert rule for the dashboard or panel where the error is occurring.
2. Set the alert condition to be triggered when an error occurs (for example, a specific error message).
3. Choose the notification channel(s) for the alert.

When the alert condition is met (that is, no data for the specified time period or an error occurs), Grafana will trigger the configured notification channel(s).

3.5.4 Notifications

Once the alert has been triggered, the Notifications group is where you determine what actions Grafana should take. Based on your configured notification channels, you can send the alert to one or more channels with the specified message.

Conclusion

Our journey through the core components of the Grafana Graph panel like Panel settings, Query Inspector button, Data Source dropdown, Alerting tab, etc., has come to an end. It is recommended that you play with connecting different data sources in different Grafana panels and start getting more familiar with distinct data visualizations.

In the next chapter, we will explore how a data source can be connected in Grafana and visualize data.

Multiple choice questions

1. Can we connect multiple data sources in a Grafana panel?

   a. Yes

   b. No

2. What style[s] are supported in Grafana panel?

   a. Lines

   b. Bars

   c. Points

   d. All of the above

3. Alerting can be configured in Grafana panel settings?

   a. Yes

   b. No

Answers

1. a

2. d

3. a

Join our book's Discord space

Join the book's Discord Workspace for Latest updates, Offers, Tech happenings around the world, New Release and Sessions with the Authors:

https://discord.bpbonline.com

CHAPTER 4
Connecting Grafana to a Data Source

Introduction

In this chapter, we will focus on implementing the skills we gained from the previous chapters. We will be utilizing real data sets, wherever applicable for visualization and analysis, which will give you a glimpse of real-world scenarios. It will help in building a dashboard that can be expected in actual production environments. As you may have realized, data is the building block for Grafana, and in this chapter, we will configure a live database that will further serve the purpose to create dashboards by providing real web service data. We will use the explorer tool to visualize the different kinds of metrics available by fetching data into Grafana as a data source.

Structure

In this chapter, we will learn the following:

- Installing the Prometheus Server
- Exploring Prometheus
- Querying the Prometheus data
- Detecting trends using aggregations
- Limitations of the Data source

Objectives

This chapter will provide information on how to connect data source to Grafana. We will be leveraging Prometheus to connect as data source, exploring how to visualize data, and understanding how to query the data source to get customized metrics and limitations associated with the data source.

4.1 Technical requirements

Apart from the installations completed so far, we will install Prometheus as a data source in this section. The following are the technical requirements for this chapter:

- Docker
- Docker-Compose
- Prometheus
- Grafana

4.2 Installing the Prometheus server

As a first step, we have to install Prometheus server so that real data can be captured as input data source for Grafana. Prometheus was built at SoundCloud in 2012; it is an open-source monitoring tool that also has an alerting mechanism. In 2016, Prometheus was the second project to be hosted after Kubernetes; after it joined Cloud Native Computing Foundation, all data collected by Prometheus is stored as time-series data. Prometheus is directly available as a first-class data source plugin in Grafana.

4.2.1 Installing Prometheus from Docker

First, we have to start Prometheus from Docker; once successfully completed, we will point it to the configuration file that is in our local folder location. To start with, create a file named *prometheus.yml* with the following details, and save it in your local directory as *ch4/prometheus*:

```
global:

scrape_interval: 15s # The target to fetch data is set for 15 seconds.

# Alerts or time series can be embedded with these labels when contacting external system

external_labels:
```

```
monitor: 'codelab-monitor'


# Config has one endpoint to fetch and it is Prometheus

scrape_configs:

#'job=<<job_name>>' label is embedded for job name to timeseries scraping

  - job_name: 'prometheus'
```

#For every 5 seconds, fetch targets and override the default set at global level

```
  scrape_interval: 5s


static_configs:

  - targets: ['localhost:9090']
```

Now we have the required basic *.yml* created. However, you are also advised to develop a better understanding about the Prometheus file format by visiting the official Prometheus website at **https://prometheus.io/docs/prometheus/latest/ configuration/configuration/**.

#creating configuration-file. Here we are working with a relatively simple file with a couple of instructions. Now, perform the following steps:

1. Set Scrape Interval to instruct how frequently Prometheus should pull the data; let's set the interval to 15 seconds.

2. Configure a job named Prometheus that can pull data from itself every 5 seconds. Here, the Target server is situated at localhost:9090.

3. The docker-**compose.yml** file should be created (downloadable file is also available from the GitHub repository of this book).

Creating docker compose file :

```
version: '3'

services:

 grafana:

 image: "grafana/grafana:${GRAF_TAG-latest}"

 ports:

 - "3000:3000"
```

```
volumes:

- "${PWD-.}/grafana:/var/lib/grafana"


prometheus:

image: "prom/prometheus:${PROM_TAG-latest}"

ports:

- "9090:9090"

volumes:

- "${PWD-.}/prometheus:/etc/prometheus"
```

The preceding docker compose file does the following:

- Starts a Grafana container and exposes its default port at 3000
- Starts a Prometheus container and exposes its default port at 9090
- Maps the **$PWD/prometheus** local directory to **/etc/prometheus** in the prometheus container

This is so that we can manage the Prometheus configuration file from outside the container. $PWD is a shell variable describing the working directory.

- The Docker Compose file is set up to start the Grafana container and then expose default port at *3000*.
- Starts the prometheus container and exposes the default port at *9090*.
- Maps the **$PWD/prometheus** local directory to **/etc/prometheus** in the **prometheus** container. This is done so that the Prometheus configuration file can be handled outside the container; here, *$PWD* is a shell variable describing the working directory.

Run the following command to start both containers:

```
> docker-compose up -d
```

Both Grafana and Prometheus containers will start in their own network so that they can communicate by executing the **docker-compose** command. If successfully executed, the following output should be displayed:

```
Starting ch4_prometheus_1 ... done

Starting ch4_grafana_1 ... done
```

Now we have to confirm that Prometheus is running correctly; in your web browser, enter http://localhost:9090/targets, and you will see a screen as shown in the following figure:

Figure 4.1: *Prometheus from web browser*

With this, we have both Grafana and Prometheus running.

4.2.2 Configuring the Prometheus data source

So far, we know that from the **docker-compose.yml** file, Prometheus will fetch data every 5 seconds, and the server host is set to **localhost** at port **9090**. Now we will set up a new data source for Prometheus:

1. In Grafana, using the left side bar, go to Configuration then click on **Data Sources**.

2. Here, you will add new Prometheus data source by filling the following information:

    ● Name: Prometheus

    ● URL: http://localhost:9090

    ● Access: Browser

3. Now, click **Save & Test**.

Now, you will have a new data source, and the screen should look like the following:

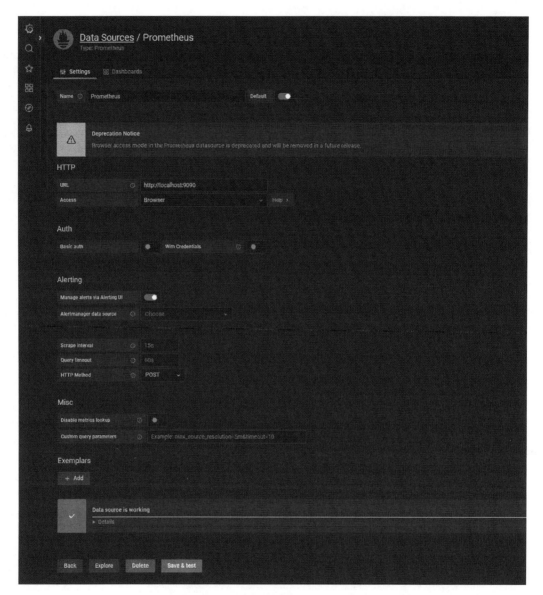

Figure 4.2: Configuring Prometheus data source in Grafana

With this, we have data source setup completed.

4.3 Exploring Prometheus

Now that data Prometheus source is set up, we have to decide what kind of data we would like to fetch. With the configuration we have done, we can get internal server metrics and store them in the Prometheus database. Let us get into the specifics.

4.3.1 Using Explore for investigation

You can start the Explorer tool by selecting it from the left-hand side of the menu. Explorer includes plugins for both **Graph and Table**, and both of them refer to the same data source. Ensure that you select data source as Prometheus from the dropdown, and then from the **Metrics** menu, select **up** to select metric data series. To begin with, this is one of the basic metrics to visualize as it shows 1 when the server is up and 0 when the server is down. The following screenshot indicates that the Prometheus server is up:

Figure 4.3: Prometheus server status

The graph shows a single series with a value of 1, and the table contains 1 in the **Value #A** field. You should also take note of the series label. In this case, it refers to the *up* metric, tagged with `localhost:9090` for the instance value and **prometheus** for the job value. Going back to the configuration file, we can see where the job label comes from:

In the previous graph, the value '1' is displayed because that is the numeric value the table holds. The 'job' label can be traced back to the configuration file, as follows:

```
# As shown below, for the timeseries the job name is appended as `job=`

job_name: 'prometheus'
```

Let us understand how Grafana knows about the data in Metrics drop-down menu and from where this metric is derived.

For the time interval of every 5 seconds, Prometheus is configured to send HTTP requests to the *http://localhost:9090/metrics* endpoint.

If you open this link in the browser, you will see metrics data populated.

The initial couple of lines would look as follows:

```
# HELP go_gc_duration_seconds will give summary related to GC initiation
duration,    TYPE    go_gc_duration_seconds    summary    go_gc_duration_
seconds{quantile="0"} 7.057e-06  go_gc_duration_seconds{quantile="0.25"}
1.2362e-05    go_gc_duration_seconds{quantile="0.5"}    2.7312e-05    go_
gc_duration_seconds{quantile="0.75"}    0.000259168    go_gc_duration_
seconds{quantile="1"} 0.001861891 go_gc_duration_seconds_sum 0.006119489
go_gc_duration_seconds_count 36

# HELP go_goroutines will give total goroutines which currently exist,
TYPE go_goroutines gauge

go_goroutines 39

# HELP go_info will provide details related to environment Go, TYPE go_
info gauge

go_info{version="go1.13.1"} 1

...
```

Metrics are a way to organize, store and retrieve data as key-value pairs. Some metrics are very simple and just consist of a value property and a name for the metric itself. Other times, there will be more information included in the key-value pair that helps qualify the result or makes it easier to compare against other metrics.

This page of data is parsed, timestamped, and stored in the Prometheus database. When you launch the Explore tool in Grafana, the Prometheus data source plug makes a service discovery query to find out what metrics are available; and based on the response, it builds a convenient menu for you.

Explore allows you to make visualizations out of your Prometheus metrics. It does this by making a service discovery query and builds a comfortable menu to choose from based on the response. We will now check how the **go_gc_duration_seconds** metric is shown in **Explore**. From the dropdown, select go, which refers to the prefix of the metric name called namespace. Then, select **gc_duration_seconds** from the submenu to visualize graph:

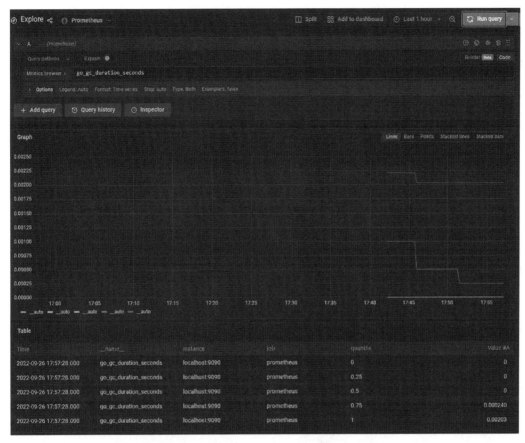

Figure 4.4: *Prometheus metrics visualization*

As you can see, all series names include quantile, instance and job.

4.3.2 Configuring Grafana metrics

Now that we have visualized metrics in Prometheus, we will look at how we can get similar visualization in Grafana. For this to happen, we have to link Grafana and Prometheus over the same network, and this is the reason why it was set as a dual container app in the Docker Compose, which shares the same network and DNS details. We have to modify **scrape_configs** in the **prometheus.yml** file to fetch metrics from the Grafana server (the downloadable file is also available in the GitHub repository of this book):

scrape_configs:

 # `job=` label is embedded as job name to timeseries fetched from this config.

- job_name: 'prometheus'

```
# For every 5 seconds, fetch targets and override the default set at
global level

scrape_interval: 5s


static_configs:

- targets: ['localhost:9090']

- job_name: 'grafana'


# For every 5 seconds, fetch targets and override the default set at
global level

scrape_interval: 5s


static_configs:

- targets: ['grafana:3000']
```

Here, we force the re-read of the configuration file on Prometheus container by sending HUP signal. In order to do that, execute the following command:

docker-compose kill -s HUP prometheus

Using the web browser, go to http://localhost:9090/targets to ensure that Grafana is set as the target:

Figure 4.5: Grafana set as target in Prometheus

4.4 Querying the Prometheus data source

It is very important to understand how querying works in Prometheus, which uses **PromQL** as the query language. Before diving into the querying time-series database of Prometheus, let us take a look at more common and traditional database queries like MYSQL. A standard basic query in MYSQL would be as follows, which fetches field data in a specified table that matches the criteria:

```
SELECT some fields
FROM some table
WHERE fields match some criteria
```

Now let us look into a standard query in a time-series database, which usually consists of three different types of information, like Timestamp, Metric Value and Key-value pairs for data characterization as shown below. Even though time-series databases can store data differently, these three types of information are usually found in some form:

```
SELECT metric
FROM some data store
WHERE metric tags match some criteria
AND in some time range
```

4.4.1 Typing in a metrics query

Now when we look into the visualization, we see both Grafana and Prometheus appear, as shown in the following image:

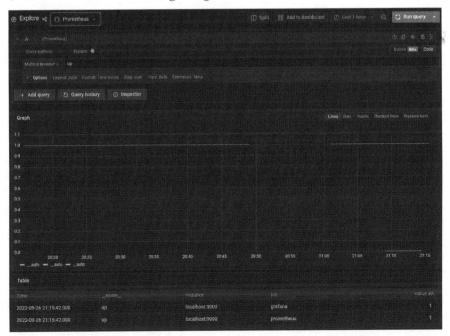

Figure 4.6: Prometheus and Grafana metrics in visualization

Let us modify the query to only fetch data from Grafana:

1. You will get a helping hand by a data source plugin that is intelligent to suggest the syntax of PromQL; start by typing the { character in the Metrics text field, and you will instantly notice the suggestion to complete brace and a label key selection option from the pop-up menu.

Figure 4.7: PromQL query suggestion

2. Enter **job=** inside braces.

3. We want to select Grafana as a job parameter; press shift key, and you will be presented with possible options; select Grafana from the list:

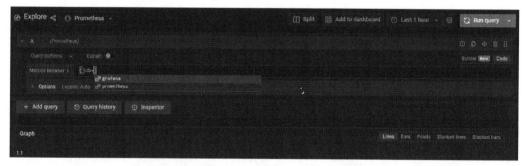

Figure 4.8: Adding Grafana as job parameter

4. To execute the query, click on **Run Query**, which is in blue color.

5. Now you will have metric from Grafana for single data series. Grafana has many metrics to visualize; we will now try to query a few of them.

4.4.2 Querying for process metrics

Now, we will query Grafana for the *go* routines, which will give us an indication of the load on the Grafana server. Here, we are interested to get data only from Grafana and not from Prometheus. Also, in the **Metrics browser** menu refer any **go** namespace, as shown in the following figure:

Figure 4.9: Querying Grafana for go routine

Another major metric to visualize is memory consumption. It indicates how servers are performing and any issue like Out of Memory error will impact the overall health. Type **process_resident_memory_bytes** in Metrics to visualize the time-series data, and you can also include alerts to indicate when memory consumption is above a threshold:

Figure 4.10: Querying Grafana for memory utilization

4.5 Detecting trends with aggregations

Now, let us analyze the web service metric as the next step. In **Metrics browser** section, type **grafana_http_request_duration_seconds_count** to visualize how many requests are received. As you see, there are many requests, and all of them cannot be visualized at the same time as they will superimpose on each other, as shown in the following figure:

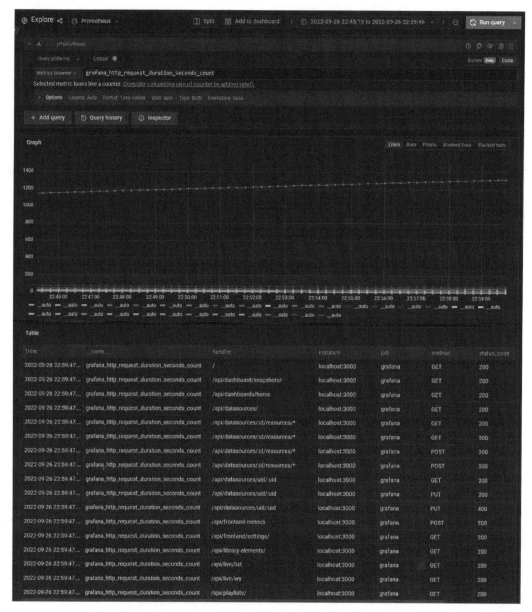

Figure 4.11: *Multiple metrics superimposing in visualization*

4.5.1 Applying aggregations to our query data

To solve the problem of multiple time series data superimposing and impacting visualization, **aggregation** is used. Here, we can instruct Prometheus to implement a function of aggregation *sum* to get the desired result; you can pass **sum** in parentheses as part of **PromQL** syntax, as shown in the following figure:

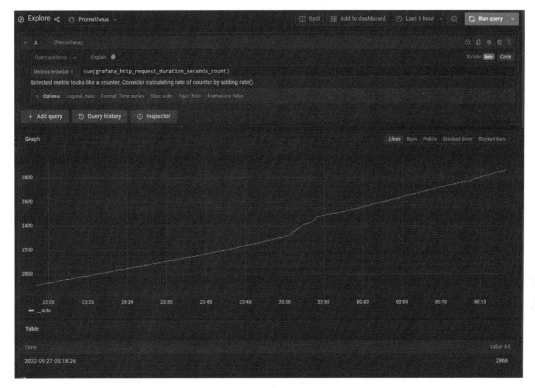

Figure 4.12: *Querying Grafana for sum*

Here, **sum** is taken as an argument, and it creates a new data series by summing up the values requested and is sent back to Grafana for visualization. PromQL is even more effective when you know how to combine multiple aggregations together and also combine them with other results to get the desired output.

But there is another problem, which is monotonic values; if you remember, we looked into **go_goroutines** as a metric and *TYPE* was a metadata string as a suffix. The **go_goroutines** metric had *gauge* at the end as shown below:

```
# HELP "go_goroutines" Total Number of goroutines which exist. & TYPE
go_goroutines gauge

go_goroutines 33
```

If you check for the same metadata for the *http_request_total*, then you will see a word: **counter**:

```
# HELP http_request_total http request counter & TYPE http_request_total
counter
```

...

Prometheus offers two distinct metrics types: *gauge* and *counter*. All time series databases may not distinguish between numerical metrics, but Prometheus does; in some way, it needs to have this differentiation between *counter* and *gauge*.

A *gauge* is a status indicator within an application, which is used to show the current value of a measure. On the other hand, an indicator typically shows a single moment in time. A gauge is similar to an air conditioner; it can fluctuate over time as new value(s) are received. A *counter* metric is among the most commonly used metrics in Prometheus and it is simply a running total value that increments by a positive amount similar to a rainfall gauge. Prometheus also has two other metric types which you can explore further, that is *histogram* and *summary*.

So, why don't we check out the rate? Unfortunately, if you try to treat the rate as a function call that you can just drop the query into, you will run into issues because it contains an aggregation. We're going to discuss issues with aggregation in the next section. For now, we'll just select a single data series and run a rate.

So, what about the rate? Is it worth utilizing it? Well, rate cannot be treated as a function that can be directly called from the query; it will result in more issues as it consists of aggregation. Issues related to aggregation is a different topic and an important one; we will discuss issues with aggregation in the next section. Let us run rate by selecting a single data series and check the outcome:

1. Select Metrics | http | http_request_total.
2. Click on the handler column cell containing */search/* in the table.
3. Click on the method column cell containing *GET*.
4. Click on the '+' button to add an additional query.
5. Also click on any handler column cell in the table.
6. Type irate(*irate{grafana_http_request_duration_seconds_ count{handler="/api/search/",method="GET"} [5m]})* into the second query.

Now the graph will look something like this:

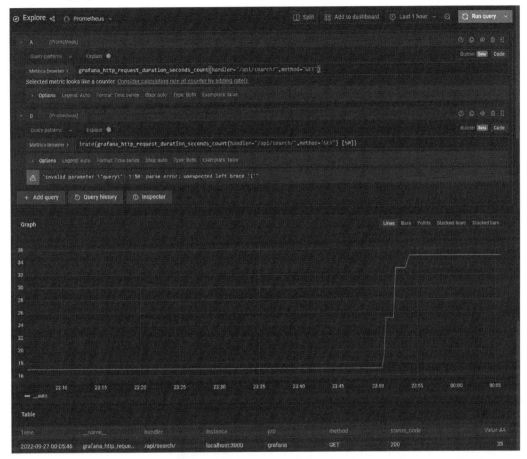

Figure 4.13: *Querying Grafana for irate*

We used the Prometheus *irate* (**instant rate**) function to find the rate that **grafana_http_request_duration_seconds_count** increased over a period of 5 minutes. *irate* was used instead of *rate* since value change was very quick, but both of them calculate in a similar manner. If you pay attention, you will realize that as the request total increased the, rate also increased momentarily.

PromQL has a number of functions and aggregations available, and what we saw is just a glimpse of it. Now, let's look at some of the aggregations captured from the Prometheus official documentation:

- *sum:* Calculates the sum of value on dimensions
- *max:* Selects the maximum value on dimensions
- *min:* Selects the minimum value on dimensions
- *avg:* Calculates the average value on dimensions
- *count:* Calculates the total number of elements present in the vector
- *count_values:* Calculates the total number of elements present with the same value
- *bottomk:* The smallest value of k elements by sample value
- *stddev:* Calculates the population standard deviation value on dimensions
- *stdvar:* Calculates the population standard variance value on dimensions
- *quantile:* Calculates the ϕ quantile ($0 \le \phi \le 1$) value over dimensions
- *topk:* The largest value of k elements by sample value

The functions list will be longer, so it is advised to refer to the documentation of Prometheus or the data source you are using for better understanding.

4.6 Limitations of data source

It is natural to think that we can query and visualize any metric we desire as PromQL is so effective. However, this comes with its own limitations based on data or the data source. It is your moral responsibility to fetch and visualize data that is accurate and not manipulated as the graph will be accessed by many users, and they will make decisions based on the Grafana dashboard. We will look at the limitations in detail in this section.

4.6.1 Querying for series aggregations

Before implementing any changes to the data, it is important to think thoroughly whether we can actually aggregate the data to get the desired output. Let's take an example of the following Grafana metrics endpoint page:

```
# HELP go_gc_duration_seconds will give summary related to GC initiation
duration, TYPE go_gc_duration_seconds summary

go_gc_duration_seconds{quantile="0"}      9.174e-06      go_gc_duration_
seconds{quantile="0.25"}1.3627e-05go_gc_duration_seconds{quantile="0.5"}
2.2022e-05  go_gc_duration_seconds{quantile="0.75"}  9.0476e-05  go_gc_
duration_seconds{quantile="1"} 0.000340337
```

go_gc_duration_seconds_sum 0.001069315

go_gc_duration_seconds_count 13

A summary is a type of Prometheus metric that refers to **go_gc_duration_seconds**, and it is a built-in metric type which is a pre-aggregated metric that can be visualized directly. It contains a histogram with the sum of all values, five quantiles (0%, 25%, 50%, 75%, and 100%) and the count. The summary should not be calculated over time because it does not contain any timestamp information. Also, when you refer to data in native condition (raw, unaggregated), you should also understand the limitations of the corresponding data source. To explain this further, we can calculate an aggregation *rate* in Prometheus as it increases in value monotonically.

It is advised to refer to the documentation of the specific data source you are using to get a good understanding of the multiple aggregation query possibilities as there could be limitations to what you can achieve. Also, it is very important to take the time to understand what you are measuring and what it means. It's also important that the aggregation of your metric makes sense for the goal you are trying to measure. Sometimes you will need to look at multiple metrics combined together to get an overall picture of performance, or a single metric that tells a story about how your application is doing.

4.6.2 Querying for time aggregations

When performing any time aggregations, it is important to consider the time interval of your data source. Prometheus identifies certain points within a time interval that you may be unaware of, and these could severely impact the accuracy of your aggregation. As an example, when a thresholding function is applied over a 15-minute interval to one data point that only exists for 10 minutes within that interval (all other data points exist for 15 minutes), the first 10-minute point is ignored entirely. You can avoid this issue by adjusting the thresholding function so that it is performed over multiple intervals or by setting a maximum amount of time for which you want to allow for latency (and confidence).

Another important factor to consider when working with time-based aggregations is choosing the correct interval. Choosing too big an interval will smooth out your data and make trends difficult to detect. Too small an interval, on the other hand, can result in anomalous values that skew results or return errors.

The Grafana display aggregation is a sophisticated algorithm that is used to determine which data points to show on the screen. If there are more data points than pixels on the screen, some of them need to be discarded. Applying a fixed interval risks this issue occurring if the interval is very small when compared to the time frame, for example, a 1-hour interval for a 1-year data set will ignore several data points and will surely impact the performance; it is really important to not do this as a rule of thumb.

Grafana does provide an option to calculate the time interval variable automatically, and it can be used instead of any fixed interval. You can achieve this by utilizing **$__interval** instead of the fixed time interval. To know more about how Grafana handles data display across time, refer to the Grafana documentation.

Any example query for time interval variable:

```
Before : irate(http_request_total{"condition"}[15m])
```

```
After: irate(http_request_total{"condition"}[$__interval])
```

Conclusion

We have come to the end of the introduction to data sources chapter, and we have learnt how to connect Grafana to a data source successfully and also create queries for them. As a treat, now go to **Configuration | Data sources**; you will be able to edit data source Prometheus configuration, you will see an additional tab named **Dashboards**. Here, you will see dashboards that work for Prometheus data source; you can import values to Grafana metrics dashboard to get it loaded with multiple pre-configured Graphs. Feel free to open these graphs and edit the queries associated; this will give you an understanding of how the data was fetched and visualized and will help you create better queries. It is recommended to refer to a pre-built dashboard from the community and analyze the logic and queries behind it to fast track your Grafana knowledge, and it is one of the best aspects of Grafana where communities can help each other by collaborating.

In the next chapter, we will explore how we can visualize data on the Graph panel.

Multiple choice questions

1. Is Prometheus a pre-configured data source in Grafana?

   a. Yes

   b. No

2. Aggregation *count_values* is used for which of the following?

   a. Counting different elements with the different value

   b. Counting different elements with the same value

   c. Counting elements with the different value

   d. Counting elements with the same value

3. Can you edit the graph panel from the Grafana dashboard to view the query?

   a. No

   b. Yes

Answers

1. a
2. d
3. b

Join our book's Discord space

Join the book's Discord Workspace for Latest updates, Offers, Tech happenings around the world, New Release and Sessions with the Authors:

https://discord.bpbonline.com

CHAPTER 5

Visualizing Data in the Graph Panel

Introduction

In this chapter, we will apply what we have learned so far about working with data sources in an advanced manner. We will investigate querying data from Prometheus, storing and displaying time series data, and utilizing y-axes in time-series Graph panels for advanced monitoring. Let's get started!

Structure

In this chapter, we will learn the following:

- Executing advanced queries
- Understanding the time series data display
- Setting vertical axes

Objectives

This chapter will provide a tour of the visualizing data in the time series graph panel of the Grafana application. It will give you information about how to use sophisticated queries to probe data from Prometheus data sources, save and visualize time-series data, and compare various units of data using multiple y-axis.

5.1 Technical requirements

Since Grafana is a web-based application, you'll need to run a few commands to get it up and running. The following are the technical requirements and prerequisites for installing and running Grafana v9.0:

- Knowledge of the command shell
- Install Grafana on the machine of your choice using a terminal application or an SSH
- Java 8 or higher
- Python 3.5 or later
- Git CLI tool
- Docker
- Docker-Compose

Optionally, you'll be able to log in as an administrator using the command line to set up and run Grafana.

5.2 Executing advanced queries

This section will provide more details about executing advanced queries to obtain data and display it on the dashboard.

5.2.1 Probing Prometheus

The dashboard and the Explore version of the Prometheus query editor are described and their features explained in the following subsections.

5.2.1.1 Dashboards' query editor

To enter edit mode for a graph, click on its title, and then select **Edit**. The following are a few configuration settings in Dashboards' Query Editor mode that can be used to query and display the data:

Name	Description
Query Expression	Refer to the Prometheus manual for further information about query expressions.
Legend Format	The name of the time series, which may be a pattern or a name, is under the control of this variable; either one is acceptable. For instance, the label value for the "hostname" would be altered to simply read "hostname".
Min Step	A lower constraint for the step parameter that can be used in Prometheus range queries, in addition to the variables `$__interval` and `$__rate` interval. The limit is absolute and does not depend on the setting for the Resolution in any way.
Resolution	The `$__interval` and step parameters of Prometheus range queries are updated by the value $1/1$ in such a way that a single data point is represented by a single pixel. This is accomplished by changing the value of the `$__interval` parameter to 1. For improved speed, you should use lesser resolutions. In the case of $1/2$, just one data point is retrieved for every other pixel, while in the case of $1/10$, one data point is retrieved for every 10 pixels. It is important to keep in mind that the maximum values of `$__interval` and step are restricted by the Min time interval and Min step constraints, respectively.
Metric Lookup	You are able to search for metric names using this box.
Format As	Choose from the available tables, time series, and heat maps. Only the table panel has any functionality. The capacity of heatmap to display measurements in the form of a histogram on a heatmap panel is a feature that is considered to be of great importance. The cumulative histograms are converted into standard ones, and the data are sorted based on the bucket bound.
Instant	To receive only the current value scraped by Prometheus for the time series of your choosing, run an "immediate" query. Instant queries deliver results faster than standard range queries, so use them in order to locate label sets.
Min Time Interval	When this number is multiplied by the denominator that is connected to the Resolution option, a lower limit is established for both the `$__interval` and step parameters that are utilized in Prometheus range queries. This restriction applies to both these parameters simultaneously. The settings of the data source serve as the primary determinant of the default Scrape interval.

Table 5.1: Configuration settings in Dashboards' Query Editor

5.2.1.2 Query editor in explore

The following are a few configuration settings of Query Editor in Explore mode that can be used to query and display the data:

Name	Description
Query Expression	For additional information regarding query expressions, refer to the Prometheus manual.
Step	The step parameter is available for use in range queries on Prometheus. In this context, the use of time units such as 5s, 1m, 3h, 1d, and 1y is acceptable. Whenever there is no alternative unit that is given, "s" will be used as the default unit (seconds).
Query Type	Different types of query types are Instant, Range, or Both of These Options. The outcomes of a Range query are presented in the form of a table in addition to a graph. Only the most current data that Prometheus has scraped for the time series that you chose will be displayed using the instant query method. This value will be retrieved and displayed in a table. When Both is chosen as the query type, both immediate and range inquiries are carried out. A graph is used to illustrate the results of a range query, whereas a table is used to show the results of an instant query.

Table 5.2: Configuration settings of Query Editor in Explore mode

5.2.1.3 Templating

You can use variables in your metric searches rather than hardcoding the names of the server, application, and sensor components. At the top of the dashboard, variables are displayed as drop-down menus. You can modify the data displayed on your dashboard using these drop-down menus. See templates and variables for more information on template variables and templating.

5.2.1.4 Query variable

It is possible to extract from Prometheus a list of metrics, label values, or the actual label values themselves. The following operations can be carried out in the Query input field, thanks to the Prometheus data source plugin:

Name	Description
label_names()	The names of the labels are returned in a list by this function.
label_values(label)	This function will return a list containing the label values for each measure.

Name	Description
`label_values(metric, label)`	This function returns a list of label values corresponding to the specified label for the specified metric.
`metrics(metric)`	This function will produce a list of metrics that are compliant with the metric regular expression that was provided.
`query_result(query)`	This function returns a collection of the results of the Prometheus query.

Table 5.3: Operations carried out in the Query input field

Refer to the Prometheus manual for details regarding metric names, label names, and label values.

5.2.1.5 Using interval and range variables

In the query variables, you have the option to use global variables like **$__interval**, **$__interval ms, $__range, $__range s**, and **$__range ms**. Because the label values function does not support queries, these can be useful with the query result function when variable queries must be filtered. In order to acquire the appropriate instances while adjusting the time range of the dashboard, the refresh trigger for the variable needs to be set to the on the time range change setting. The following piece of code provides an example of how to populate a variable with the five busiest request instances based on the dashboard's average QPS for the amount of time that was specified in the expression. This piece of code also serves as an illustration of how to do so:

Query: `query_result(topk(5, sum(rate(http_requests_total[$_range])) by (instance)))`

Regex: `/"([^"]+)"/`

The following code explains how to populate a variable with the instances that had a certain state inside the time range presented on the dashboard by showing how to use the **$__range s** variable. This may be done using the **$__range s** variable.

Query: `query_result(max_over_time(<metric>[${_range_s}s]) != <state>)`

5.2.1.6 Using the $__rate_interval variable

Within the scope of the rate function, the **$__rate interval** variable is meant to be used. It is determined by taking the greatest value from the expressions (**$__ interval + Scrape interval**) and (Scrape interval * 4). If there is no such setting, the Scrape interval is determined by the interval that is specified in the Prometheus data source.

5.2.1.7 Using variables in queries

There are two syntaxes:

`$<varname>`

Example: `rate(http_requests_total{job=~"$job"}[5m])`

`[[varname]]`

Example: `rate(http_requests_total{job=~"[[job]]"}[5m])`

Why are there not just one but two options to select from instead? The first syntax is less difficult to read and write, but it does not allow the usage of variables within the confines of individual words. When using the multi-value or including all value options in Grafana, the plaintext labels are converted to a string that is compatible with regular expressions. This can be done either manually or automatically.

5.2.1.8 Annotations

The addition of layers of granular event data to graphs is made possible via annotations. You can add annotation questions either by viewing them in the Annotation view or by utilizing the menu that is located on the Dashboard. For extra information, please refer to the annotations. There are two different approaches to query annotations when using Prometheus:

- A routine metric inquiry
- A Prometheus query for pending and active notifications; see examining alarms during execution for additional information

The step parameter is important for limiting the number of results returned by a query.

5.2.2 Sample queries

This section will have the details about examples of sample queries:

- Give back all the time series that contain the measure that tracks the total number of HTTP requests.

    `http_requests_total`

- Return all time series that have the names of the provided job and handler, along with the total metric for http requests in the result set.

  ```
  http_requests_total{job="apiserver", handler="/api/comments"}
  ```

- Returning the entire time range for the same vector (in this case, 5 minutes up to the query time) is the first step in the process of creating a range vector.

  ```
  http_requests_total{job="apiserver", handler="/api/comments"}[5m]
  ```

  Note that expressions that produce range vectors cannot be graphed directly but can be investigated using the expression browser's tabular ("`Console`") mode.

- You could use regular expressions to restrict your selection of time series to only include jobs whose names match a particular pattern; for example, you could choose time series only for tasks whose names end with server. This would be an example of an appropriate pattern:

  ```
  http_request_total{job=~".*server"}
  ```

- The RE2 syntax is used in each and every regular expression that can be created using Prometheus. You can use the run command to pick all HTTP status codes other than 4xx ones:

  ```
  http_requests_total{status!~"4.."}
  ```

5.2.3 Advanced queries

This section will have details about structure and examples of advanced queries:

- Return the 30-minute 5-minute rate of the http requests total metric with a resolution of 1 minute:

  ```
  rate(http_requests_total[5m])[30m:1m]
  ```

- An example of a subquery that is nested within another query is presented here. The derive function will use the default resolution for the subquery that it employs in order to perform its operations. Consider the fact that it is not a good idea to employ subqueries when not really necessary.

  ```
  max_over_time(deriv(rate(distance_covered_total[5s])[30s:5s])
  [10m:])
  ```

- Return the rate in seconds for the all time series associated with the total metric name for HTTP requests based on the measures made during the past 5 minutes. This rate should be based on the total number of http requests.

  ```
  rate(http_requests_total[5m])
  ```

- Assuming that all the http requests total time series have the labels job and instance, we might want to sum over the rate of all instances in order to decrease the number of output time series while still maintaining the job dimension. This can be accomplished by summing over the rates of all the requests:

```
sum by (job) (

    rate(http_requests_total[5m])

)
```

- If it were to be summed up by application, the same expression could be phrased as follows:

```
sum by (app, proc) (

    instance_memory_limit_bytes - instance_memory_usage_bytes

) / 1024 / 1024
```

- The following is one possible method for determining the three applications and processes that utilize the most CPU:

```
topk(3, sum by (app, proc) (rate(instance_cpu_time_ns[5m])))
```

- 90th Percentile Latency

```
histogram_quantile(0.9,rate(demo_api_request_duration_seconds_
bucket{job="demo"}[5m])) > 0.05 and rate(demo_api_request_duration_
seconds_count{job="demo"}[5m] > 1
```

Select HTTP endpoints with a 90th percentile latency greater than 50ms (0.05s), but only for dimensional combinations that receive several requests per second. We utilize the histogram **quantile()** function to calculate the percentile here. It computes the 90th percentile latency for each dimension subtype. To filter problematic latencies and maintain just those that receive several requests per second, histogram quantile can only be utilized in conjunction with a Histogram metric.

- HTTP request rate, per second an hour ago

```
rate(api_http_requests_total{status=500}[5m] offset 1h)
```

- The **rate()** function computes the per-second average rate of time series in a range vector. Using a combination of the mentioned instruments, we can determine the HTTP request rates for a given time period. The query computes the per-second rates of all HTTP requests made in the last 5 minutes and 1 hour ago.

```
topk(10, count by (__name__) ({__name__=~".+"}))
```

Above query can be used to monitor your most expensive Prometheus metrics while tuning and is resource-intensive to execute.

5.3 Understanding time series data display

Let us say you were curious about the way in which the temperature varies throughout the course of the day. You were to check the thermometer once every hour and make a note of both the time and the temperature displayed. In the end, you would have something that looks like this:

Time	Temperature Value
09:00	24°C
10:00	26°C
11:00	27°C

Table 5.4: Temperatures at different time interval

This data on temperature is an example of what is known as a time series, which is a set of measurements that are arranged in a specific order. A single reading was obtained from the sensor at the time and location specified in the row of the table. Tables are an indispensable tool for determining specific measurements, but their presence makes it more difficult to grasp the bigger picture. The presentation of time series is most commonly done through the use of graphs, which plot each measurement along an axis that represents time. The identification of patterns and qualities of the data, which would otherwise be difficult to see, is made easier with the use of visual representations of the data, such as the graph. Other instances of time series include the following:

- CPU and memory utilization
- Stock market index
- Sensor data

In spite of every one of these examples is a list of measurements being presented in reverse chronological order, they have the following characteristics: At predetermined times, such as the beginning of each hour at 9:00, 10:00, and 11:00, and so on, new data is appended to the end of the file.

Measurements are rarely updated once they have been added; for example, the temperature did no change since yesterday. A succession of timestamps may demonstrate that the server crashed not long after there was no more free space on the disk. The patterns that are revealed by time series can also be used to make predictions about the future. You should be able to make an educated guess about the size of your user base by the end of the year if the number of users who have registered for an account has increased by 4% per month over the past several months. There are time series with patterns that continue to appear after a certain period of time has passed. One common phenomenon is that the temperature during the day is typically higher than the temperature at night. It is feasible to make an accurate forecast of the following period by first identifying any periodic or seasonal time series. If you know that the system load is at its highest every day at 6:00, you can add more computers approximately one hour before that time.

5.3.1 Aggregating time series

By utilizing aggregating time series option, we can observe the condition of the system at any given time, which enables you to gain a better understanding of what happened in the past. The accumulation of timestamps may provide evidence that the server became inaccessible shortly after the total amount of free disk space was exhausted. By analyzing patterns in the data that they produce, time series can also be used to make predictions about the future. You should be able to estimate the size of your user base toward the end of the year if the number of people who have registered for an account has increased by 4% on a monthly basis over the preceding several months. There are some time series that exhibit repeated patterns throughout the course of a specific time range. The average temperature during the day is significantly higher than the average temperature during the night. It is possible to make an accurate prediction of the era that will follow if one takes the time to recognize certain time series that occur on a periodic or seasonal basis. If you know that the peak load on the system occurs every day at 8:00 in the evening, you can add more machines around one hour before that time.

- The result that the **average** function gives back is the sum of all the values, divided by the total number of the values.

- Min and max are functions that return the lowest and highest values in the collection, respectively.

- The result of calling *Sum* on a collection is the collection's total value.

The **count** method returns the total number of elements in the collection.

For instance, by taking an average of the data for a specific month, we can conclude that the month of August 2017 was, on average, warmer than it was in August 2016. This conclusion may be drawn by comparing the average temperatures over the 2 years. Instead, a comparison would be made between the highest temperature reached during each month to determine which months had the highest average temperature. This comparison would be made so that the highest average temperature could be determined. The narrative that you plan to construct with the help of the data will significantly impact one of the most critical decisions you will have to make, which is deciding how to aggregate the time series data that you have collected. It is standard practice to use various aggregations to display the same time series data in different formats. This is done in order to maximize clarity and readability.

5.3.2 Time series and monitoring

In the field of information technology, collecting time series data is commonly necessary in order to monitor infrastructure, hardware, and application activities. Time series data that is typically created by a machine is collected at short intervals. This allows you to react to any unplanned changes that have occurred within seconds of their occurrence. As a result, data is rapidly accumulated, which necessitates a system that is both effective at storing data and retrieving it. As a direct result of this, databases that are designed for time series data have seen a rise in popularity over the past few years.

5.3.3 Time series databases

A database that was developed expressly for the storage of time series data is referred to as a **Time Series Database** (**TSDB**). While it is possible to store measurements in any regular database, **Transaction-Specific Databases** (**TSDBs**) offer certain features that are to the user's advantage. Databases that are used to store modern time series use the fact that measurements are practically never altered and are only ever added to. For example, because the timestamps associated with each measurement shift only little over the course of time, duplicate data must be stored:

```
1572524345, 1572524375, 1572524404, 1572524434, 1572524464
```

This results in an inefficient usage of storage space because all these timestamps start with the number 1572524. Instead, we might store each subsequent timestamp as the delta, often known as the difference, between the starting timestamp and the current one:

```
1572524345, +30, +29, +30, +30
```

Further, we might compute the deltas of these deltas, which are as follows:

```
1572524345, +30, -1, +1, +0
```

If measurements are carried out at consistent intervals, the vast majority of these delta-of-deltas will equal zero. Because of these improvements, the space utilized by TSDBs is much lesser than that utilized by other databases. In addition to this, a TSDB provides the ability to filter measurements by utilizing tags. Every single data point has some contextual information attached to it, such as the place where the measurement was really taken.

The following is a list of TSDBs that Grafana is compatible with:

- Prometheus
- InfluxDB
- Graphite

5.3.4 Collecting time series data

Now that we have a place to store the measurements for our time series, what is the best way for us to collect them? In most cases, in order to acquire time series data, you will need to install a collector on the monitored device, machine, or instance. While some collectors are developed specifically with a certain database in mind, others can accept several different output destinations.

The following are a few instances of collectors:

- Prometheus exporters
- Collectd
- Telegraf
- Statsd

Either a collector will provide data to a database, or the database will be allowed to pull data from the collector. Each strategy has its own benefits and drawbacks, as listed in the following table:

	Pros	Cons
Push	It is easier to replicate data to several destinations.	The TSDB does not have any influence or control over the amount of data that is sent.
Pull	There is a more precise command over the quantity and authenticity of the data that is taken in.	It's possible that firewalls, VPNs, or load balancers will prevent you from accessing the agents.

Table 5.5: Benefits and drawbacks

The data collectors pre-aggregate the information before writing it to the time series database. This is done since writing each measurement individually to the database would be inefficient.

5.4 Setting vertical axes

After seeing how data points are graphed horizontally in time, let's move on to looking at how they are graphed vertically on their respective Y axes. As with any other tool, the freedom offered by Grafana's Y-axes display can be exploited in inappropriate ways. In this section, we will discuss the opportunities that exist for using the Y-axes display to maybe make our data more understandable or illuminating.

5.4.1 Right Y-axis

There are times when it can be helpful to graph time series that have significant differences between them but are still connected or associated in some way, for example, the amount of RAM and CPU that is being used. Grafana enables users to attach series to a second (right) Y-axis, which can have a different unit and scale depending on the user's preferences. You can assign a series to the right Y-Axis of the graph by clicking on the colored line icon that is located to the left of the series' name in the graph legend, as demonstrated in *Figure 5.1*:

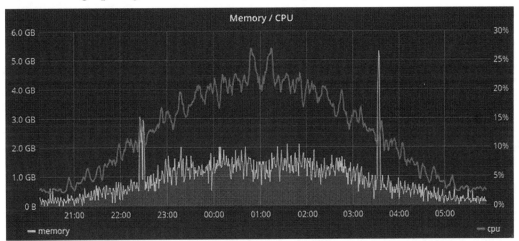

Figure 5.1: Memory vs CPU

5.4.2 Log scale

Another way for displaying series that differ by orders of magnitude is to use a logarithmic scale, as demonstrated in *Figure 5.2*. This method comes in quite handy when calculating latency and measuring data consumption. It is important to accomplish this task so that a single series does not come to dominate the graph and push all the other series to the bottom.

Figure 5.2: *Log Base 32 Scale*

5.4.3 Setting up a dual axis graph

Dual axis graphs enable users to study patterns between time series that have different magnitudes or units by using a second Y axis, as demonstrated in *Figure 5.3*:

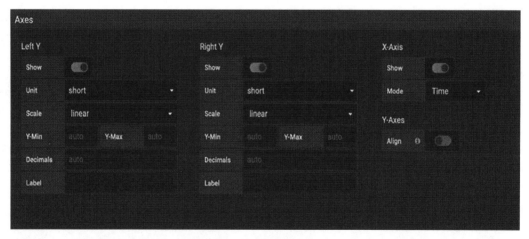

Figure 5.3: *Dual Y-Axis*

Suppose you are interested in determining whether or not there is a connection between the amount of CPU work being done by a machine and the amount of time it takes for a service to respond. You can get the answers to questions like *Does a CPU load more than 1.0 per core influence reaction time?* by utilizing the left axis for response time and the right axis for load.

It is necessary to designate a time series to the right Y axis in order to produce a graph with two axes. In the panel legend, click the colorful line next to the time series' name.

Click the **Y-Axis** tab in the **Colors** dialog box, and then check the box that appears. Employ the correct Y-axis. In this panel, the legend for the series has been moved to the right, and the right Y axis has been drawn. Additionally, the unit and range of each axis can be set independently from one another.

Now that you understand how to create a graph with two axes, let's take a look at a few scenarios in which using such a graph could prove to be beneficial.

5.4.4 Finding correlation

When you are looking into performance concerns, you are curious about whether or not an increase in traffic has a negative impact on the latency. You set up your graph in such a way that the left axis denotes the amount of traffic, while the right axis denotes the amount of lag. On the graph labeled 5.5, the number of requests is depicted as a collection of points, while the latency is shown as a line fill. Even though there is a consistent rate of 1600 per minute, there are certain inquiries that take more than 2 seconds.

Figure 5.4: *Traffic vs. latency*

Another scenario is when you are interested in determining whether or not the amount of CPU load and the amount of memory consumed are related.

5.4.5 Resource utilization

An additional use case is the visualization of resource usage in conjunction with its utilization. For example, the disk is 80% full. On the left side of the example shown below is a representation of absolute memory utilization measured in bytes, while on the right side is a representation of relative memory utilization measured in percentage. As illustrated in *Figure 5.5*, this gives you the ability to maximize the vertical resolution of presenting absolute resource consumption while also giving you the ability to grasp at a glance how much of it is relative to the entire number of resources that are accessible.

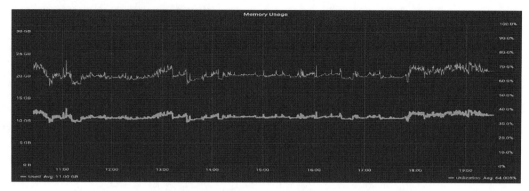

Figure 5.5: Absolute vs. relative memory usage

If you only monitor one machine, you can accomplish the same thing by adjusting the Y-max value on the left axis to equal the entire amount of memory that is installed on that system. This will give you the same result. It is possible that you will not be able to establish a single Y-max value for all the resources that are contained inside a cluster of computers that have varying memory configurations.

5.4.6 Dangers of using dual axis graphs

Dual axis graphs can be helpful, but they lack the intuitiveness of other types of graphs and are devilishly easy to misuse. If you include an excessive quantity of data in your graphs, you are at risk of making your message difficult to understand. The presence of two axes doubles the potential for harm. It may be challenging to identify which series belongs to which axis when you are effectively generating two graphs on top of one another. Even though dual axis graphs can be difficult to comprehend, there are a few things we can do to remedy the situation.

5.4.7 Increase contrast between series

Make it easier to determine which series belong to which axis by employing unique graphic options for each axis. For the right Y-axis series, you might want to think about utilizing points or a different line width. The vast majority of Grafana's display options are applicable to each and every series contained within a graph. Consult the section on series overrides if you want to make changes to the visualization parameters for series.

5.4.8 Align baselines

The scale and baseline of each axis can change independently of one another; they can tell incredibly diverse stories for the same data set, which can result in the appearance of a link where none actually exists. It is possible, for instance, to give the impression that the two series are growing at the same pace by altering the scale and the baseline of the graph. The graph can be adapted to almost any narrative by just modifying the scales to fit the data. Charts with multiple axes should only be used with extreme caution. The magnitudes and minimum values of each axis are subject to arbitrary change, which means they have the potential to rapidly become misleading. To make things clearer, axes can be aligned with the number 0. To enable Align, go to the Visualization options menu, then select Axes, then Y-axis.

Conclusion

We've covered a lot of ground in this chapter. We learned key concepts of simple to advanced queries to probe data from Prometheus, storing and visualizing data in time series graph panels.

We also set axis units and displayed multiple series with different units on the same graph.

Multiple choice questions

1. Can multiple y-axis be enabled in time series graph panel?

    a. Yes

    b. No

2. Does Grafana Graph panel support multiple data sources to query data from?

    a. Yes

    b. No

Answers

1. a

2. a

Join our book's Discord space

Join the book's Discord Workspace for Latest updates, Offers, Tech happenings around the world, New Release and Sessions with the Authors:

https://discord.bpbonline.com

CHAPTER 6
Creating Your First Dashboard

Introduction

In this chapter, we will learn how to create a dashboard in Grafana. Dashboards are a type of graphic user interface that usually offer a glance at the essential performance indicators related to a specific goal or business activity. Grafana dashboard has the ability to provide greater insights into the application and the components that should be monitored; so, it also helps in driving technical, business and user decisions. Multiple visualization panels can be included in a single view on a Grafana dashboard, results from several data sources can be visualized and configured simultaneously.

Structure

In this chapter, we will cover the following topics:

- How to install TestData DB
- How to create a dashboard
- Different settings and options in dashboard
- How to view dashboard query
- Creating an information-heavy dashboard

Objectives

This chapter will provide a step-by-step guide to creating your first dashboard. We will install TestData DB as a data source to fetch sample data sets. We will also understand the different settings and visualization options available in the dashboard, along with viewing the query that is responsible for pulling the required data on the dashboard. Additionally, we will investigate how an information-heavy Grafana dashboard can be created and viewed.

6.1 Technical requirements

The technical requirement for this chapter are listed as follows:

- Grafana
- Admin Access to Grafana
- Data source

6.2 Designing a dashboard

Dashboard is the main element of the Grafana software that can visually tell the story and the status of an application, before we create a dashboard it is essential to have a plan of purpose. Start by pondering about who will be the users of this dashboard. What details do I want to convey? What is the most important and least important aspect of the dashboard, and how should I visually represent both of them? Answers to these questions will help you design a dashboard that best suits your purpose. The following conditions should be addressed when developing the dashboard:

- Information and statistics
- Visual impact and placement
- Prioritizing crucial metrics

6.2.1 Target audience for your dashboard

Each user will have different interests and requirements to view the dashboard. You have to start by knowing your target audience and capture the exact requirements even before you think of any design. *Table 6.1* depicts how a user role will have different points of concern to be addressed and what exact dashboard objective is expected to be fulfilled:

Role	Concern	Dashboard Objective
Engineer	What is broken? I cannot find the exact problem to troubleshoot.	Provide relevant data ASAP to identify the issues faster.
Product Owner	I have a lot of data of my product but cannot compare or have a single view.	Display pre-calculated and neatly designed metrics that highlight the current product status.
Client	Is everything working fine?	Display the product health and whether any regular maintenance action is needed.

Table 6.1: Grafana dashboard objectives based on user roles

6.2.2 Installing TestData DB

You need a data source for Grafana to publish statistics in the dashboard; based on the project setup, you can use one or multiple data sources. Grafana provides connection to many popular data sources like AWS CloudWatch, Azure Monitor, Elasticsearch, Google Cloud Monitoring, Influx DB, Loki, and MySQL. For our purpose of explanation and creating a dashboard, we will install and use TestData DB, which is a data source provided by Grafana, with mocked-up data for the purpose of verifying the functionalities and options before designing the dashboard with actual data source:

1. On the Grafana home page, click **Configuration** | **Plugins**, as shown in *Figure 6.1*:

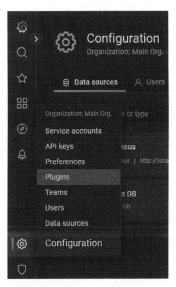

Figure 6.1: Grafana plugins selection

2. In the search bar, enter **TestData DB** and then click on the **TestData DB Tile**, as shown in *Figure 6.2*:

Figure 6.2: Grafana TestData DB

3. Click **Install**, as shown in *Figure 6.3*:

Figure 6.3: Plugins Install

4. Once installed, it will show up in the list of **Data sources**, as shown in *Figure 6.4*:

Figure 6.4: TestData DB listed in Data sources

Now you are ready to use TestData DB as a data source to design a dashboard in Grafana; you do not have to be concerned about data set generation for this activity. Instead, you will focus on creating and trying different options in the dashboard.

6.2.3 Creating a dashboard

Now that we have the required setup, we are ready to create our first dashboard! Follow these steps:

1. On the Grafana home page, click **Dashboards | + New dashboard**, as shown in *Figure 6.5*:

Figure 6.5: Grafana Dashboards

- **+ New dashboard**: To create a new dashboard
- **+ New folder**: To create a new folder under which multiple dashboards can be created
- **+ Import**: To import pre-built dashboards using ID or JSON (Many pre-built dashboards are available at Grafana Labs: **https://grafana.com/grafana/dashboards/**)

2. Click on **Add a new Panel**, as shown in *Figure 6.6*:

Figure 6.6: Dashboard Panel

3. You should see the screen shown in *Figure 6.7*; at this point, it is not publishing any metrics. From here, we have to configure as per our project needs to view relevant details.

Figure 6.7: Dashboard default panel view

6.2.3.1 Select data source

Grafana has some of the widely used data sources built-in, like Influx DB, Prometheus, My SQL, and AWS CloudWatch. The dashboard is put together with data collected by an external source like a database; in the previous section, we installed TestData DB as our data source. Now, let us look at how we can access that in the dashboard:

1. Click on the **Data** source search bar; here, you should see a list of data sources that you have configured. Select **TestData DB**, as shown in *Figure 6.8*:

Figure 6.8: *TestData DB as data source in dashboard*

2. Now you should see the screen shown in *Figure 6.9*; here, the graph is plotted for the Random Walk data set from **TestData DB** (hit the **Refresh** button on the panel if the graph does not load):

Figure 6.9: *Panel graphs*

6.2.3.2 Visualization

Visualization can make or break your dashboard; it is very important to select the right visualization method to showcase your data:

1. On the right side of the panel, click on **Visualization** to see multiple options available, as shown in *Figure 6.10*:

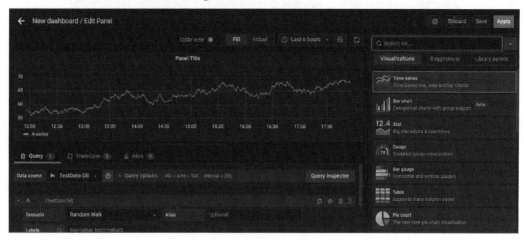

Figure 6.10: Panel visualization

2. Grafana provides many visualization options by default, as shown in *Figure 6.11*. Based on the data type and the message you want to convey, a visualization option should be selected. Time series works well for showing historical trend, Geomap to show the data distribution geographically, and so on. Another most important point is that you can download additional visualization from the plugins:

Figure 6.11: Visualization list

6.2.3.3 Title change

Title for your panel should be appropriately set; you can also add a short description to provide relevant information to the user, as shown in *Figure 6.12*:

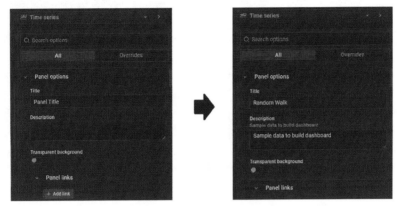

Figure 6.12: *Panel title*

6.2.3.4 Panel standard options

Panel comes with pre-set standard options, which can be altered based on the requirements; these standard options convey the relevant information, but we can further enhance user experience by updating with appropriate labels and colors:

1. Keeping most of the options same, we have updated **Display name** to **Random Walk Stats** here, as shown in *Figure 6.13*:

Figure 6.13: *Display name update*

The display panel will update as shown in *Figure 6.14*:

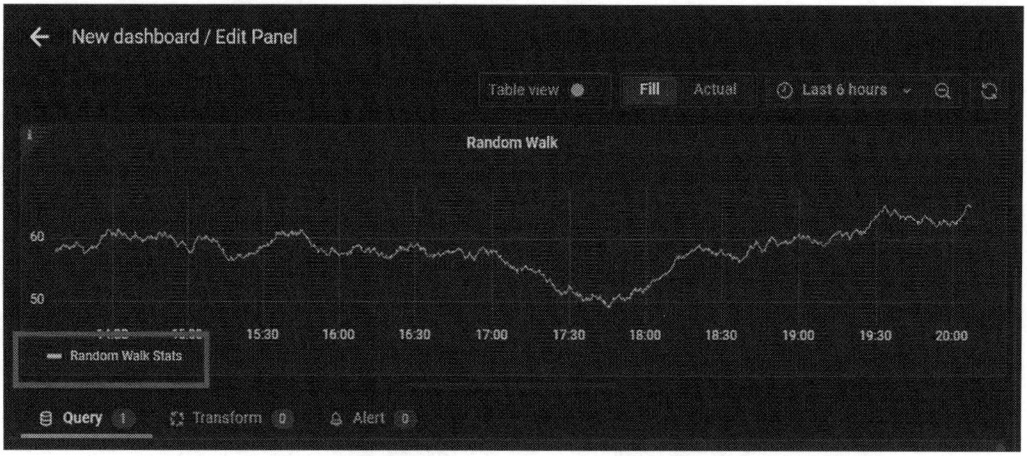

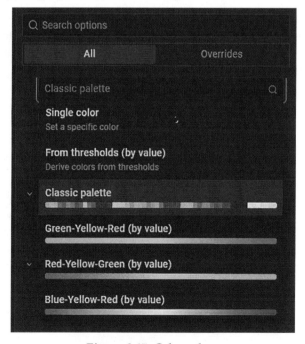

Figure 6.14: *Display name update*

2. Color palette in standard options is another parameter to try and enhance dashboard appearance. Try different color combinations to finalize the one best suits your project, as shown in *Figure 6.15*:

Figure 6.15: *Color palette*

6.2.3.5 Panel link for external website

You can add a link to the external website. If you are publishing any information from different website or you want your user to navigate to the website you desire for further understanding you can provide appropriate links that will show up in the dashboard panel (remember to save the panel and dashboard after you make changes):

1. From the **Panel** option under the **Panel** links, click + **Add** link, as shown in *Figure 6.16*:

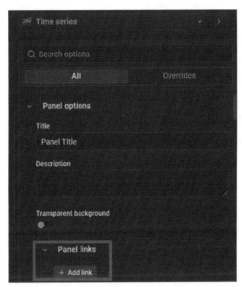

Figure 6.16: Panel links

2. Provide **Title** and **Target URL**, and click **Save**, as shown in *Figure 6.17*:

Figure 6.17: Adding URL

3. You should see the website link, as shown in *Figure 6.18*, on the graph **i (info)** button:

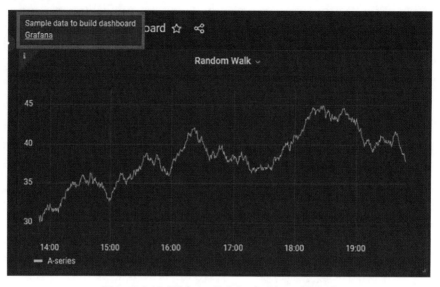

Figure 6.18: Website link in dashboard panel

6.2.3.6 Threshold

Threshold is another metric you can configure in the panel, as shown in *Figure 6.19*, to visually know at any given point in the set timeframe whether the value has breached the threshold value; this will help in getting a quick understanding of the application overall health and troubleshooting. It is also possible to alter threshold value and color as desired. Alerts can also be set when the threshold value is breached; that will be discussed in the later sections:

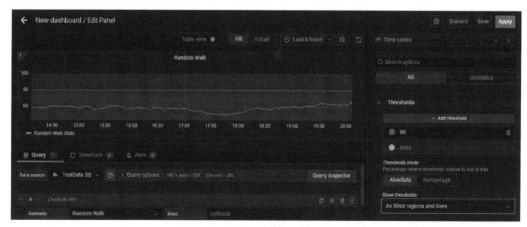

Figure 6.19: Threshold values

6.2.3.7 Query inspector

So far, we have seen how we can set up a panel using different configurations; if you think deeper, you will realize that Grafana is pulling these values by actually querying the data source. Most times, when the expected metric is not displayed, validating the query is the first option you should try. In this section, we will look at how a query inspector can give you a better understanding of behind-the-scenes operation in your panel:

1. Click on **Query Inspector** in the panel, as shown in *Figure 6.20*:

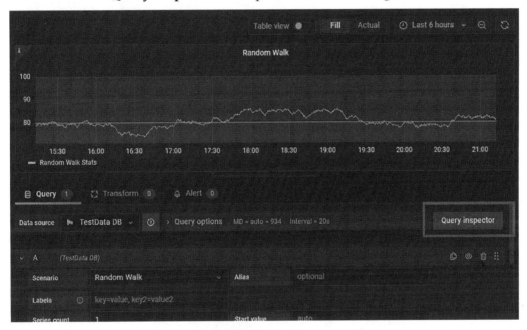

Figure 6.20: *Query inspector*

2. Query inspector provides four different pieces of information, as listed below and shown in *Figure 6.21* and *Figure 6.22*:

   - **Query**: Request query (hit refresh if query is not loaded)
   - **JSON**: Query in JSON format
   - **Stats**: Statistics of the query
   - **Data**: List of data set collected

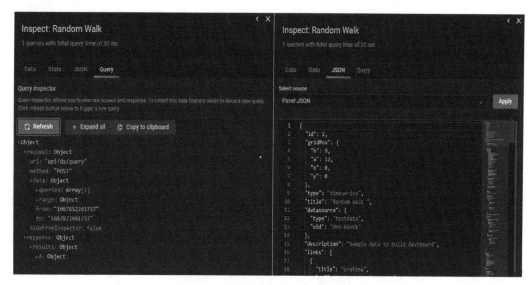

Figure 6.21: Viewing query and JSON

You can see the **Stats** and **Data** in *Figure 6.22*:

Figure 6.22: Viewing Stats and Data

6.2.3.8 Saving panel and dashboard

After making the changes on the panel, you can click **Apply** to view the updated metrics, but you must **Save** the panel to confirm the changes, as shown in *Figure 6.23*. You can also provide a description of the changes that will be maintained as a version and can be restored later if required. Similarly, any changes to the dashboard should also be saved to reflect as permanent changes, as shown in *Figure 6.23*:

Figure 6.23: Saving panel

1. Saving the newly created dashboard:

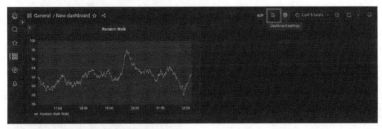

Figure 6.24: Saving Dashboard

6.2.3.9 Time range on dashboard

All the dashboard metrics are derived for a specific time range; by default, it may take the last 6 hours duration, but this can be changed as per the requirement. Click on **Time Range**, and Grafana will present you with many pre-set options to choose from, or you can provide the exact time duration in the **From** and **To** section, as shown in *Figure 6.25*:

Figure 6.25: Dashboard time range

Pro-tip: Using cursor, you can select a time range directly on the panel, and grafana will automatically set the start and end duration, as shown in *Figure 6.26*:

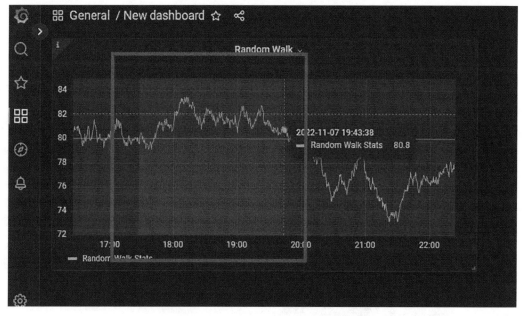

Figure 6.26: Selecting time range from graph

6.2.3.10 Dashboard refresh frequency

The Grafana dashboard has a refresh button that will enable you to refresh the data set on demand, but you can also set refresh frequency, which will automatically refresh the dashboard on a fixed interval to provide up-to-date information, as shown in *Figure 6.27*:

Figure 6.27: Dashboard refresh time

6.3 Information-heavy Grafana dashboard

Now that you know how to build a panel, let us look into how we can design a dashboard with more visualization. Grafana dashboard can accommodate many panels in a dashboard. When combined together, it can visually provide a spectacular view of the system in one glance. Think of an airplane cockpit; it will have many indicators in the dashboard, and the crucial ones are always placed in the center and emphasized more. Similarly, a high information Grafana dashboard can be developed to provide end-to-end observability of your system.

6.3.1 Multiple panels

Each panel has a story to tell, message to convey and metric to show. Multiple panels with different indicators and visualization will provide a dashboard with a lot of information, as depicted in *Figure 6.28*. Here, we have multiple panel visualization like time series, gauge, pie chart, bar graph which convey the important monitoring metrics to user. You can also easily resize the panel using the cursor and rearrange the panel in any order as per the need; try different visualization patterns to identify the one that suits best; also, take feedback from the users to redesign where required for a perfect dashboard:

Figure 6.28: Multiple dashboard panels

6.3.2 Graphs placement

When creating a dashboard, you can incorporate aspects of human psychology to enhance user experience. Adding too many panels can make your dashboard undesirable and may not convey the right message. It is important to keep the dashboard crisp and easily readable for successful implementation. Some of the best practices to follow while designing high information dashboards are as follows:

- **Alignment**: When someone looks at the dashboard, usually they scan it in the Z pattern. So, always place important panels that need attention in these areas, as shown in *Figure 6.29*:

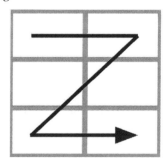

Figure 6.29: Dashboard alignment

- **Panel Size**: Having a way bigger panel will completely fill up the dashboard. On the other hand, having a panel that is too small may not be readable at all. Generally, panels that are bigger in size convey the message that the information there is important and should be viewed first, as shown in *Figure 6.30*:

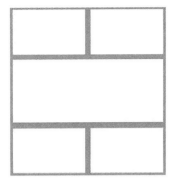

Figure 6.30: Dashboard panel size

- **Color**: Color plays a major role in driving the user toward dashboard panels; any metric in Green is considered positive, and Red is usually an indication of something wrong, so naturally, that panel will be analyzed first, as shown in *Figure 6.31*:

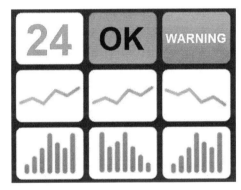

Figure 6.31: Dashboard color

Conclusion

You should now be able to create your first dashboard and see all the metrics getting populated. Grafana dashboard is like a blank canvas on which you can create a dashboard with many panel combinations and data sets. Identify your target audience and the metrics that need to be presented, and frequently get feedback from the stakeholders and update the dashboard as the project matures.

Now that you are also familiar with the different options you can choose from for visualization, try different combinations to see which one is more suitable for your project needs. Understand the query that the dashboard uses to pull the metrics, that is, the basis on which the dashboard is displayed. Try to alter the dashboard view by providing additional conditions, time frames and transforming the data that will help you ensure better dashboard visualization. Grafana provides the ability to share your dashboard with others via a URL. You can also provide elevated privileges to others to collaboratively create and update the dashboard; we will discuss this in upcoming chapters.

In the next chapter, we will explain Grafana`s advanced dashboard features.

Multiple choice questions

1. Can you create multiple Grafana Dashboards with the same name?

    a. Yes

    b. No

2. Which of the following option is not available in the Query Inspector?

    a. JSON

    b. Data

    c. Count

    d. Stats

3. Which of the following is not an option in the visualization panel?

    a. Cold map

    b. Time series

    c. Gauge

    d. Bar chart

Answers

1. b

2. c

3. a

Join our book's Discord space

Join the book's Discord Workspace for Latest updates, Offers, Tech happenings around the world, New Release and Sessions with the Authors:

https://discord.bpbonline.com

## CHAPTER 7

Visualization Panels in Grafana

Introduction

In the previous chapters, we examined the graph panel in depth and looked at some of its powerful capabilities. In this chapter, we will (largely) abandon the Graph panel in favor of some of Grafana's other visualization options. While the Graph panel is strong and adaptable, it is not the only option to present data in Grafana. Sometimes you need a new approach to show your data, and other times you just want to break the monotony of looking at a grid of graphs. For these reasons, Grafana provides panels that depict data in several ways, and we will examine each of them in this chapter. First, we will look at panels that condense the data, such as the Stat and Gauge panels. Next, we will display geographically distributed data with the World map panel; and finally, we will look at depicting our data sets in spreadsheet form with the Table panel.

Structure

The following topics will be covered in this chapter:

- Introducing the Stat panel
- Introducing the Gauge panel

- Introducing the World Map panel
- Introducing the Table panel

Objectives

This chapter will provide you with a tour of the visualizing data in stat, gauge, world map and table panels. It will give you the information about queries to probe data from data source and visualize data in different panels in various styles.

7.1 Technical requirements

Since Grafana is a web-based application, you will need to run a few commands to get it up and running. The following are the technical requirements and prerequisites for installing and running Grafana v9.0:

- Knowledge of the command shell
- Install Grafana on the machine of your choice using a terminal application or an SSH
- Java 8 or higher
- Python 3.5 or later
- Git CLI tool
- Docker
- Docker-Compose

Optionally, you will be able to log in as an administrator using the command line to set up and run Grafana.

7.2 Introducing the Stat panel

To navigate to the Stat panel in Grafana, you can follow these steps:

1. First, make sure you are logged in to your Grafana account and have the necessary permissions to access the dashboard.

2. Once you are on the dashboard, locate the panel that you want to view as a Stat panel. The panel should have a set of options in the top-right corner, including a **gear** icon, a share icon, and a panel menu icon (three horizontal lines).

3. Click on the **panel** menu icon (three horizontal lines) and select the "**Edit**" option.

4. This will take you to the panel editor, where you can customize the panel settings. Look for the **Visualization** section and click on the drop-down menu.

5. From the drop-down menu, select the **Stat** option, as shown in *Figure 7.1*. This will change the visualization type of the panel to a **Stat** panel:

Figure 7.1: *Stat Panel Selection*

6. You can now customize the **Stat panel** settings, such as the data source, query, and display options, to show the information you want to see.

7. Once you have configured the Stat panel to your liking, click on the **Save** button in the top-right corner of the editor to save your changes.

One or more big stat numbers are displayed in the Stat panel visualization. Using thresholds, you can change the color of the background or the value, as demonstrated in *Figure 7.2*:

Figure 7.2: Stat Panel

One of the following is what the Stat panel shows by default:

- Only one series or field
- Both the value and the name are necessary for multiple series or fields

The arrangement of the panel is automatically adjusted based on the dashboard's available width and height. If the panel grows too small, it conceals the graph automatically.

7.2.1 Value options

You can use the following settings to modify the way the value is shown:

1. Pick and choose which metrics to show off in Grafana:

   Calculate

2. Display a sum total calculated from all the data in the rows.

   All Values

3. Display a different statistic for each row. Using this setting, you can specify a maximum number of rows to show.

   - **Limit**: Display Row Limit Specifies how many rows can be shown at once.
   - **Fields**: Choose the tabs that show up in the panel.

7.2.2 Stat styles

The following are different stat styles that are available in the Stat panel of Grafana:

- **Direction mode**: Following are the direction modes we can choose from to stack and display data in stat panel:
  - o **Auto**: Grafana chooses the orientation that it deems to be optimal.
  - o **Horizontal**: The bars go from left to right horizontally.
  - o **Vertical**: From top to bottom, the bars are vertically positioned.
- **Text mode**: You may manage the text that the panel displays using the Text mode option. If the value is irrelevant and just the name and color matter, go from Text mode to Name mode. The value will be shown in a tooltip and used to choose the color going forward. Following are the text modes available to choose from and stack data in stat panel:
  - o **Auto**: The name and value should be shown if the data is divided into several series or fields.
  - o **Value**: Never show the name, only the value; instead, a tooltip appears when you hover over a name.
  - o **Value and name**: Name and value should always be displayed.
  - o **Name**: Rather than value, display name; when hovered over, the value is shown in the tooltip.
  - o **None**: Name and value are shown in the tooltip.
- **Color mode**: Following are the color modes available to choose from and stack data in stat panel:
  - o **Value**: The only colored areas are the value and graph area.
  - o **Background**: The background is also colored.
- **Graph mode**: Following are the graph modes available to choose from and stack data in stat panel:
  - o **None**: Without the graph, simply the value is shown.
  - o **Area**: Under the value, it displays the area chart; this requires the results of your query to include a time column.

- **Text alignment**: Following are the text alignment modes available to choose from and stack data in stat panel:
  - ○ **Auto**: The value is centered if there is only one value displayed. The value is aligned to the left if there are several series or rows displayed.
  - ○ **Centre**: Value of a centering stat.
- **Text size**: Following are the text size modes available to choose from and stack data in stat panel:
  - ○ **Title**: For the size of the gauge title, provide a numerical value.
  - ○ **Value**: Enter a number as the gauge size value.

7.3 Introducing the Gauge panel

To navigate to the Gauge panel in Grafana, you can follow these steps:

1. First, make sure you are logged in to your Grafana account and have the necessary permissions to access the dashboard.

2. Once you are on the dashboard, locate the panel that you want to view as a Gauge panel. The panel should have a set of options in the top-right corner, including a **gear** icon, a share icon, and a panel menu icon (three horizontal lines).

3. Click on the **panel** menu icon (three horizontal lines) and select the **Edit** option.

4. This will take you to the panel editor, where you can customize the panel settings. Look for the **Visualization** section and click on the drop-down menu.

5. From the drop-down menu and select the **Gauge** option. This will change the visualization type of the panel to a **Gauge** panel, as shown in *Figure 7.3*:

Figure 7.3: *Gauge Panel Selection*

6. You can now customize the **Gauge panel settings**, such as the data source, query, and display options, to show the information you want to see.

7. Once you have configured the Gauge panel to your liking, click on the **Save** button in the top-right corner of the editor to save your changes.

A Gauge is a single-value depiction that may be repeated for each series, column, and row, as demonstrated in *Figure 7.4*:

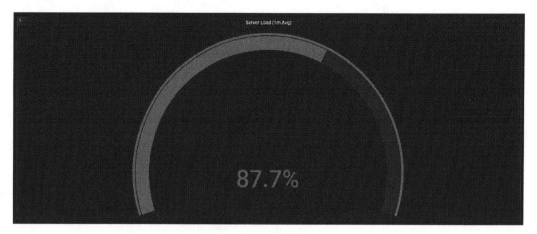

Figure 7.4: Gauge Panel

7.3.1 Value options

Use the following options to modify how your visualization displays the value:

- **Show**: Adapt the way your data is displayed in Grafana.
- **Calculate**: Display a value derived from all rows:
  - **Calculation**: Choose a reducer function that Grafana will employ to condense a number of fields down to a single value.
  - **Fields**: Pick one of the options from the panel's list.
- **All values**: Display a different statistic for each table row. You may optionally set the maximum number of rows shown if you select this option.
  - **Limit**: Establishes the maximum number of rows that can be shown; the default value is 5,000.
  - **Fields**: Pick which field the panel displays.
- **Gauge**: Change how the gauge is shown.
  - **Show threshold labels**: Specifies whether threshold values should be shown
  - **Show threshold markers**: Controls whether a threshold band is seen outside of the inner gauge value band
- **Text size**: Make the necessary adjustments to the gauge text sizes.
  - **Title**: Enter a numeric value to alter the gauge title's size
  - **Value**: Entering a numeric value will cause the size of the gauge title to be adjusted accordingly

7.4 Introducing the World Map panel

Following are the steps for World Map panel selction:

1. First, make sure you are logged in to your Grafana account and have the necessary permissions to access the dashboard.

2. Once you are on the dashboard, locate the panel that you want to view as a World Map panel. The panel should have a set of options in the top-right corner, including a **gear** icon, a share icon, and a panel menu icon (three horizontal lines).

3. Click on the **panel** menu icon (three horizontal lines) and select the **Edit** option.

4. This will take you to the panel editor, where you can customize the panel settings. Look for the **Visualization** section and click on the drop-down menu.

5. From the drop-down menu, select the **World Map** option. This will change the visualization type of the panel to a **World Map** panel, as shown in *Figure 7.5*:

Figure 7.5: *World Map Panel Selection*

6. You can now customize the **World Map panel settings**, such as the data source, query, and display options, to show the information you want to see.

7. Once you have configured the World Map panel to your liking, click on the **Save** button in the top-right corner of the editor to save your changes.

The World Map Panel is a tile map of the world that allows users to superimpose circles that represent data points from a query on top of the map. It is compatible with time series metrics, geohash data from Elasticsearch, and table-formatted data, among other types of information.

7.4.1 Data sources format

Two different data sources are required for the World map panel; they are as follows:

- **Time Series Format**: If it is in the time series format, then the name of the metric needs to correspond to a key that comes from a list of different locations. Typically, this key will be a country code or the name of a city. Either a file or an HTTP endpoint may serve as the source for the location list.

- **Table Format**: If the information is presented in table format, each row should include either one column containing a geohash or two columns containing the latitude and longitude coordinates. Tabular data, also known as table data, is organized into columns and rows.

7.5 Introducing the Table panel

Following are the steps for the Table panel:

1. First, make sure you are logged in to your Grafana account and have the necessary permissions to access the dashboard.

2. Once you are on the dashboard, locate the panel that you want to view as a Table panel. The panel should have a set of options in the top-right corner, including a **gear** icon, a share icon, and a panel menu icon (three horizontal lines).

3. Click on the panel menu icon (three horizontal lines) and select the **Edit** option.

4. This will take you to the panel editor, where you can customize the panel settings. Look for the **Visualization** section and click on the drop-down menu.

5. From the drop-down menu, select the **Table** option. This will change the visualization type of the panel to a **Table** panel, as shown in *Figure 7.6*:

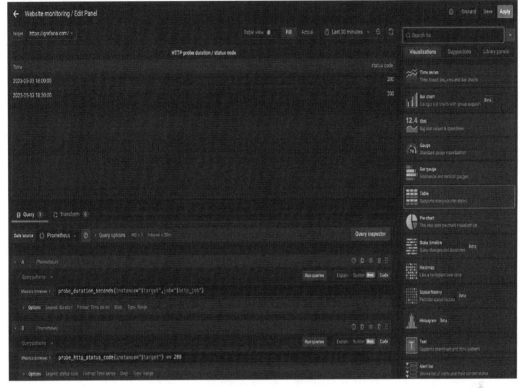

Figure 7.6: *Table Panel*

6. You can now customize the **Table panel settings**, such as the data source, query, and display options, to show the information you want to see.

7. Once you have configured the Table panel to your liking, click on the **Save** button in the top-right corner of the editor to save your changes.

As shown in *Figure 7.7*, the table panel visualization has a wide range of display options for time series, tables, annotation, and raw JSON data. This panel also gives you the option to format dates and values, and it gives you coloring options as well.

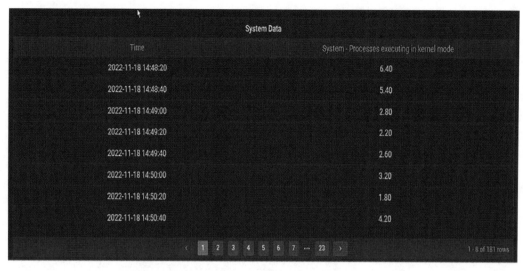

Figure 7.7: Table Visualization

Following are a few settings of the Table panel:

- **Show column header**: You have the option of displaying or hiding the column names that were imported from your data source.

- **Minimum column width**: The column width in a Grafana table is automatically calculated depending on the table size and the minimum column width by default. This field option can override the default and determine the width in pixels for each column.

- **Column alignment**: You can choose how Grafana should align cell contents from the following options:
  - Auto (default)
  - Left
  - Centre
  - Right

- **Cell display mode**: Grafana will, by default, select the appropriate display settings for you. You can override the settings by selecting one of the following options to make all the fields different.

- **Color text**: If thresholds are configured, the field text will be displayed in the color designated for that threshold.

Conclusion

In this chapter, we looked at many of the most important plugin panels that are pre-installed with Grafana. We looked at the Stat and Gauge panels, which condense the complexity of each data series into a single graphical or textual representation. These panels also provide you with various style options, which you may use to enhance the aesthetic appeal and importance of your data.

In addition to that, we looked at the optional World Map panel, which is only one of the several panels that can be downloaded from Grafana Labs. The World map panel is helpful for presenting data that has been tagged with the coordinates of latitude and longitude. We also demonstrated how to graphically display data values by assigning them to a certain size and/or color. This was done by mapping the values.

In the final step, we investigated a few of the options available in the Table panel. The Table panel is a gridded data panel that displays time series data by row or column or in aggregate, or it simply displays tabular data. Its look is comparable to that of a spreadsheet. We saw how to utilize regular expressions to match column headers to simplify the formatting of the data contained inside the cells. Our journey through a selection of the available Grafana plugin panels has come to an end.

In the next chapter, you will learn how to organize the dashboard for a sophisticated view by outlining how to effectively name a dashboard, how to create a new folder and map the dashboard to the folder, how to start and tag the dashboard for easier grouping, and how to view and alter the dashboard list panel.

Multiple choice questions

1. Which of the following panels are supported in Grafana for visualization?

   a. Table

   b. Gauge

   c. World Map

   d. All of the above

2. Does Grafana World Map panel support multiple data sources to query data from?

   a. Yes

   b. No

Answers

1. d
2. a

Join our book's Discord space

Join the book's Discord Workspace for Latest updates, Offers, Tech happenings around the world, New Release and Sessions with the Authors:

https://discord.bpbonline.com

CHAPTER 8
Organizing Dashboards

Introduction

You are already accustomed to developing dashboards and dashboard panels. It is important to categorize them well when there is a requirement to develop several dashboards and manage them among teams. In this chapter, we shall organize the dashboards and design folders to easily identify them for quick reference. Grafana dashboard will be easier to use once it is started, tagged, and mapped under the appropriate folders. Tips for naming the dashboard for the optimal outcome will be shared in this chapter, along with instructions on how to organize it effectively.

Structure

In this chapter, we will learn the following topics:

- Dashboard naming
- Dashboard folders
- Dashboard starring and tagging
- List panel in dashboard

Objectives

This chapter will help you understand how to organize the dashboard for a sophisticated view by outlining, and how to effectively name a dashboard and create a new folder. You will also learn to map the dashboard to a folder, and start and tag the dashboard for easier grouping. Additionally, you will learn to view and alter the dashboard list panel.

8.1 Technical requirements

All the required installations have already been done; no additional software installation is required for this chapter.

8.2 Dashboard naming

Organizing the Grafana dashboards starts with giving your dashboard an effective name. When you have multiple dashboards created, it will be difficult to instantly identify the dashboard you have to access if dashboard naming is not proper, especially when someone from your team is accessing the dashboard and has no idea about the dashboard content.

In this section of the chapter, we will look at how to name or rename the dashboard and the best practices to keep in mind when naming them.

8.2.1 Naming a dashboard

Follow these steps to name (or rename) a dashboard:

1. Open the dashboard.
2. Click on the **gear** icon to open dashboard settings.
3. In the **Name** field, enter the dashboard name.
4. Provide comments and click on the **Save** dashboard. As shown in *Figure 8.1*, the dashboard name is saved as `Sample Dashboard`:

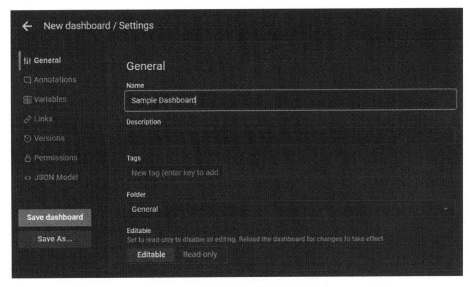

Figure 8.1: Dashboard Name Update

5. It is strongly suggested to add relevant comments in the **Details** section before saving the dashboard, as shown in *Figure 8.2*; Grafana will keep track of these changes, and you will have an option to roll back if required:

Figure 8.2: Saving Dashboard with details

8.2.2 Dashboard naming best practices

You will have started organizing your dashboard when you name it correctly; a decision should be made at this point to effectively choose a relevant name. Initially, we tend to use names that are the least creative, such as Dashboard1, Dashboard copy, and Dashboard new. These names do not state the exact content of the dashboard and often confuse users. Follow the given tips to find an effective name for the dashboard that is highly recognizable:

1. Use a name that accurately describes your dashboard content, for example, Weather monitor for USA, COVID-19 real time bed availability in India, etc.

2. Start with a broader naming convention and then move to a specific subname; this way, you can easily identify which broader category it belongs to, for example, `Sales_Customer_List`, `Sales_Revenue`, `Sales_Forecase`, and so on.

3. Avoid using comparisons or versions, for example, Airline Profits 2022.V1, Airline Profits 2022 v/s 2023, and so on.

Grafana tracks all the dashboard changes and maintains versions. You will always have the option to revert to an older version or rename the dashbaord from dashboard settings.

8.3 Dashboard folders

By now, you have already created a dashboard and named it appropriately. Now, you have to create multiple dashboards based on the requirements and organizational needs. The more dashboards you create, the more difficult it will be to easily identify them and access them seamlessly. The best way to efficiently manage dashboards is by mapping them to related folders. In this section, we will create a new folder for our dashboard management and look at the best practices for folder creation.

8.3.1 Creating a dashboard folder

Follow these steps to create a new dashboard folder:

1. On the sidebar, click on **Dashboard** and then on **+New folder**, as shown in *Figure 8.3*:

Figure 8.3: *Adding New Folder from Dashboard Sidebar*

2. In the name field, enter the folder name and click on **Create**, as shown in *Figure 8.4*. A new folder named `Sample Folder` will be created:

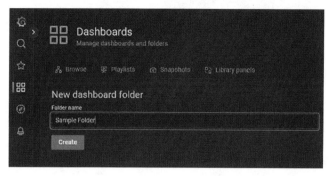

Figure 8.4: *Saving New Dashboard Folder*

8.3.2 Adding dashboards to a folder

After creating a folder, it is important to identify the relevant dashboards and move them into the folder. Grafana also provides the option to select multiple dashboards at once and move them in bulk. You will always have the option to move dashboards from one folder to another as the need arises.

Follow these steps to move the dashboard to a folder:

1. On the sidebar, click on **Dashboard**; you will land in the **Browse** section. Select the **Dashboard(s)** you want to move, as shown in *Figure 8.5*:

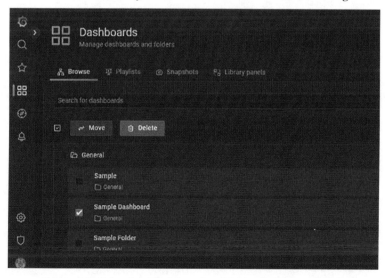

Figure 8.5: *Selecting Dashboard to Move to Different Folder*

2. Select the destination folder and click on **Move**, as shown in *Figure 8.6*:

Figure 8.6: Selecting Destination Folder for moving Dashboard

3. The `Sample Dashboard` will be moved from the **General** folder to the **Sample Folder**, as shown in *Figure 8.7*:

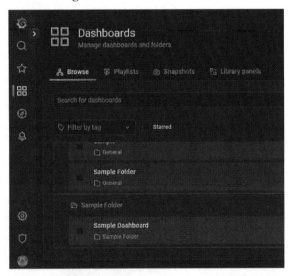

Figure 8.7: Dashboard moved to Destination Folder

8.3.3 Deleting folders

Deleting folders is a part of organizing Grafana dashboards. There will be times when you have to re-map the relevant dashboards to different folders or simply have no need to continue using the folder and dashboards created in it. When deleting a folder, use extreme caution because it will also delete all the data in it. Consider re-evaluating and moving dashboard(s) that should be in different folders before deleting it.

Follow these steps to delete a folder:

1. On the sidebar, click on **Dashboard**; you will land in the **Browse** section. Select the folder you want to delete and click on **Delete**, as shown in *Figure 8.8*:

Figure 8.8: Selecting Dashboard Folder to Delete

2. A confirmation message will pop up; click on **Delete**, as shown in *Figure 8.9*. `Sample Folder2` will be deleted:

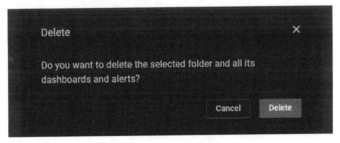

Figure 8.9: Deleting Dashboard Folder

8.3.4 Folder management best practices

Similar to dashboard, folders also should be named and managed well for easier accessibility. Here are a few best practices to follow when creating dashboard folders:

- Do not create too many folders; have fewer folders for easy identification and drill-down.

- Decide on the folder structure before creating it. It is suggested to have folders based on departments for large organizations and folders based on project for smaller teams.

- Avoid having duplicate dashboards in different folders; it will be a maintenance nightmare when you have to make any changes.

8.4 Dashboard starring and tagging

Starring and tagging in Grafana serve two main purposes: organization and accessibility. By starring panels and dashboards, users can mark the ones that are most important or frequently used, making it easier to find and access them later. Tagging, on the other hand, allows users to categorize their panels and dashboards, making it easier to search and filter through large numbers of panels and dashboards.

8.4.1 Marking dashboards as favorites

Frequently used dashboards can be starred, and it is part of individual user experience; starring a dashboard will not make it starred to other users.

Follow these steps to start a dashboard:

1. Open the dashboard to be starred. Click on start next to the dashboard name on the title to **Mark as Favorite**, as shown in *Figure 8.10*:

Figure 8.10: Starring Dashboard

2. On the left sidebar, click on **Starred** to see the newly added dashboard, as shown in *Figure 8.11*. The `Sample Dashboard` will be starred:

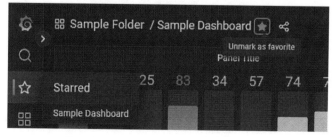

Figure 8.11: Viewing starred dashboard

8.4.2 Tagging dashboards

Tags on the dashboard have much more impact than stars. Grafana allows multiple tags for each dashboard, and they can be used in various ways, like filtering, grouping, and searching. In this section of the chapter, we will explain how to add tags on the dashboard and delete them.

8.4.2.1 Adding tags

Tags can be added directly on the dashboard; you will always have the option to alter the tag, add new tags or delete them in the dashboard settings.

Follow these steps to start a dashboard:

1. Open the dashboard and go to **Settings**.
2. Make sure you are on the **General** tab.
3. In the **Tags** text field, add the tag as desired and click on **Add**, as shown in *Figure 8.12*.
4. The newly created tag will show up in the list; add more tags if required.
5. Click on **Save dashboard** to save the changes.

The **learning** tag will be created on **Sample Dashboard**.

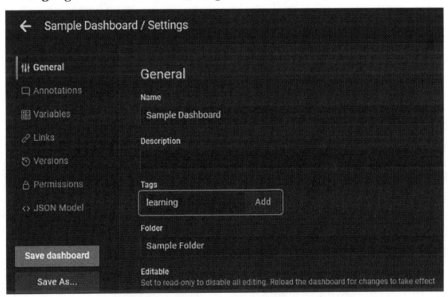

Figure 8.12: Adding Tag on Dashboard

8.4.2.2 Deleting tags

You can delete redundant tag(s) in the dashboard to keep it organized and well maintained. Open the dashboard settings and delete a tag by clicking on **x** next to it, as shown in *Figure 8.13*:

Figure 8.13: *Deleting Dashboard Tag*

8.5 List panel in dashboard

You may have had a glimpse of the List panel if you have looked at the Grafana Home. List panel will show the list of starred dashboards and dashboards that have been viewed recently for quick reference, as shown in *Figure 8.14:*

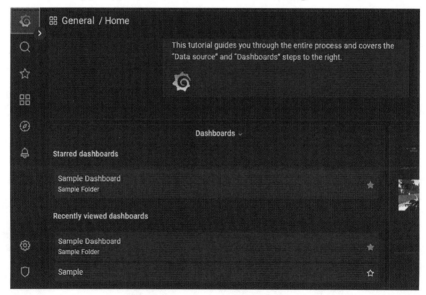

Figure 8.14: *Grafana List Panel*

We can further customize these list as per the user's need. Toggle switches are provided to enable or disable the display of starred, recently viewed, search and show headings, as shown in *Figure 8.15*:

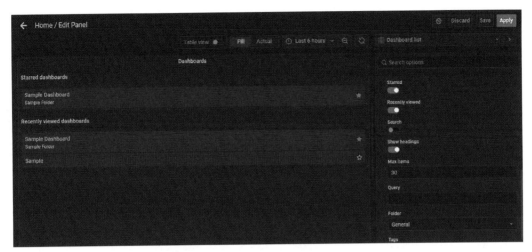

Figure 8.15: Configuring Grafana List Panel

Conclusion

Creating dashboards is the foundation for good monitoring but organizing them well gives the holistic presentation approach for easy navigation and enhanced user experience. In this chapter, we started with naming the dashboards and the best practices to follow while naming the dashboards, creating the folders, adding dashboards into the folder and deleting the dashboards.. Then, we proceeded to learn how to star and tag the dashboards for quick reference. Finally, we explored the dashboard panel and options to customize the panels. You will have other users accessing the dashboards and continuously monitoring it, so you must provide the best dashboard experience by directing them to the destination without much hassle. Regularly maintain the dashboard and folders, and explore options related to tagging and list panel to maximize Grafana monitoring potential.

In the next chapter, we will explore how we can create Alerts.

Multiple choice questions

1. When you delete a folder, will all the dashboard inside the folder also get deleted?

    a. Yes

    b. No

2. Which of the following examples is the preferred way to name a dashboard?

   a. Sales_Past Year_Compared to Current Year

   b. Sales_2023_V1.67_Updated_Latest

   c. Sales_AI Product_2023

   d. Sales_View for CEO_Need Clarification

3. Can you create multiple tags in a single dashboard?

   a. No

   b. Yes

Answers

1. a

2. c

3. b

Join our book's Discord space

Join the book's Discord Workspace for Latest updates, Offers, Tech happenings around the world, New Release and Sessions with the Authors:

https://discord.bpbonline.com

CHAPTER 9
Grafana Alerting

Introduction

In the previous chapters, we looked at Grafana's analytical features. In this chapter, we will explore one of Grafana's key components: alerting. This allows users to receive notifications when certain conditions are met within their data. It is acceptable to focus solely on visualization in many applications. However, in certain situations, it is important to take action based on the monitoring statistics you receive, and alerting is highly beneficial in such cases. We will explore the various options for setting up and managing alerts within Grafana, which will help you stay informed about important changes or trends in your data and take timely action.

Structure

In this chapter, we will learn about the following:

- Threshold setup
- Alerts configuration
- Alerts to notification channel
- Alert state history and management

Objectives

This chapter will familiarize you with creating and configuring alerts, managing alert rules and notifications, and viewing alert state history. By this end of the chapter, you should have understand how to use Grafana's alerting capabilities to stay informed about your data and take timely action when needed.

9.1 Technical requirements

Most of the required installations are already done; for this chapter, apart from it you will only need an active email account to receive alert notifications (Gmail used in the illustration).

9.2 Threshold setup

Grafana allows users to set threshold-based alerts, which trigger notifications when a metric exceeds or falls below a certain value. These alerts can be set to trigger only once, or to repeat at regular intervals. Threshold-based alerts can be extremely useful for monitoring critical systems and ensuring that they are operating within acceptable limits. Open panel in **edit** mode from a dashboard; from the right-hand options menu, you can access and set threshold value as shown in *Figure 9.1*:

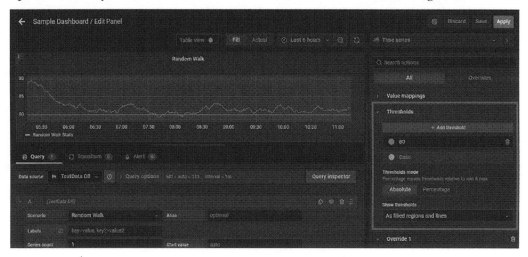

Figure 9.1: Setting Threshold from Dashboard Panel

Grafana also provides the option to change the color of the alert indicator as desired and the set threshold value will be indicated in the graph for visual aesthetics. Grafana provides alerting functionality for time series-based graph panels.

9.3 Alerts configuration

Monitoring applications and visualizing the statistics is a great start, but what if you must make a decision based on these statistics? Consider a situation wherein you are monitoring an application web server and the CPU or memory utilization suddenly exceeded the threshold and remained above 90%; at that point, some action is required to bring the utilization back below the threshold. Otherwise, the application will experience slowness, or the server may crash. We cannot continuously monitor the statistics, and this is where alerts come in and help trigger a notification so that additional action can be taken.

9.3.1 Accessing alerts

Alerts can be accessed from Grafana dashboard panel **Alert** section, as shown in *Figure 9.2*:

Figure 9.2: Accessing Alert from Dashboard Panel

Another way to access alerts from Grafana home screen is by clicking on the **Alerting** menu, as shown in *Figure 9.3*:

Figure 9.3: *Accessing Alert from Home Page*

Both options will land you in the **Alert rule** section, as shown in *Figure 9.4*; click on **New Alert Rule** to create a new rule:

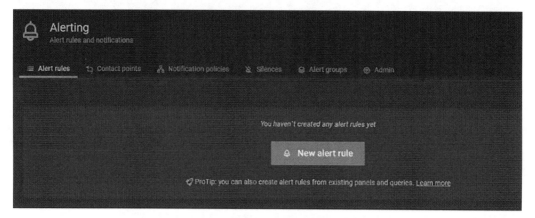

Figure 9.4: *Alert rules section*

9.3.2 Setting up alerts

Utmost caution should be exercised when setting up alert rules as it forms the base on which alerts get triggered. In section A, select the data source (TestData DB is selected for our illustration) and then the scenario for which an alert should be created. The graph will be displayed based on your selection in section A, as shown in *Figure 9.5*:

Figure 9.5: *Alert Data Source and Scenario selection*

Section B sets the condition for which the alert should be triggered. As illustrated in *Figure 9.6*, the alert will be triggered if the last value of Random Walk scenario is above 10:

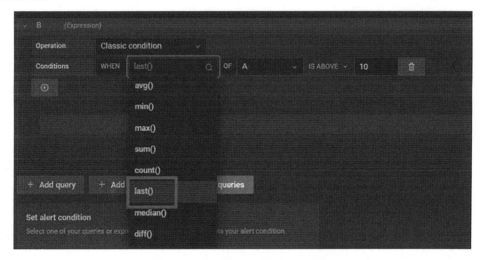

Figure 9.6: *Setting Alert condition*

Section 2 **Alert evaluation behavior** defines a rule for the frequency at which the condition should be checked. As illustrated in *Figure 9.7*, alert condition is validated every 10 seconds, and if the condition is true for 1 min, then the alert is triggered. You can also preview the alert value by clicking on **Preview alerts**:

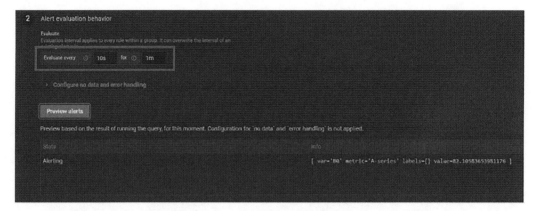

Figure 9.7: Alert Evaluation Behavior set up

In Section 3 **Add details for your alert**, you can configure the alert details to be triggered, like **Summary**, description, and so on, as shown in *Figure 9.8*:

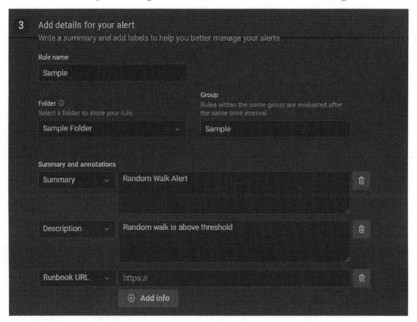

Figure 9.8: Alert Details set up

9.4 Alerts to notification channel

Where alerts should be sent is specified in the notification channel; if alerts are triggered but not received at the correct end channels, then the alerting system will not be useful. Grafana provides several communication channels, like email, Slack, PagerDuty, and so on.

9.4.1 Setting up notification

In our illustration, we will set up a notification to email (Gmail). We also need to update the SMTP configuration setting in the local Grafana folder and give the required access to receive the email notifications. As shown in *Figure 9.9*, Grafana has a default notification policy for all alerts:

Figure 9.9: Default Grafana Notification Policies

Click on the **Contact points** tab and then click on the edit icon of **Grafana default email**, as shown in *Figure 9.10*:

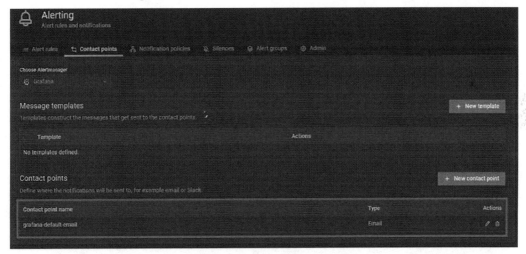

Figure 9.10: Contact points on Grafana

Provide the email ID for which you want to receive alerts in the **Addresses** section, as shown in *Figure 9.11*, and then click **Save**. You can provide multiple email IDs if desired and verify that the email alert can be successfully received by clicking on **Test**:

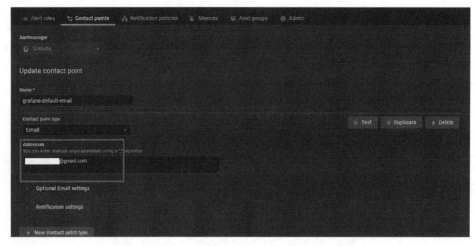

Figure 9.11: *Adding Email ID for notification*

9.4.2 Alert triggers

Now that you are done with setting the alerts and notifications, we have to monitor the alerts to ensure that everything is working as desired. Expand the alert rule to see the status of the alert; if the condition is partially met, then the alert will be in **Pending,** as shown in *Figure 9.12.* In our example, we have set up a condition that **Random walk** value should stay above 10 for 1 minute, now it will continue to check for 1 minute before triggering the alert.

Figure 9.12: *Alert in Pending Status*

Once all conditions are met, the alert status will change to **Firing,** as shown in *Figure 9.13*. If the condition is met partially, the alert will not be triggered:

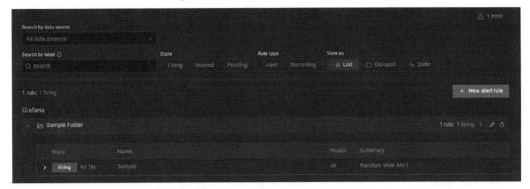

Figure 9.13: *Alert in Firing Status*

An email notification will be received for the alert, as shown in *Figure 9.14*. This communication can be used to take immediate action:

Figure 9.14: *Email Notification of the Alert*

9.5 Alert state history and management

Now that we have set up alerts and notification channel and also received an email notification successfully, let us look into a few more useful options in Grafana, like viewing the history of the alerts and how we can manage the notifications.

9.5.1 Viewing alert state history

Grafana constantly logs and tracks the history of all alerts in the **State History** section. From the alerts rule section, click on **Show State History**, as shown in *Figure 9.15*:

Figure 9.15: Alert History tab from Alert Rules Section

The state history details will be displayed for the previous alerts, as shown in *Figure 9.16*:

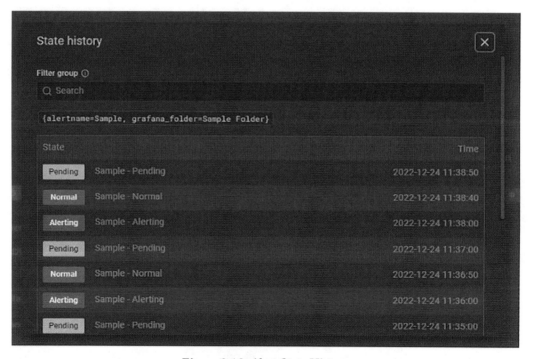

Figure 9.16: Alert State History

9.5.2 Alerts silences

Grafana alert silences let users disable alert notifications for a certain period or until a predetermined event occurs. This is helpful when maintenance or other tasks are being carried out and alerts are not required, or when an alert is raised due to a known problem already being fixed. Through the alerting menu in Grafana, alert silences can be set for a particular dashboard, panel, or even an entire data source. This helps users avoid being inundated with unnecessary notifications and focus on the most important alerts:

Figure 9.17: Setting Up Alert Silences

Conclusion

Grafana alerts and notification extend the capability of Grafana beyond monitoring. It enables the team to have a sense of assurance that a notification will be received if something critical happens. In this chapter, we started with setting the threshold on the graph panel, and then we created detailed alert rules and conditions for which alert should be triggered and set up a Gmail ID to receive email alert notifications. Finally, we explored additional aspects of Grafana alerting, including viewing alert state history and how to set up alert silences. It is advised to try different alert options to get familiarized with alerting and regularly maintain, adjust or delete the alerts that are no longer required.

In the next chapter, we will explore logs using Grafana Loki.

Multiple choice questions

1. Can threshold be set to any type of graph?
    a. Yes
    b. No
2. Which of the following is NOT a status of alert in state history?
    a. Pending
    b. Normal
    c. Alerting
    d. Assigned
3. Can an alert notification be sent to multiple email IDs?
    a. Yes
    b. No

Answers

1. b
2. d
3. a

Join our book's Discord space

Join the book's Discord Workspace for Latest updates, Offers, Tech happenings around the world, New Release and Sessions with the Authors:

https://discord.bpbonline.com

CHAPTER 10
Working with Advanced Dashboard Features

Introduction

At this point, you are likely comfortable using Grafana, but you must have valid concerns regarding the associated work. You may be concerned that the prospect of writing a great deal of code to handle **Extract, Transform, and Load** (**ETL**) activities may consume your budgeted time for creating dashboards. The number of panels you will need to create and manage across several dashboards may appear tiresome and error-prone.

Using template variables, this chapter will examine ways to lessen the ETL effort. We will also demonstrate how annotations enable the examination of individual data points inside aggregated data. Then, we will utilize simple UI components to connect our dashboards. We will then examine techniques for sharing our dashboards with others.

Structure

The following topics will be covered in this chapter:
- Using template variables to interactively visualize data
- Developing links for the dashboard and panels to facilitate navigation

- Annotating data points for examination
- Exporting dashboards for distribution and backup

Objectives

This chapter provides details of variables, annotations, links and config export for better usage of dashboard features and for saving time and effort during work.

10.1 Technical requirements

Since Grafana is a web-based application, you will need to run a few commands to get it up and running. The following are the technical requirements and prerequisites for installing and running Grafana v9.0:

- Knowledge of the command shell
- Install Grafana on the machine of your choice using a terminal application or an SSH
- Java 8 or higher
- Python 3.5 or later
- Git CLI tool
- Docker
- Docker-Compose

Optionally, you will be able to log in as an administrator using the command line to set up and run Grafana.

10.2 Templating dashboards using Grafana variables

The following table lists the types of variables included with Grafana that can be used to template Grafana dashboards:

Variable Type	Description
Query	A collection of information returned by a query, which may contain references to data centers, metrics, servers, and sensor IDs
Chained variables	A variable query may also include a further variable
Custom	Make use of a comma-separated list to define the available values for the variable

Variable Type	Description
Global variables	Variables predefined for usage in the query editor's expressions
Text box	Show a blank text box that can have a starter value typed in
Ad hoc filters	Automatic key/value filters applied to every data source metric query (Prometheus, InfluxDB and Elasticsearch only)
Constant	Establish a secret constant
Interval	Timing intervals represented by interval variables
Data source	In a short amount of time, you may switch the dashboard's data source

Table 10.1: Variables Details

To access the Grafana dashboard's variable's area, click the **Gear** icon in the top-right corner, and then click the **Variables** section on the left, as shown in *Figure 10.1*:

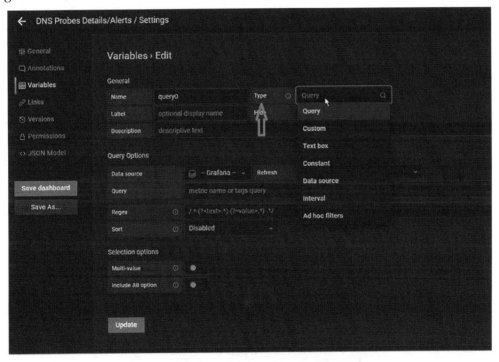

Figure 10.1: Variables Creation

10.3 Linking dashboards

When you add links to your dashboard, they appear at the very top of your dashboard. This is a great way to connect many dashboards into one cohesive whole. An example would be a dashboard that provides an overview of all the nodes reporting in, with links to more granular dashboards where you can check statistics for individual hosts, network statistics, or other dashboards. While you can always return to the Browse or Home menus, narrowing the emphasis like this might help streamline your job.

You can add links to the dashboard in two ways: using a regular link (`Type=Link`) or by using dashboard tags (`Type=Dashboard`). Whenever you add a tag to a dashboard in Grafana, all dashboards with that tag will be automatically included to this dashboard.

10.3.1 Grafana dashboard hierarchy

The goal is to have one dashboard that compiles all the information from the others. We also want a method to access the additional dashboards at the second level should we require further information on a certain system. Here, we will look at the Grafana link builder in action. Grafana allows you to construct connections between panels and between dashboards.

Panel links

Grafana dashboards may be seen via their URLs in any web browser. As you can see in the following figure, this details the real name in addition to a unique ID. Go ahead and open the *second* level dashboard now so that you can write down its URL; you will need it later. You can then define a link on the **Storage** stat panel of the Top-level dashboard once you have the URL in hand. Then, as shown in *Figure 10.2*, select **Panel links** and then **Add link** from the **Options** section of the right pane:

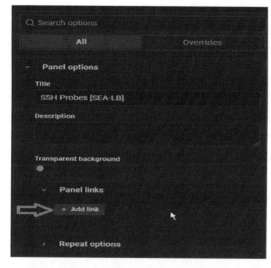

Figure 10.2: Add Panel Link

In this section, you can give your link a title and provide the location where the secondary dashboard we created in the previous step is saved. In addition, you have the option of switching to a different tab to see the other dashboard. You may exit edit mode by clicking **Save**, as shown in *Figure 10.3*:

Figure 10.3: *Storage Link Creation*

You will notice a little arrow indicator in the upper-left corner of the *Stat panel* in the *Top*-level dashboard now. You can view the title of the link you supplied by hovering over it. Clicking on it, as shown in *Figure 10.4*, will bring up the upper-level dashboard:

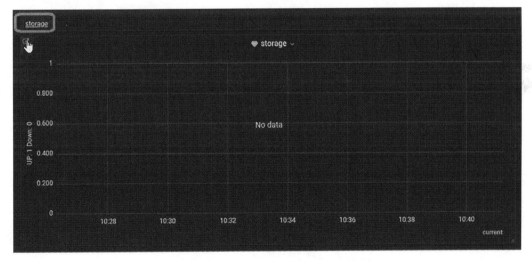

Figure 10.4: *Storage Panel Link Shortcut*

Dashboard links

A second choice is to set up dashboard integrations. Your dashboard's upper-right corner will always display them. Proceed with the creation of two dashboard links:

- You can connect to other monitors by following the links
- Reference an external resource

To get started, head to your dashboard's preferences. From the settings cog in the top-right corner, choose **Links** and then **New Link** on the left side of the dashboard. The term **Dashboards** should be used as the link's label. To be specific, the clickable text will be the **Title** string. We choose **Dashboards** for the **Type** drop-down menu. All your dashboards will appear on one continuous line if you have just a few. *Figure 10.5* shows how to make things more organized by selecting the **Show as dropdown** option if you want to have several:

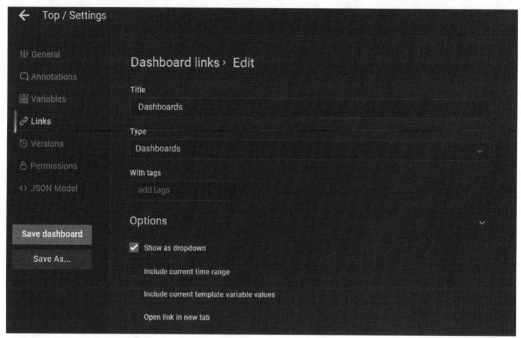

Figure 10.5: Dashboards Dropdown Creation

Given that this top-level dashboard would most likely be shown in an operations center, another possible use is a dashboard link relating to support, such as a customer care system. Let us make a connection that takes us to the vendor's customer care website so that we can submit a ticket. This time, we will use the **Link** format and specify the link's destination URL. As seen in *Figure 10.6*, you can alter the link's appearance by replacing the default icon with one of your own choosing:

Figure 10.6: Dashboard Link Customization

As shown in *Figure 10.7*, after a link has been configured, it will appear in the **Links** option under the dashboard's **Settings**:

Figure 10.7: Dashboard Link Details

The next step is to click **Save Dashboard**, after which you will arrive at a screen similar to the following in the dashboard. You can see in *Figure 10.8* that clicking on the **Dashboards** option brings up the pre-existing dashboards (just *second* in this case):

Figure 10.8: Dashboard Link Shortcut

10.4 Annotations

Using annotations, you can label specific nodes on the network as having significant events. Hovering over an annotation will provide the description and tags for that particular occurrence. You can insert external links to more comprehensive databases into the text box. Clicking the cog symbol in the dashboard's upper-right corner, as shown in *Figure 10.9*, will take you to the **Annotations** settings page:

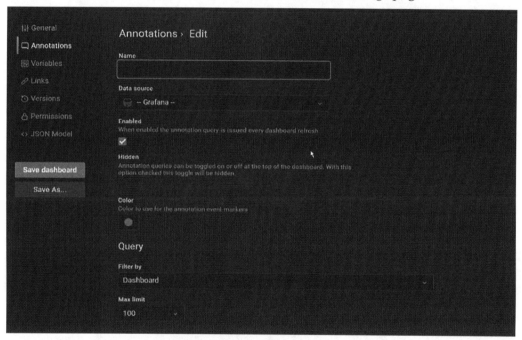

Figure 10.9: Annotation Creation

Give the annotation query a name. This is the label for the checkbox that allows you to select whether or not to display annotation events based on this query. There may be two annotation queries, one named **Deploys** and the other **Outages**, to illustrate. Using the switch, you can select which kind of annotations to view.

10.4.1 Use annotations in dashboards

Dashboard annotations may provide a wealth of additional, time-specific insights into the data you are already collecting. It is possible that annotating data can help your team spot activities or abnormalities that need special attention. You can make changes to an existing annotation, such as changing the content or adding a new date, or you can remove the annotation entirely.

Creating an annotation

In Grafana, annotations are used to mark specific events or time periods on a graph or panel in a dashboard. Annotations can be used to provide context to a graph, explain unusual spikes or dips in data, or mark important events like outages or deployments. Follow these steps to create an annotation in Grafana dashboard:

1. To access the boards, use the left-hand menu and click on Dashboards option.

2. To add an annotation, either choose a dashboard that already exists or make a new one, and then click the **Annotations** option:

    a. To add a time stamp to the graph, hold down the Shift key and click on the specific point you would like to mark.

    b. Select the time period you want to annotate by holding down the Shift key while you click the beginning of the range and drag the mouse to its finish.

    c. You can edit the time range or specific time on the **Add Annotation** page.

    d. Specify a note (up to 255 characters) to be linked to the period or time range you've chosen.

    e. Simply choose **Save Annotation**. It is annotated right in the cell (dotted lines indicate the selected time or time range).

Edit an annotation

Follow these steps to edit an existing annotation in a Grafana dashboard:

1. Select **Boards** from the sidebar menu (**Dashboards**).

2. To make changes to an annotation, access the dashboard containing the annotation, and then click the annotation to open it.

3. You may edit the annotation by typing new text (up to 255 characters) or adding a timestamp and then clicking the **Save Annotation** button.

View or hide annotations

In most cases, annotations will be shown to the public:

1. Boards can be accessed from the left-hand menu (**Dashboards**).

2. Launch an annotated dashboard:

    a. Annotations can be hidden by using the Hide Annotations button. To indicate that annotations are hidden, the button turns gray.

    b. Click the **Annotations** button to reveal the annotations. If you can see annotations, the button will be purple.

Delete an annotation

Take these steps to delete an existing annotation in a Grafana dashboard:

1. Boards can be accessed from the left-hand menu (**Dashboards**).

2. To remove an annotation from a dashboard, open the dashboard in question, click the annotation's dotted line, and then click **Delete Annotation**.

10.5 Exporting dashboards

With Grafana, you can publish your dashboards and panels to the web for the benefit of your whole business or to the public eye, as appropriate. The following methods of dissemination are available to you:

*   A direct link

*   A snapshot

*   An embedded link (for panels only)

*   An export link (for dashboards only)

To view a picture through a direct link, you must be an approved viewer. If you do not have admin privileges or have anonymous access enabled on your Grafana instance, you will need the same authority to read embedded links.

> **Note: Grafana Cloud no longer supports anonymous access authorization as of version 8.0. Snapshots (which are copies of the panel or dashboard at the time the snapshot was taken) are made available online once they have been shared. The information is available to everyone who has the link. As snapshots may be viewed by anybody, regardless of permissions, Grafana scrubs them clean of account details and other sensitive information.**

10.5.1 Sharing a dashboard

Either a snapshot or a live link to a dashboard can be shared with others. As can be seen in *Figure 10.10*, exporting a dashboard is also possible using the following steps:

1. Go to your Grafana installation's landing page.

2. To share content, use the **Share** button located on the main menu.

3. When you click the **Share** button, a dialogue box will display, and you can select the **Link** tab to begin sharing:

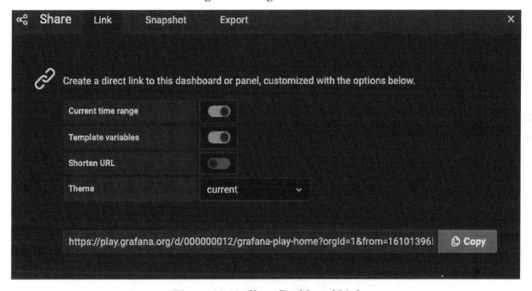

Figure 10.10: Share Dashboard Link

> **Note: In case you decide to modify a dashboard and then share it, remember to save your modifications.**

10.5.2 Sharing a direct link

On the Link page, you can see the active time frame, template variables, and the active design. A shortened link is another option:

1. You should then select **Copy** from the menu.

2. The URL is copied to the clipboard.

3. Just share the copied link with a person in Grafana who has access to it.

10.5.3 Publishing a snapshot

Sharing a dashboard snapshot grants others access to its data. When using Grafana, confidential information like queries (metric, template, and annotation) and panel connections are removed, leaving only the viewable metric data and series names. Once you know the URL, anybody can access the dashboard as it was saved at a certain time. You can choose between publishing to your local instance and snapshots. raintank.io. As a second choice, you can take advantage of Grafana Labs' free service for sharing screenshots of your dashboard on a remote instance of Grafana. Anyone in possession of the link can see it. If you just need the snapshot for a certain amount of time, you can provide an expiration date and time.

Following are the steps to create a snapshot:

1. Select either **Local Snapshot** or **Publish to snapshots.raintank.io**.

2. A snapshot connection is automatically created by Grafana.

3. Take a screenshot and send it around the office or post it online for everyone to see.

4. Snapshots can be removed from your Grafana installation by clicking the **delete snapsho**t button if you happen to have accidentally produced one.

Creating a snapshot is depicted in *Figure 10.11*:

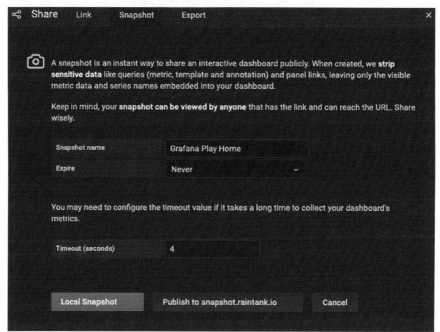

Figure 10.11: Dashboard Snapshot Creation

10.5.4 Exporting a dashboard

Any dashboard may be exported to PDF format and saved for later viewing. *Figure 10.12* demonstrates how straightforward it is to export a Grafana dashboard:

Figure 10.12: Exporting Dashboard

Conclusion

In conclusion, this chapter has explored various aspects of utilizing dashboard features effectively. By incorporating template variables, users can visualize data interactively, enhancing their understanding and analysis. The development of links within the dashboard and panels streamlines navigation, improving user experience. The ability to annotate data points provides a valuable tool for examination and deeper insights. Lastly, the option to export dashboards ensures easy distribution and backup, saving time and effort. By mastering these techniques, users can maximize the potential of their dashboards, optimizing their workflow and achieving greater efficiency in their work. In the next chapter, reader will learn how to explore logs with Grafana Loki.

Multiple choice questions

1. Which of the following variable types are supported in Grafana dashboards?

   a. Query

   b. Custom

   c. Interval

   d. All of the above

2. Does Grafana support importing and exporting dashboard?

   a. Yes

   b. No

Answers

1. d
2. a

Join our book's Discord space

Join the book's Discord Workspace for Latest updates, Offers, Tech happenings around the world, New Release and Sessions with the Authors:

https://discord.bpbonline.com

## Chapter 11

Exploring Logs with Grafana Loki

Introduction

So far, we have delved into the dashboard capabilities of Grafana. This chapter will look into a key concept of data-driven workflow. One of the main challenges in log analysis is the sheer volume of data generated, which can quickly reach gigabytes. This makes accessing and analyzing logs difficult and time-consuming. A more streamlined and cost-effective solution is needed to overcome this challenge. This is where Loki comes into play; it is designed to make searching and filtering logs easier and more structured. The basic concept behind Loki is to label the logs, which enables users to quickly locate and analyze the required information. This helps make log analysis more manageable, reducing the time and effort required to extract meaningful insights from the data.

Structure

In this chapter, we will learn the following:

- Loki architecture
- Installing Loki and Promtail

- Setting-up config files for Loki and Promtail
- Loki log visualization in Grafana

Objectives

This chapter will provide you with an understanding of Loki architecture, a detailed step-by-step explanation on downloading and installing Loki and Promtail, and an understanding of modifying the config files to collect logs and further visualize them in Grafana. By the end of this chapter, you should have a thorough understanding of how to collect logs from a local windows machine using Loki and Promtail and how to effectively visualize the logs in Grafana.

11.1 Technical requirements

Majority of the required installations have already been done. For this chapter, you will need the following apart from that:

- Windows Machine (suggested - Windows 10, 16 GB for 32-bit OS, 2GB RAM)
- Loki and Promtail installed from GitHub (**https://github.com/grafana/loki/releases**)

11.2 Loki architecture

Loki is a decentralized, privacy-focused cryptocurrency that utilizes a service node network for privacy and security, as shown in *Figure 11.1*. It has features like private transactions, session transactions and Lokinet. Promtail is a log data collection agent and part of the Loki logging stack; it is responsible for collecting log data from various sources and shipping it to a centralized Loki server for storage and indexing. Promtail is designed to be highly scalable, efficient, and flexible, making it an ideal solution for log data collection and management. Together, Loki and Promtail provide a powerful and secure log management and analysis solution.

Loki uniquely indexes on metadata instead of accessing entire text in the log lines. Some of the key advantages of Loki are privacy, scalability and efficiency. Once Promtail has collected and shipped log data to a centralized Loki server, the log data can be queried and visualized in Grafana.

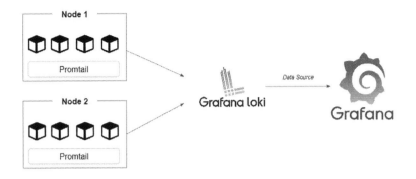

Figure 11.1: *Loki Architecture*

11.3 Installing Loki and Promtail

Visit the GitHub link **https://github.com/grafana/loki/releases** to download the relevant files. For the purpose of demonstration, we will install Loki (loki-windows-amd64) and Promtail (promtail-windows-amd64) on a local Windows machine. The stable version used in the demonstration is v2.7.1. This version has been tested and has proven to be reliable. To visualize the logs in Grafana, we will be reading the log data from a local folder. This allows us to work with the log data in a familiar environment, making it easier to understand the log collection and visualization process using Loki and Promtail. The resources for Loki and Promtail are maintained on a GitHub repository, as shown in *Figure 11.2*, making it easy to download the latest stable version:

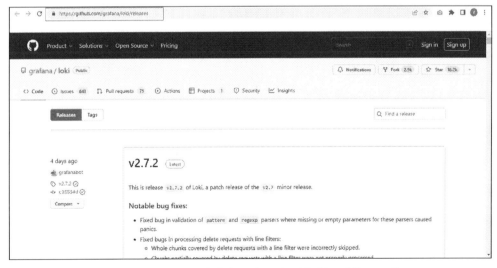

Figure 11.2: *GitHub link to download Loki and Promtail*

Following are the steps to download standard config files for Loki and Promtail:

1. Download Loki and Promtail ZIP files from GitHub.

2. Unzip both **.exe** files in a same directory.

3. Download standard config files for Loki and Promtail from the following link:

   - Loki: **https://raw.githubusercontent.com/grafana/loki/main/cmd/loki/loki-local-config.yaml**

   - Promtail: **https://raw.githubusercontent.com/grafana/loki/main/clients/cmd/promtail/promtail-local-config.yaml**

Now you have all the required files to start using Loki and Promtail locally. But to collect logs, we need to make some changes to the **.yaml** file. In the upcoming sections, we will achieve this and start generating and visualizing logs in Grafana.

11.4 Setting-up config files for Loki and Promtail

The standard configuration files you downloaded serve as useful templates, but it is necessary to customize them to meet your specific requirements to make the logs visible in Grafana. These configuration files play a crucial role in the functioning of Loki and Promtail, as all the conditions and configurations for log collection and visualization are derived from these files.

11.4.1 Updating .yaml files

Open config files for both Loki and Promtail from the local folder location and replace existing config file with the following content; open the files in notepad to make changes and save them

```
Loki:


auth_enabled: false


server:

  http_listen_port: 3100


ingester:
```

```
lifecycler:

  address: 127.0.0.1

  ring:

    kvstore:

      store: inmemory

    replication_factor: 1

  final_sleep: 0s

chunk_idle_period: 1h          # Any chunk not receiving new logs in this
                               time will be flushed

max_chunk_age: 1h              # All chunks will be flushed when they hit
                               this age, default is 1h

chunk_target_size: 1048576     # Loki will attempt to build chunks up to
                               1.5MB, flushing first if chunk_idle_period or
                               max_chunk_age is reached first

chunk_retain_period: 30s       # Must be greater than index read cache TTL
                               if using an index cache (Default index read
                               cache TTL is 5m)

max_transfer_retries: 0        # Chunk transfers disabled


schema_config:

  configs:

    - from: 2020-10-24

      store: boltdb-shipper

      object_store: filesystem

      schema: v11

      index:

        prefix: index_

        period: 24h
```

```yaml
storage_config:

  boltdb_shipper:

    active_index_directory: ./data/loki/boltdb-shipper-active

    cache_location: ./data/loki/boltdb-shipper-cache

    cache_ttl: 24h          # Can be increased for faster performance over
                            longer query periods, uses more disk space

    shared_store: filesystem

  filesystem:

    directory: ./data/loki/chunks


compactor:

  working_directory: ./data/loki/boltdb-shipper-compactor

  shared_store: filesystem


limits_config:

  reject_old_samples: true

  reject_old_samples_max_age: 168h


chunk_store_config:

  max_look_back_period: 0s


table_manager:

  retention_deletes_enabled: false

  retention_period: 0s


ruler:

  storage:

    type: local

    local:
```

```
    directory: ./data/loki/rules

  rule_path: ./data/loki/rules-temp

  alertmanager_url: http://localhost:9093

  ring:

    kvstore:

      store: inmemory

  enable_api: true
```

Promtail:

```
server:

  http_listen_port: 9080

  grpc_listen_port: 0


positions:

  filename: ./positions.yaml


clients:

  - url: http://localhost:3100/loki/api/v1/push


scrape_configs:

- job_name: grafana

  static_configs:

  - targets:

      - localhost

    labels:

      job: grafana

      __path__: C:\Program Files\GrafanaLabs\grafana\data\log\*.log
# Above path should be location of grafana log in your local system
```

11.4.2 Run Loki and Promtail locally

Follow these steps to execute Loki and Promtail locally to collect logs:

1. Open two different instances of command prompt.

2. Navigate to the folder where Loki and Promtail is installed.

3. Execute the command shown in *Figure 11.3* for Loki:

   Loki: `loki-windows-amd64.exe --config.file=loki-local-config.yaml`

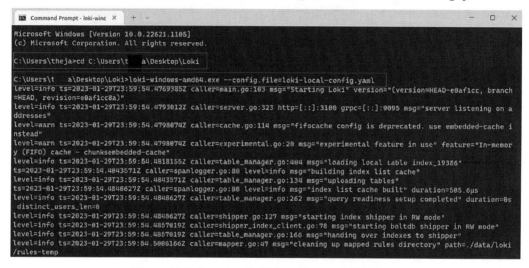

Figure 11.3: Running Loki from Command-Prompt

4. Execute the command for Promtail, as shown in *Figure 11.4*:

   Promtail: `promtail-windows-amd64.exe --config.file=promtail-local-config.yaml`

Figure 11.4: Running Promtail from Command-Prompt

5. To view metrics locally, access the URL **http://localhost:3100/metrics**, as shown in *Figure 11.5*:

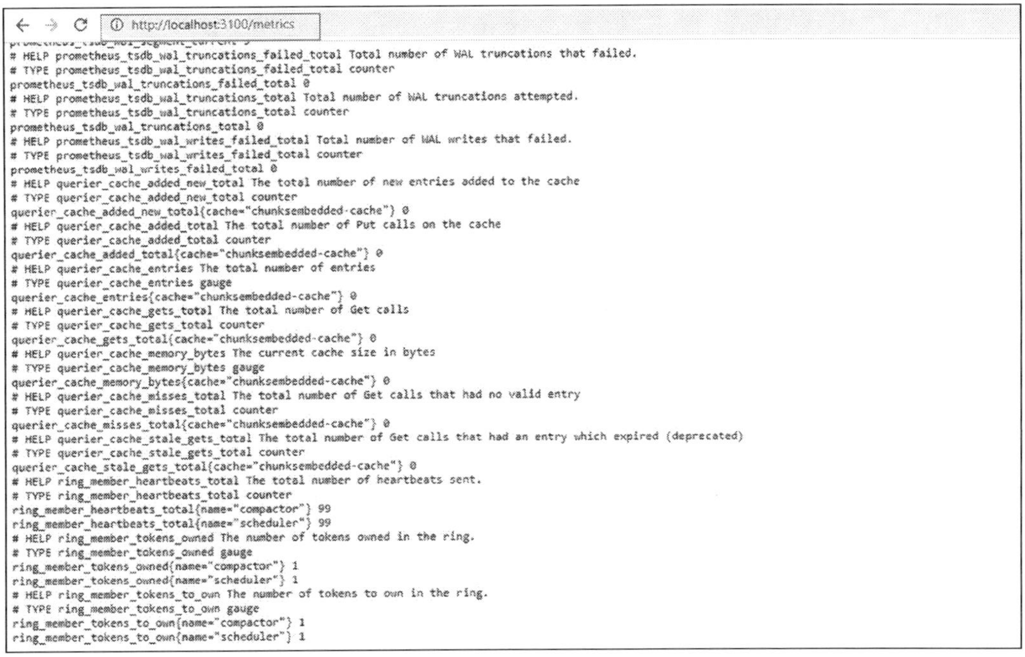

```
←  →  C  ⓘ http://localhost:3100/metrics
pt........._t.db_w.._.egm.nt_cut.... 5
# HELP prometheus_tsdb_wal_truncations_failed_total Total number of WAL truncations that failed.
# TYPE prometheus_tsdb_wal_truncations_failed_total counter
prometheus_tsdb_wal_truncations_failed_total 0
# HELP prometheus_tsdb_wal_truncations_total Total number of WAL truncations attempted.
# TYPE prometheus_tsdb_wal_truncations_total counter
prometheus_tsdb_wal_truncations_total 0
# HELP prometheus_tsdb_wal_writes_failed_total Total number of WAL writes that failed.
# TYPE prometheus_tsdb_wal_writes_failed_total counter
prometheus_tsdb_wal_writes_failed_total 0
# HELP querier_cache_added_new_total The total number of new entries added to the cache
# TYPE querier_cache_added_new_total counter
querier_cache_added_new_total{cache="chunksembedded-cache"} 0
# HELP querier_cache_added_total The total number of Put calls on the cache
# TYPE querier_cache_added_total counter
querier_cache_added_total{cache="chunksembedded-cache"} 0
# HELP querier_cache_entries The total number of entries
# TYPE querier_cache_entries gauge
querier_cache_entries{cache="chunksembedded-cache"} 0
# HELP querier_cache_gets_total The total number of Get calls
# TYPE querier_cache_gets_total counter
querier_cache_gets_total{cache="chunksembedded-cache"} 0
# HELP querier_cache_memory_bytes The current cache size in bytes
# TYPE querier_cache_memory_bytes gauge
querier_cache_memory_bytes{cache="chunksembedded-cache"} 0
# HELP querier_cache_misses_total The total number of Get calls that had no valid entry
# TYPE querier_cache_misses_total counter
querier_cache_misses_total{cache="chunksembedded-cache"} 0
# HELP querier_cache_stale_gets_total The total number of Get calls that had an entry which expired (deprecated)
# TYPE querier_cache_stale_gets_total counter
querier_cache_stale_gets_total{cache="chunksembedded-cache"} 0
# HELP ring_member_heartbeats_total The total number of heartbeats sent.
# TYPE ring_member_heartbeats_total counter
ring_member_heartbeats_total{name="compactor"} 99
ring_member_heartbeats_total{name="scheduler"} 99
# HELP ring_member_tokens_owned The number of tokens owned in the ring.
# TYPE ring_member_tokens_owned gauge
ring_member_tokens_owned{name="compactor"} 1
ring_member_tokens_owned{name="scheduler"} 1
# HELP ring_member_tokens_to_own The number of tokens to own in the ring.
# TYPE ring_member_tokens_to_own gauge
ring_member_tokens_to_own{name="compactor"} 1
ring_member_tokens_to_own{name="scheduler"} 1
```

Figure 11.5: *Viewing metrics from localhost*

Now that you are successfully running Loki and Promtail from your local windows server, in the next section, we will explore how we can visualize these logs in Grafana.

11.5 Loki log visualization in Grafana

In order to effectively visualize log data, it is necessary to connect Loki as a data source within Grafana. By doing so, we can access the logs and use Grafana's powerful querying capabilities to modify and customize the visual representation of the data. This allows us to tailor the visualization to our needs and requirements.

11.5.1 Adding Loki as data source

Open Grafana directly from the home page and click on **Configuration** in the right-hand panel. Now click on **Data Source**, as shown in *Figure 11.6*:

Figure 11.6*: Open Data sources from Grafana home page*

From the list of available data sources, select **Loki,** as shown in *Figure 11.7*:

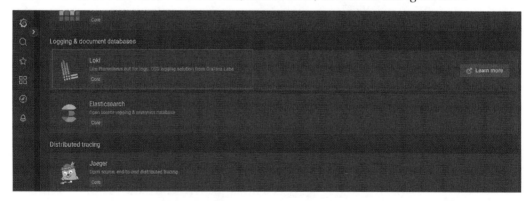

Figure 11.7*: Selecting Loki as Data source*

In the Loki data source, fill the HTTP details as `http://localhost:3100`. Click on **Save & test**; you should get a success message saying **Data source connected and labels found**, as shown in *Figure 11.8*:

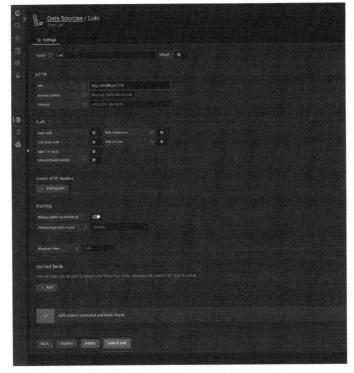

Figure 11.8: *Setting-up Loki configuration*

11.5.2 Visualizing logs in Grafana

You can click on **Explore** from the Loki data source page or from the Grafana home page right-hand panel click on **Explore**, as shown in *Figure 11.9*:

Figure 11.9: *Accessing Explore from Grafana home page*

Make sure the data source is selected as **Loki**. You should see the relevant labels based on the logs and config file. For the purpose of demonstration, label **job** is selected, as shown in *Figure 11.10*:

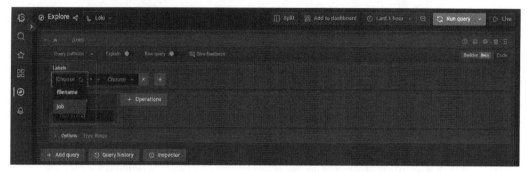

Figure 11.10: Selecting Labels to visualize in Grafana

Visualization graph is displayed as shown in *Figure 11.11*; you can select different labels and timeframe to view the corresponding logs:

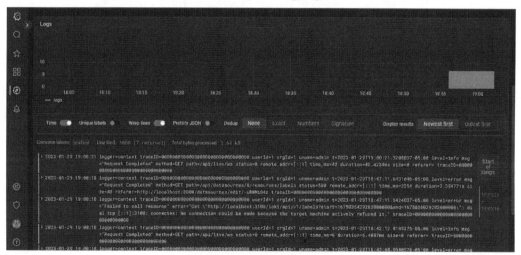

Figure 11.11: Grafana Visualization

Conclusion

Loki has made log aggregation and analysis really effective and affordable. It can host multi-tenant and is highly scalable. A step-by-step process for installing both Loki and Promtail, which are the two critical components of the system, was demonstrated in this chapter. We also downloaded and modified the config files as a necessary step. With the help of Promtail and Loki, we saw how we can set up log visualization in Grafana; these are very prominent combinations and can make way for more innovation in log aggregation and visualization process. You are encouraged to further explore the Loki capabilities, collect and visualize logs from different systems, modify Grafana query to fetch different values, and so on.

The next chapter will explore how we can manage authorization and authentication for users and teams.

Multiple choice questions

1. What is Loki in Grafana used as?

    a. A database management system

    b. A log aggregation system

    c. A machine learning model

2. What type of data can be ingested into Loki in Grafana?

    a. Binary data

    b. Text data

    c. Audio data

3. What are the benefits of using Loki in Grafana for log analysis?

    a. Scalability

    b. Real-time querying

    c. High availability

    d. All of the above

Answers

1. b
2. b
3. d

Join our book's Discord space

Join the book's Discord Workspace for Latest updates, Offers, Tech happenings around the world, New Release and Sessions with the Authors:

https://discord.bpbonline.com

## CHAPTER 12

Managing Authorization and Authentication

Introduction

This chapter examines how people, teams, and organizations manage access to Grafana resources like dashboards, folders, and data sources. We will begin by examining how to add users to a Grafana site and how to manage the permissions for those users. Once we have covered the principles of user permissions, we will examine how combining users into teams can effectively manage permissions on a wider scale. Finally, we will examine how to divide a Grafana site into organizations with different users, data sources, and dashboards, allowing the security benefits of isolation to be provided without the need to maintain additional servers.

Structure

This chapter will address the following topics:

- Understanding critical permissions ideas
- Establishing teams
- User management in Grafana organization
- User and organization administration

- Configure Google OAuth2 authentication
- Analyze the Google OAuth2 configuration

Objectives

This chapter explains the authentication and authorization of Grafana users and teams for successful management. Authentication verifies the identity of a user, and authorization determines user access rights.

12.1 Technical requirements

Since Grafana is a web-based application, you will need to run a few commands to get it up and running. The following are the technical requirements and other prerequisites for installing and running Grafana of version v9.0:

- Knowledge of the command shell
- Install Grafana on the machine of your choice using a terminal application or an SSH
- Java 8 or higher
- Python 3.5 or later
- Git CLI tool
- Docker
- Docker-Compose

Optionally, you will be able to log in as an administrator using the command line to set up and run Grafana.

12.2 Understanding key permissions concepts

Permissions are represented in Grafana by the following fundamental concepts:

- **Organizations**: Grafana permits the formation of many organizations, each with its own set of users and rights.
- **Roles**: Grafana includes four predefined user roles: Viewer, Editor, Admin, and Super Admin. Each position has its own set of privileges, such as the ability to build and change dashboards and manage users.

- o   **Admin role**: Can do all tasks within the organization's purview according to the points listed here:
    - ▪ Add and edit source data
    - ▪ Users and teams can be added and edited.
    - ▪ Configure application plugins and organization settings
- o   **Editor role**: Create and change dashboards and notification rules; this feature may be deactivated for particular folders and dashboards.
    - ▪ Not permitted to establish or update data sources or invite new users
- o   **Viewer role**: Explore any dashboard; this feature may be deactivated for particular folders and dashboards.
    - ▪ Not permitted to build or modify dashboards or data sources
- **Permissions**: Permissions in Grafana dictate users' activities inside an organization. For instance, a user with the **View** permission can only view dashboards, but a person with the **Update** access will be able to create and edit dashboards.
- **Inheritance**: Roles and permissions can be inherited from one level of the organization to the next, such that users at lower levels automatically inherit the permissions of their parent.
- **Teams**: Grafana allows users to be grouped into teams, to which responsibilities and permissions may be provided.
- **Dashboard-level permissions**: Grafana also enables dashboard-level permission settings, enabling granular control over who can see and change certain dashboards.
- **Folder-level permissions**: Grafana has folder-level permission settings, enabling granular control over who can see and update certain folders.
- **Data source-level permissions**: Grafana permits the setup of permissions at the data source level, enabling fine-grained control over who can see and update certain data sources.
- **Panel-level permissions**: Users who have authority to build and update dashboards can establish and manage panel-level permissions. This enables them to regulate the degree of access other users have to panels and the data they show.

12.3 Managing users in Grafana organization

Users can be added to a Grafana organization through the server admin interface. The initial user added to an organization is configured as an administrator by default. Grafana has three types of organizational functions:

- **Grafana admin:** This is a global role held by the default administrator user. Grafana admin can administer organizations, users, and server-wide configurations.

- **Organization administrator:** This job can handle the organization's data sources, teams, and users.

- **Editors and viewers:** These positions have restricted access to resources, including dashboards, data sources, and alarms.

To add a user to an organization, you must navigate to Server Admin via the **Configuration** menu and create new users under the user's tab. You can also invite individuals to the organization; this is the only method for adding new users. The invitees will get an email with instructions for creating their accounts.

It is important to note that establishing a new user in Grafana and setting a password can be done via the Server Admin panel's **Configuration** menu, under the **Users** tab.

12.4 Establishing teams in Grafana

Teams can be created in Grafana in the Configuration section as shown in *Figure 12.1*:

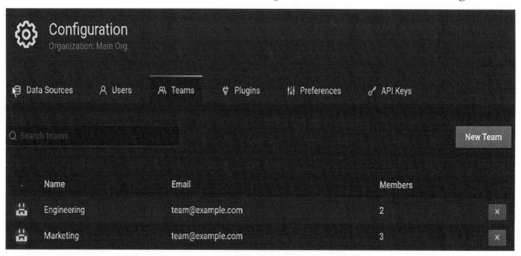

Figure 12.1: Teams creation

There are numerous steps a Grafana System Administrator may take to form teams in Grafana:

1. **Assign Roles to Users:** Grafana's organization roles consist of Grafana Admin, Organization Administrator, and Viewer. The Grafana Admin position permits the management of organizations, users, and server-wide settings, whereas the Organization Administrator role permits management of data sources, teams, and users inside an organization. Users should be assigned the appropriate role depending on their duties.

2. **Create Teams:** To create a team, click the **New team** button in the Configuration | Teams area of the sidebar, and then input the team's name and optional email address. Next, click the **Create** button.

3. **Add Users to Teams:** Add users to the relevant team after creating teams. This can be accomplished by modifying the user's profile and choosing the desired team from the drop-down menu.

4. **Synchronize with external groups:** In addition, a Grafana team's activity may be coordinated with that of an external group. In order to synchronize with an IAM Identity Center group, navigate to the **Configuration** section of the Grafana interface, click on Teams, and then enter the IAM Identity Center group ID. Insert the attribute value supplied in the **Assertion** attribute so that you can synchronize with a group derived from a SAML-based identity provider.

5. **Configure Alerting:** Use the Grafana alerting tool to set your notifications. You can build and manage alerting rules for Grafana, set up alert groups, disable alert notifications for Prometheus data sources, connect with contact points, use messaging templates, and manage notification policies.

By building teams and delegating responsibilities, you can ensure that only authorized individuals have access to sensitive data and are able to complete the necessary duties.

12.5 Administering users and organizations in Grafana

Managing access to the system and ensuring that only authorized users have access to critical information depends on the administration of users and organizations in Grafana. The Super Admin job is required to manage users. This job allows you to create and assign roles to users, as shown in *Figure 12.2*. Follow these steps to assign a user certain role:

1. Choose **Configuration** ǀ **Users** from the sidebar.
2. Using the sidebar, navigate to **Configuration** ǀ **Users**.
3. Locate the user account for which you wish to modify the role.
4. Find the user in the list, then under the **Role** column, click the person's role.
5. Select the desired assignment role.

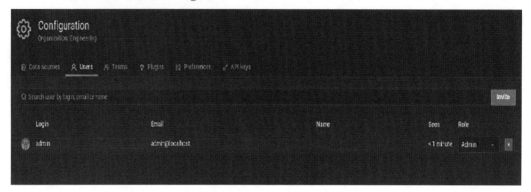

Figure 12.2: Users Creation

You may use the same procedure to administrate organizations. Organizations are the responsibility of Grafana Server Administrators, as shown in *Figure 12.3*:

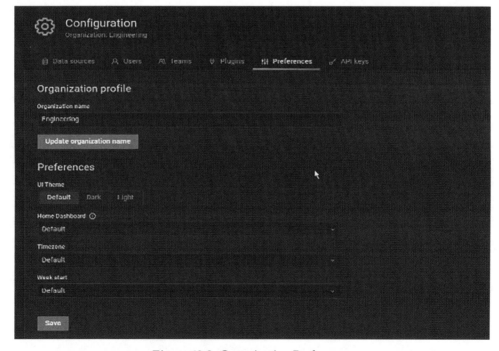

Figure 12.3: Organization Preferences

Organizations are used to partition resources, such as dashboards, so that members of one organization cannot access dashboards allocated to another organization. Nevertheless, a user can be a member of many organizations. It is vital to note that users can only access dashboards that have been allocated to their company. This ensures that only authorized parties have access to sensitive information. By managing users and organizations in Grafana, you can control access to resources and guarantee that only authorized users have access to sensitive data.

12.6 Configuring Google OAuth2 authentication

The following steps will help in configuring Google OAuth2 authentication mechanism in Grafana.

1. **Generate your own Google OAuth keys**

   To get started, you must configure a Google OAuth Client by following these steps:

   a. Navigate to **https://console.developers.google.com/apis/credentials**.

   b. After clicking the button labeled **Create Credentials**, select **OAuth Client ID** from the drop-down menu.

   c. The following should be entered:

      i. Type of Application: Web

      ii. Name of Application: Grafana

      iii. JavaScript Origins Can Be Found At: **https://<your-custom-grafana-endpoint-hostname>**

      iv. Authorized Redirect URLs: **https://<your-custom-grafana-endpoint-hostname >/login/google**

   d. Select from the drop-down the option labeled create **x**.

   e. It is important to make a copy of the Client Secret and Client ID generated.

2. **Configure Google OAuth in Grafana**

   You must incorporate the Client ID and the Secret into the Grafana configuration file you are using. Take just one illustration out of a great number of others:

   ```
   [auth.google]
   client_secret = CLIENT_SECRET
   enabled = true
   ```

```
client_id = CLIENT_ID

allow_sign_up = true

scopes = https://www.googleapis.com/auth/userinfo.email  https://
www.googleapis.com/auth/userinfo.profile

auth_url = https://accounts.google.com/o/oauth2/auth

token_url = https://accounts.google.com/o/oauth2/token

allowed_domains = <your-company>.org <your-company>.com
```

A button to sign in with Google should now be present on the login page. Signing in or creating an account may now be done using a Google account. The authorized domains parameter is entirely discretionary, and the domains themselves are separated by spaces. By setting the enable sign up option to the true value, you can make it feasible for people to sign up using Google OAuth2 authentication. This may be done by changing the Boolean value of the option. Any user who authenticates themselves using Google authentication and has this option set to true will have their participation in the program immediately added to their account if the option is enabled.

12.7 Testing the Google OAuth2 authentication configuration

To test the Google OAuth2 configuration in Grafana v9.0 and later, you must follow the given steps:

1. In the Grafana interface, navigate to Configuration | Authentication.

2. Select Google from the available service providers.

3. Enter the Client ID and the Client Secret that you acquired from the Google API Console.

4. Configure the remaining parameters as necessary, including the Allowed Domains and Scopes.

5. Save the modifications and test the setup by signing into Grafana with your Google account.

If the setting is right, you should be able to log in to Grafana using your Google account and be allowed access to the necessary resources depending on the defined scopes. Note that the methods for configuring Google OAuth2 may vary based on the version of Grafana and the exact parameters you need to specify.

Conclusion

In conclusion, managing authentication and authorization in Grafana is crucial to ensure the security of your Grafana instance and the data it displays. This chapter covered OAuth authentication method that can be used in Grafana. Additionally, we explored various authorization mechanisms, such as role-based access control, user-based access control, team-based access control and organization wide permissions. Finally, it is important to carefully consider the needs of your organization and the level of security required when selecting an authentication and authorization method for your Grafana instance. A well-designed authentication and authorization strategy can help ensure that only authorized users have access to sensitive data and features within Grafana.

In the next chapter, we will discuss Blackbox exporter, which can be used to perform different health checks.

Multiple choice questions

1. GitHub OAuth2 Authentication is not supported in Grafana.

    a. True

    b. False

2. Multiple user roles are supported in Grafana.

    a. True

    b. False

3. Teams can be created to manage user permissions.

    a. True

    b. False

Answers

1. b

2. a

3. a

Join our book's Discord space

Join the book's Discord Workspace for Latest updates, Offers, Tech happenings around the world, New Release and Sessions with the Authors:

https://discord.bpbonline.com

CHAPTER 13
Blackbox Exporter

Introduction

Till now, we have monitored logs from local system; now, let us look into monitoring external sources like websites. It is also one of the highly used capabilities in Grafana monitoring. In the following chapter, we will look at how we can leverage Blackbox Exporter in connection with Prometheus and Grafana to probe website information and visualize it. A Blackbox Exporter is a powerful tool that allows you to monitor the availability and performance of endpoints and services, including their response time, availability and error rate. Blackbox Exporter provides valuable insights into the health and performance of websites and has seamless integration with Grafana for visualizing and analyzing the data, which helps in quickly identifying and resolving performance issues.

Structure

In this chapter, we will learn about the following:

- What is Blackbox Exporter?
- Installing Blackbox Exporter

- Setting-up Blackbox and .yml files
- Monitoring websites performance in Grafana

Objectives

This chapter will provide understanding of Blackbox Exporter architecture, detailed step-by-step explanation on downloading and installing Blackbox Exporter, modifying the config files to probe website status and further visualize them in Grafana. By the end of this chapter, you will have a good understanding of how to probe website information from local windows machine using Blackbox Exporter and how to effectively visualize the statistics in Grafana.

13.1 Technical requirements

In addition to the installations already done so far, you will need the following for this chapter:

- Windows machine with admin privileges
- Prometheus pre-installed
- Blackbox Exporter to be installed from GitHub

13.2 What is Blackbox Exporter?

Blackbox Exporter is a tool mainly utilized for the purpose of monitoring and troubleshooting network endpoints like websites, servers and applications. It provides a simple yet powerful interface for performing various types of probes, such as HTTP, TCP, DNS, and ICMP. With Blackbox Exporter, you can gather critical information about the performance, availability, and accessibility of your network endpoints, which can be used to optimize their performance and prevent outages. Additionally, Blackbox Exporter allows you to define custom probes and alerts to better monitor your infrastructure. Blackbox Exporter is an essential tool for ensuring the reliability of network infrastructure and integrates well with Prometheus and Grafana.

As shown in *Figure 13.1*, Blackbox Exporter has a simple architecture: it is installed in the target machine, from where it makes the intended HTTP requests and collects required statistics and send it to Prometheus. From Prometheus, the statistics are fetched by Grafana for visualization.

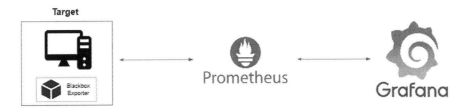

Figure 13.1: *Blackbox Exporter Architecture*

13.3 Installing Blackbox Exporter

It is necessary to have Prometheus installed on the target machine as a prerequisite; the steps to install Prometheus are stated earlier in the book. Visit the GitHub link at **https://GitHub.com/prometheus/blackbox_exporter/releases** to download the relevant files. For the purpose of demonstration, we will install Blackbox Exporter (`blackbox_exporter-0.23.0.windows-amd64`) on a local Windows machine. The resources to download Blackbox Exporter are maintained on a GitHub repository, as shown in *Figure 13.2*:

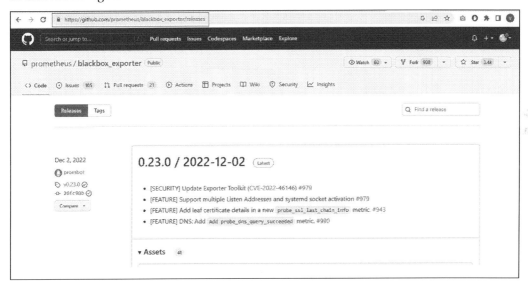

Figure 13.2: *GitHub link to download Blackbox Exporter*

Here are the steps to acquire the required setup:

1. Download Blackbox Exporter ZIP file from GitHub.

2. Unzip on a local directory.

3. Make sure you have **blackbox_exporter.exe** and **blackbox.yml** files.

Now, you have the required setup to run Blackbox Exporter locally. But to probe websites and collect statistics, we need to make some changes to the **.yal** file for both Prometheus and Blackbox Exporter. In the upcoming sections, we will achieve this and start probing and visualizing website performance in Grafana.

13.4 Setting-up Blackbox and .yml files

In order to successfully probe websites using the Blackbox Exporter, we need to ensure that the required **blackbox.yml** file is present in the Blackbox Exporter directory. However, it is important to note that simply having the file is not enough. The configuration file must be updated appropriately to accurately instruct the rules and for the visualization.

It is crucial to pay close attention to the contents of the **blackbox.yml** file as it plays a vital role in determining the success of the probing process. Properly updating the file will ensure that you get the desired results and can visualize the data in an effective manner. Failing to update the file appropriately could result in inaccurate results or even failure of the probing process.

13.4.1 Updating .yml files

We have to make changes to both Prometheus and Blackbox **.yml** files. First, let us open the **blackbox.yml** file from the local **Blackbox** folder location and replace the **blackbox.yml** file with the following content; then, open the file in notepad to make changes and save it:

```
modules:

  http_2xx:

    http:

      fail_if_not_ssl: true

      ip_protocol_fallback: false

      method: GET

      no_follow_redirects: false

      preferred_ip_protocol: ip4

      valid_http_versions:

        - HTTP/1.1
```

```
    - HTTP/2.0

  prober: http

  timeout: 15s
```

Now, open the **prometheus.yml** file from the local Prometheus folder location and add the following content in the **Static_Configs** section of the file. Open the file in the notepad to make changes and save it. In the **targets** section, you can provide additional websites you want to collect statistics for visualization.

```
static_configs:

    - targets: ["localhost:9090"]


  - job_name: 'blackbox'

    metrics_path: /probe

    params:

      module: [http_2xx]  # Look for a HTTP 200 response.

    static_configs:

      - targets:

        - http://prometheus.io     # Target to probe with http.

        - https://prometheus.io    # Target to probe with https.

       - http://example.com:8080 # Target to probe with http on port 8080.

        - https://www.aaitp.org   # Target to probe with https.

       - http://www.youtube.com # Target to probe with http on port 8080.

    relabel_configs:

      - source_labels: [__address__]

        target_label: __param_target

      - source_labels: [__param_target]

        target_label: instance

      - target_label: __address__
```

```
replacement: localhost:9115  # The blackbox exporter's real
hostname:port.
```

13.4.2 Run Prometheus and Blackbox Exporter locally

Follow these steps to execute Prometheus and Blackbox Exporter to start probing websites:

1. Open two different instances of Command-prompt.

2. Navigate to the folder where Prometheus and Blackbox Exporter are installed.

3. Execute the following command for Prometheus, as shown in *Figure 13.3*:

   Prometheus: **prometheus.exe --config.file prometheus.yml --web.listen-address ":9090" --storage.tsdb.path "data"**

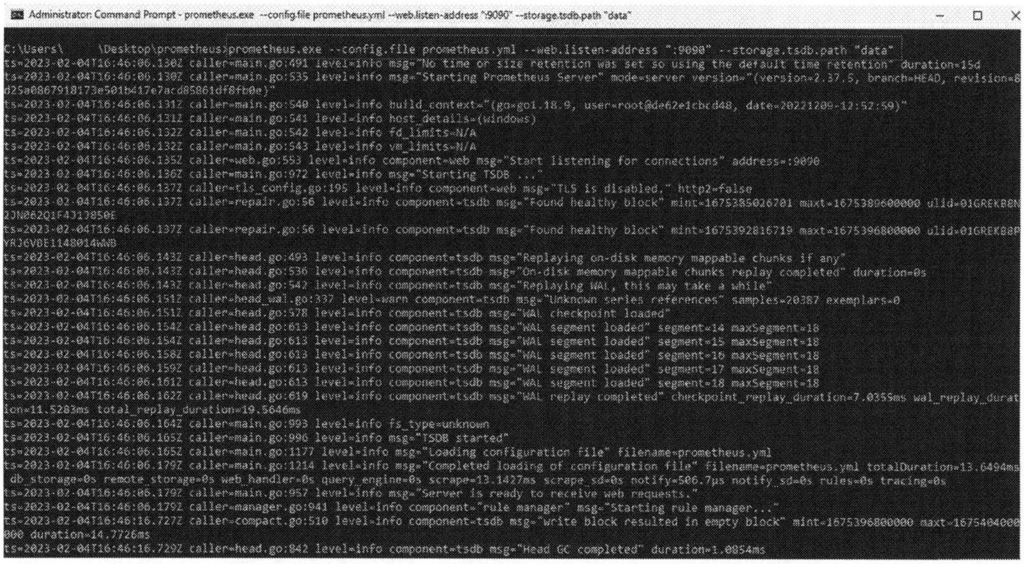

Figure 13.3: Running Prometheus from Command-Prompt

4. Execute the following command for Blackbox, as shown in *Figure 13.4*:

   Blackbox Exporter: **blackbox_exporter.exe --config.file blackbox.yml**

Figure 13.4: Running Blackbox Exporter from Command-Prompt

5. To view Blackbox Exporter information locally, access the URL `http://localhost:9115`, as shown in *Figure 13.5*:

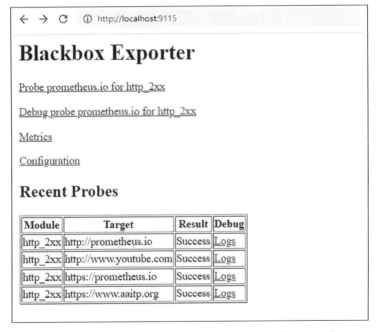

Figure 13.5: Viewing Blackbox Exporter metrics from localhost

6. Access Prometheus locally at `http://localhost:9090/targets?search=` to ensure that Blackbox Exporter is listed in **Targets**, as shown in *Figure 13.6*:

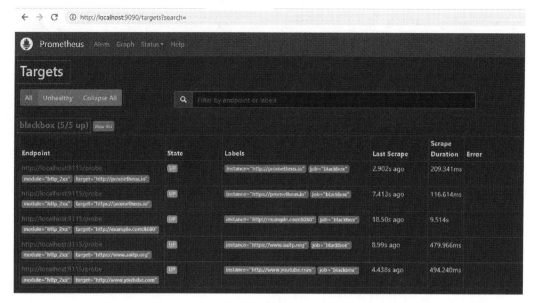

Figure 13.6: Viewing Blackbox Exporter in Prometheus Targets

Now that you are successfully running Prometheus and Blackbox Exporter from your local windows server, in the next section, we will look at how we can visualize them in Grafana.

13.5 Monitoring websites performance in Grafana

In this section, we will look at how monitoring data is transferred between Blackbox Exporter and Prometheus and finally, visualized in Grafana.

13.5.1 Prerequisites

Before proceeding with the visualization process in Grafana, it is important to ensure that Prometheus is capturing the desired statistics correctly. Prometheus acts as the source of data that is fed into Grafana for visualization. To check whether the expected statistics are being captured by Prometheus, simply navigate to the **Graph** tab in Prometheus, as shown in *Figure 13.7*. Then, select any HTTP parameter of your choice. For demonstration purposes, let us consider `probe_http_status_code`. The expected statistics should be retrieved if everything is set up correctly.

It is crucial to take the time to verify that Prometheus is capturing the desired statistics, as this will ensure that the visualization process in Grafana is accurate and effective. Failing to do so may result in incomplete or incorrect visualizations.

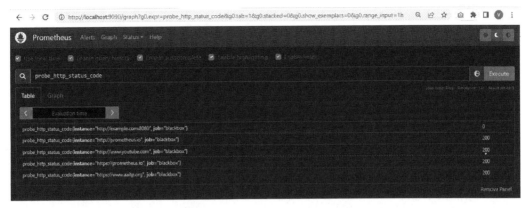

Figure 13.7: *Viewing Blackbox Exporter probe (http status code) in Prometheus*

13.5.2 Visualizing in Grafana

To start visualizing the website metrics, go to the Grafana home page and click on **Dashboards** in the right-hand panel and then **+ New Dashboard**, followed by **Add a new panel**. Before adding any metrics, it is important to select **Prometheus** as the data source, as shown in *Figure 13.8*. Once you have selected the correct data source, navigate to the *Metrics'* section and enter the term **http**. This will give you a list of HTTP-related metrics that can be visualized in Grafana.

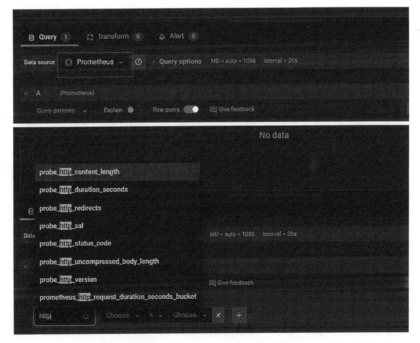

Figure 13.8: *Grafana Panel setup*

For demonstration purposes, we have selected the `probe_http_status_code` metric. To have a clear and concise view of the metrics, it is recommended to choose the visualization type as **Table** and format it as **Table**. Additionally, by selecting the **Type** as **Instant**, we will obtain the latest result of the probe. This setup will provide us with a tabular representation of the data, making it easier to understand and analyze the metrics, as demonstrated in *Figure 13.9*. By using the table visualization, we will have a clear view of the status of the website being probed.

Figure 13.9: *Dashboard setup for Website HTTP Status Code Probe*

Now we can see the expected metrics in the dashboard; to further enhance the visualization aspect, we will add **Value Mapping**, which will add the rule to display metrics in specific color for easy identification. Select **Value Mapping** from the left-hand panel and add rules; in our visualization, we set code 200 to be displayed in **Green** and any other range of response code to be displayed in **Red**, as shown in *Figure 13.10*. HTTP status codes are three-digit codes that serve as a means of communication between a server and a client. These codes help inform the client about the result of their request, including whether it was successful in retrieving the requested resource or an error occurred. The most frequently encountered HTTP status code is `200 OK`, which signifies that the server has successfully processed the request and is returning the requested resource to the client.

Also, note that the **Display** text is set to **PASS** or **FAIL** based on the response code; this will help communicate the status of the website clearly for any user.

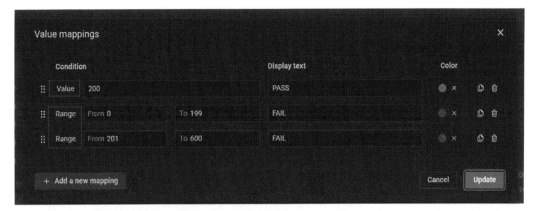

Figure 13.10: Value mappings setup

Now the dashboard will look more presentable, as shown in *Figure 13.11*. We will further enhance the overall appearance by setting up **Cell display mode** as **Color text** from dashboard options for greater impact from the visualization:

Figure 13.11: Color display mode

The dashboard is now ready for monitoring, but sometimes it is good to remove additional display information and keep only the relevant details for quick monitoring. Some of the information displayed may not be relevant for all users or may be in-general repetitive; use the Grafana **Transform** tab and expand the **Filter by name** section to select only the relevant display columns, as shown in *Figure 13.12*:

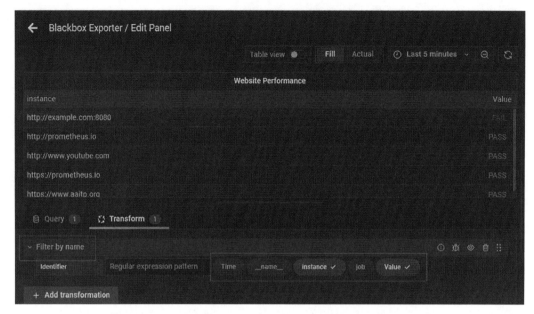

Figure 13.12: Displaying only relevant columns in dashboard

Conclusion

As you have witnessed till now, Blackbox Exporter is indeed a vital tool for monitoring the performance and availability of endpoints and services. When coupled with Prometheus and Grafana, it provides a comprehensive monitoring solution. In this chapter, we discussed how to install and configure the Blackbox Exporter, and how to set up website status visualization in Grafana. This powerful combination opens up endless possibilities for monitoring and visualization. We encourage you to continue exploring the full capabilities of the Blackbox Exporter and Grafana, including collecting and visualizing statistics from multiple websites, and modifying Grafana dashboard.

In the next chapter, we will explore how to perform synthetic monitoring in Grafana.

Multiple choice questions

1. What is the purpose of Grafana Blackbox Exporter?

    a. To monitor network traffic

    b. To monitor database performance

    c. To monitor the availability and performance of endpoints and services

    d. To monitor system resource usage

2. How does the Grafana Blackbox Exporter gather data?

   a. By sending probes to target endpoints and services

   b. By monitoring network traffic

   c. By analyzing system logs

   d. By querying databases

3. What type of data can be collected and analyzed using the Grafana Blackbox Exporter?

   a. Network traffic data

   b. Availability and performance data of endpoints and services

   c. System log data

   d. Database performance data

Answers

1. c

2. a

3. b

Join our book's Discord space

Join the book's Discord Workspace for Latest updates, Offers, Tech happenings around the world, New Release and Sessions with the Authors:

https://discord.bpbonline.com

CHAPTER 14
Synthetic Monitoring

Introduction

In this chapter, we will cover the basics of understanding, installing, and configuring synthetic monitoring in Grafana, and we will look at the recommended practices for alerting. We will start with the installation of the synthetic monitoring plugin, and then we will talk about the various kinds of synthetic monitoring tests. In the final part of this chapter, we will talk about how to configure alerts for synthetic monitoring tests, including the best practices to be followed while establishing alerts for synthetic monitoring checks.

Structure

This chapter will address the following topics:

- Understanding synthetic monitoring
- Initialization of synthetic monitoring
- Synthetic monitoring check configuration
- Recommended practices for synthetic monitoring alerts

Objectives

This chapter explains various checks that can be configured as part of synthetic monitoring.

14.1 Technical requirements

Since Grafana is a web-based application, you will need to run a few commands to get it up and running. The following are the technical requirements, prerequisites for installing and running Grafana v9.0:

- Knowledge of the command shell
- Install Grafana on the machine of your choice using a terminal application or an SSH
- Java 8 or higher
- Python 3.5 or later
- Git CLI tool
- Docker
- Docker-Compose

Optionally, you will be able to log in as an administrator using the command line to set up and run Grafana.

14.2 Introduction of synthetic monitoring

Synthetic monitoring is a black box monitoring service offered by Grafana Cloud. It provides visibility into how your apps and services behave from an outside perspective. You can design tests to continuously test distant targets from probe sites across the globe and evaluate the availability, performance and accuracy of services. The home dashboard of synthetic monitoring is displayed in the following figure:

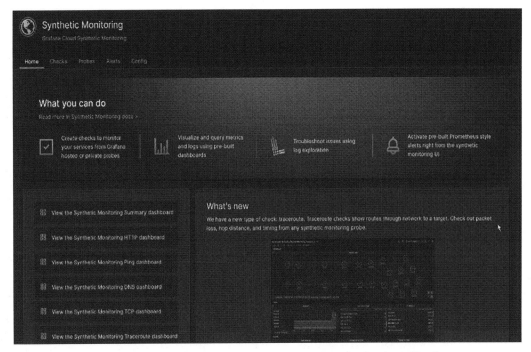

Figure 14.1: Synthetic Monitoring Home Page in Grafana Cloud

The following types of checks are supported by Synthetic monitoring:

- **Ping**: Ping is the quickest and most straightforward method for determining whether an endpoint is accessible. The probe's network must be able to communicate with the target servers, and those servers must be able to set themselves to respond to ICMP echo queries. The amount of time it takes for the endpoint to reply is what is considered when calculating the latency from each probe site.

- **HTTP and HTTPS**: Checks using HTTP and HTTPS are used to evaluate websites. Both uptime and response latency are monitored just like the other types of checks. These checks can also be customized to conduct more complex tests, such as determining whether a website uses a certain version of SSL, whether an SSL certificate has expired, or whether HTTP automatically redirects to HTTPS.

- **DNS**: Domain name servers, often known as DNS, are responsible for translating domain names like grafana.com into their corresponding IP addresses. This check verifies that a domain resolves successfully and calculates the typical amount of time required for this to be done. DNS checks may be configured to validate against a certain DNS server and look for a particular form of answer. This can be done at any time.

- **TCP**: A TCP check establishes a connection to an endpoint using the IP address or hostname that is specified, along with a port. This verifies that the server accepts the connection and evaluates the response latency and the uptime.

- **Traceroute**: During a Traceroute check, the traceroute protocol is executed from probes to targets. You can track the journey a request takes across the internet and obtain further information on the path that your requests take as they go over the internet. A traceroute check can be helpful for seeing the path taken by a network, tracking how that path shifts over time, and figuring out how data gets to its destination.

The following are two distinct kinds of probes that may be utilized to carry out examinations on synthetic materials from various geographical locations:

- **Public probes**: Public probes are implementations of the open-source Synthetic Monitoring Agent that are managed by Grafana Labs and located in various parts of the world. Checks are executed from the locations that have been defined, and the results are written immediately to your Grafana Cloud account.

- **Private probes**: You also have the option to set up your private probes and conduct checks from within your own environment or from any other location of your choice.

14.3 Initialization of synthetic monitoring

Synthetic monitoring is pre-installed in every Grafana Cloud Stack, and an installation of synthetic monitoring may be added to each stack in Grafana Cloud Org:

- Go to **Synthetic Monitoring | Home** in the menu bar.
- Click the **Initialize the Plugin** button.

This will configure synthetic monitoring on your Grafana Cloud Stack. The Grafana Cloud Free Tier provides all the tools necessary to build a fundamental synthetic monitoring system.

14.4 Configuring synthetic monitoring check

First, *HTTP* a target system to determine whether it's reachable. This can be done by sending a network packet to the host and waiting for a response. The availability of the system may be quickly and easily checked using this method, which is also the quickest and easiest.

HTTP check creation

1. Inside your Grafana instance, navigate to **the Synthetic Monitoring |
   Checks** menu item.

2. Choose New **Check** from the drop-down menu.

3. Ensure that HTTP is chosen in the **Check type** drop-down menu.

4. Provide **Job Name**.

5. Provide **Target** details with the website's endpoint URL that must be
   examined.

6. Choose which **Probe Locations** you want to test from or select **All** to test
   from all the available places.

7. Adjust the **Checks Frequency** and **Execution Timeouts** according to the
   requirements.

8. Other settings, such as HTTP, TLS config, authentication, validation, alerting,
   and other advanced options, can be customized according to the user's
   preferences.

9. Hit **Save**.

The following figure has the details of HTTP Check creation details:

Figure 14.2: *Configuring HTTP Check*

The check is dispersed to all the selected probes by means of the synthetic monitoring back end. Each probe will ping the target that has been specified and will send metrics and logging data back to the account that you have set up with Grafana Cloud. Your data is shown on the Grafana dashboards as panels in the form of rows. You have the option of creating your own dashboards from scratch or using the predefined dashboards that come with synthetic monitoring. Just clicking save button will take you to the default dashboard for HTTP Check, which may also be modified as shown in the following figure:

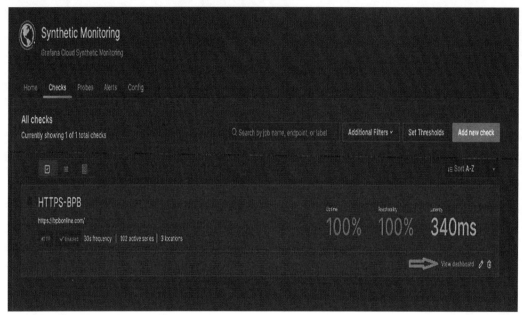

Figure 14.3: Synthetic Monitoring Checks View

This dashboard displays the specifics of the HTTP check you have put up, as shown in the following figure; you will see a figure of a globe at the bottom of the panel:

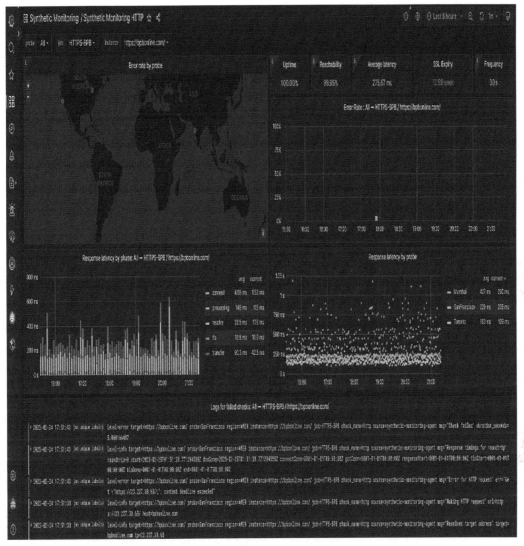

Figure 14.4: *HTTP Check Dashboard*

14.4.1 Recommended practices for synthetic monitoring alerts

The best practices that you should follow to enhance the alerts generated by the Synthetic Monitoring app for Grafana Cloud are mentioned here.

Recording rules

Following are a few details about recording rules in Grafana:

- When you wish to establish numerous alerts on a measure with various thresholds, you will need to first construct a recording rule. By recording rules, it will be possible for you to avoid repeating the entire query phrase in each of the alert rules, which will make it much simpler for you to manage the alerts. Recording rules also allows you to save time.

- When there are several warnings on the same underlying measure, it is advisable to use recording rules to speed up the review of alerts.

- As a result of the recording rules, metrics will be generated, and then those measurements will be included into active series for the purpose of invoicing. Use sum by on labels you use in alerts to prevent recording rules with high cardinality. This will allow you to circumvent the need to record such rules. The remaining labels can be eliminated by removing them from the sum by expression.

Alert expressions

Following are a few details about alert expressions in Grafana:

- You should steer clear of alert phrases that have limited range. You face the danger of obtaining false alerts because of missing or late data if you employ a narrow range in an alert that has a low frequency of checks (for example, once every 120 seconds).

- It is suggested that you use percentiles whenever alerting on latency measurements.

- Use the sum by operator () in alert expressions to restrict the number of series that are generated. Nevertheless, just sum the alert labels you want to display.

- Avoid alerting on particular probes and exclude the Probe label from synthetic monitoring alerts, as removing the Probe label from the total prevents false positives.

- Use the for clause in the alert rules to delay the activation of an alert for a set period before declaring it to be active.

- If possible, you should refrain from delivering an alert that is directly based on a gauge measure (for example, the probe success metric). At this time, the flapping gauge will clear its readings, and no warnings will go off.

Alerting on probes

- It is not suggested to set up an alert at the probe level. Because of potential network difficulties between a probe and a target, notifications at the probe level can be erroneous.

- For reliable alarms, incorporate at least three probes into your checks. It is not suggested to raise alerts for checks that are running on a single probe.

- Filtering on probes in alert expressions is not something that we advocate doing. Because of this, the notifications may be unreliable or inconsistent.

Testing alert expressions

- Try out different alert words using Grafana Explore. It is a quick approach for looking at previous data to determine what conditions your alert would have been activated under.

- You may check the ALERTS Prometheus time series to see which alerts are active (whether they are pending or firing) and which ones were active in the past.

Conclusion

In conclusion, this chapter has provided an overview of synthetic monitoring, focusing on its understanding, initialization, check configuration, and recommended practices for alerts. By explaining the various checks that can be configured, readers have gained insights into the crucial aspects of synthetic monitoring. With a clear understanding of synthetic monitoring's purpose and benefits, organizations can effectively initialize the monitoring process and configure appropriate checks to ensure the performance and availability of their applications. By following the recommended practices for synthetic monitoring alerts, organizations can proactively identify and address potential issues, ultimately optimizing the user experience and achieving their monitoring objectives. In the next chapter, reader will learn how to maximize Grafana plugin.

Multiple choice questions

1. Which of the following checks are supported as part of synthetic monitoring?

   a. HTTP

   b. TCP

   c. DNS

    d. Traceroute

    e. All of the above

2. Log's view is available in HTTP Check Default Dashboard.

    a. True

    b. False

3. Alerts can be configured for synthetic monitoring checks.

    a. True

    b. False

Answers

1. e

2. a

3. a

Join our book's Discord space

Join the book's Discord Workspace for Latest updates, Offers, Tech happenings around the world, New Release and Sessions with the Authors:

https://discord.bpbonline.com

CHAPTER 15

Maximizing the Grafana Plug-in

Introduction

We briefly talked about the Grafana plugin in the previous chapters, but the capabilities go far beyond what we have discussed. We will talk about plugins in greater detail in this chapter. While the core Grafana features are extensive and allow you to build their own dashboards and panels, utilizing plugins can take your visualization and analysis to the next level. Using the existing plugins, you can open an array of visualization dimensions that cannot be achieved using standard Grafana features. Plugins can help you showcase your data in new ways, such as using pictures or colors to make it easier to understand. Additionally, they can help you connect to new data sources you might not have access to, like monitoring data from a different app or website. Think of plugins as similar to adding a new app to your phone, allowing you to add new capabilities and features to your Grafana platform. Plugins can be developed by users, third-party developers or by Grafana labs itself; and with the help of the community, these plugins are made available for easy adoption and usage. It is important to note that building a useful plugin takes a lot of time and effort. However, by utilizing the existing plugins available through the Grafana platform and the community, users can quickly enhance the functionality of their dashboards and panels, without having to create new plugins themselves.

Structure

In this chapter, we will learn the following:

- What is the Grafana plugin?
- Types of Grafana plugins
- Best Grafana plugins to download
- Building your own plugin

Objectives

This chapter aims to familiarize you with the importance of using plugins in the Grafana tool and how it can elevate your overall monitoring and visualizing capabilities. By the end of this chapter, you will have a good understanding of Grafana plugins, the different types of plugins groups, few of the most popular plugins to try, and resources to access if you want to build your own plugins.

15.1 Technical requirements

Most of the required installations are already done so far; no additional installation is required for this chapter. All plugins can be downloaded directly from Grafana home page.

15.2 What is the Grafana plugin?

A plugin is a software component that integrates with Grafana to add new features or enhance the existing ones. It is an essential part of the platform that enables users to extend the core functionality of Grafana. It allows developers and users to customize the functionality of a platform based on their requirements. Grafana plugins are developed using web technologies like **Hypertext Markup Language** (**HTML**), **Cascading Style Sheets** (**CSS**) and JavaScript. The Grafana plugin architecture is based on a modular system that consists of a plugin at the front end and a plugin at the back end. The front end is responsible for rendering the plugin UI elements in the dashboard, while the back end provides the necessary data and logic to interact with the data sources. The availability of a large number of plugins is one of the key strengths of Grafana.

The platform provides a plugin marketplace where users can find and download various plugins developed by the community. The plugin marketplace contains plugins for various data sources like databases, cloud services and IoT devices. The plugin architecture enables the creation of various types of plugins, including data source plugins, app plugins and panel plugins.

There are also plugins for various visualization components, such as graphs, charts and maps. As shown in *Figure 15.1*, you can access Grafana's list of available plugins at **https://grafana.com/grafana/plugins/**. You can decide on the plugin you want to use by thoroughly understanding your current monitoring requirements and existing dashboard view, and brainstorming what components can add more overall impact along with exploring existing plugins which are available in Grafana by default. You will always have the flexibility to uninstall a plugin and try different ones:

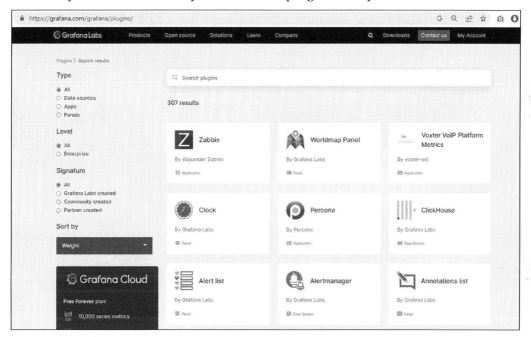

Figure 15.1: Grafana Plugins

15.3 Types of Grafana plugins

Grafana has hundreds of plugins available on the platform; from the feasibility point of view, these are divided into 3 broad types: data source plugins, apps plugins and panels plugins. Now, let us deep dive into each type and understand its capabilities.

15.3.1 Data source plugins

Data source plugins are a key component of the Grafana platform, allowing users to connect to various data sources and integrate them into their dashboards. These plugins act as a bridge between Grafana and the data source, allowing data to be queried and visualized in real time. Data source plugins support various data sources, including time-series databases like InfluxDB and Prometheus, log aggregators like Elasticsearch and Loki, and relational databases like MySQL and PostgreSQL. Each data source plugin implements a specific **application programming interface (API)** for querying and returning data, and Grafana provides a consistent user interface for working with these APIs. Using data source plugins, users can create visualizations and dashboards that monitor and analyze data from multiple sources in a single view. This is particularly useful in complex environments with several systems generating data.

Additionally, data source plugins can be used to set up alerts and notifications based on specific metrics. With the availability of many plugins, users can easily connect and visualize data from almost any data source. As shown in *Figure 15.2*, you can filter for **Data sources** on the **Type** to see all plugins specifically related to the data sources:

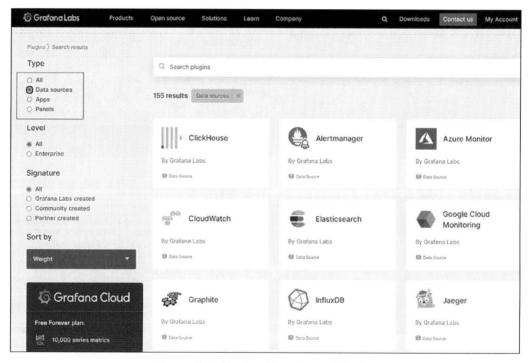

Figure 15.2: Grafana Data Source Plugins

15.3.2 Apps plugins

Apps plugins are a type of Grafana plugin that extend the platform's functionality by providing additional features and integrations with other systems. They are designed to integrate Grafana with other third-party tools and services, making it easier for users to monitor and manage their systems at a centralized location. Some examples of app plugins are the GitLab app plugin, which allows users to view and manage GitLab issues and pipelines directly within Grafana, and the InfluxDB app plugin, which provides additional features for working with InfluxDB data sources. Other app plugins enable users to authenticate with external identity providers, such as Auth0 or Okta, to send notifications and alerts to external systems like Slack or PagerDuty. App plugins are typically installed and managed through Grafana's built-in plugin manager, which provides a streamlined process for finding and installing new plugins. They can be installed individually or as part of larger plugin bundles, which provide a set of related plugins that work together to provide a specific set of features.

By providing additional integrations and features, app plugins help users to more effectively monitor and manage their systems, ultimately leading to improved performance and reliability. As shown in *Figure 15.3*, you can filter for **Apps** on the **Type** to see all plugins specifically related to the apps:

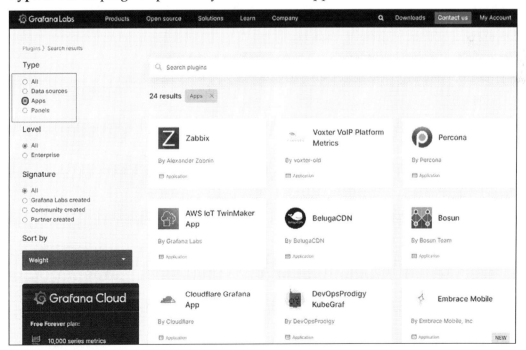

Figure 15.3: *Grafana Apps Plugins*

15.3.3 Panels plugins

Panel plugins are a type of Grafana plugin that provide new visualizations and data representations that can be added to Grafana dashboards. They are designed to enable users to visualize their data in new and innovative ways, providing new insights and helping uncover trends and patterns that might otherwise go unnoticed. Grafana supports a wide variety of panel plugins, each of which provides a different type of visualization. Some examples of popular panel plugins are the Graph panel plugin, which provides a line or bar chart visualization; the **Worldmap panel** plugin, which provides a geographic visualization; and the Gauge panel plugin, which provides a dial or gauge visualization.

Panel plugins are designed to be highly configurable, with a range of settings and options that enable users to customize the visualization to their needs. This includes the ability to customize colors, axis labels and legend information, and to specify how data is displayed and aggregated. As shown in *Figure 15.4*, you can filter for **Panels** on the **Type** to see all plugins specifically related to the panels:

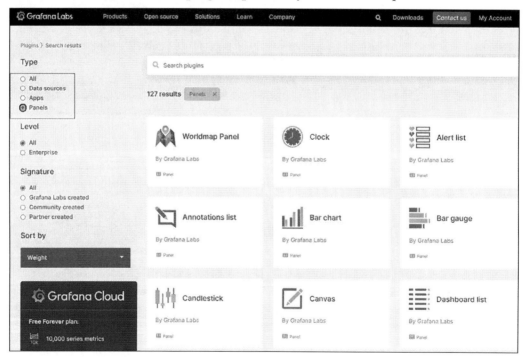

Figure 15.4: Grafana Panels Plugins

15.4 Best Grafana plugins to download

Grafana's vast array of over 300 plugins can make it challenging to identify the best ones for your needs. To help simplify the process, we have compiled a list of five plugins that are popular within the Grafana community. These plugins are tried-and-tested, with a high level of stability and performance, making them a great starting point for your data visualization and monitoring needs. By starting with these popular plugins and carefully evaluating their features and capabilities, you can create effective dashboards that provide valuable insights into your data. As you become more familiar with the Grafana platform, you can gradually explore additional plugins and find the ones that meet your specific needs.

15.4.1 Boom table

The boom table plugin is one of the most popular Grafana panel plugins and provides a flexible and customizable table visualization for data presentation. It has dynamic styling and advanced features like filtering and sorting, making it a great tool for displaying large amounts of data in an easily digestible format, as shown in *Figure 15.5*:

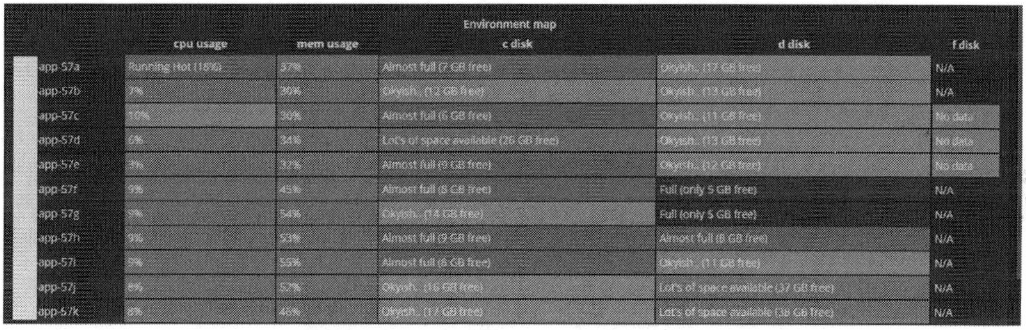

Figure 15.5: Grafana Boom Table Plugin

15.4.2 FlowCharting

The flow-charting plugin is a Grafana panel plugin that allows users to create custom flow charts to visualize and analyze complex data. As shown in *Figure 15.6*, with its drag-and-drop interface and powerful features like conditional formatting and interactive drilldowns, this plugin is a great tool for creating insightful and visually appealing flow charts for your data:

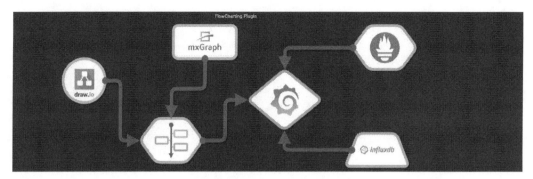

Figure 15.6: *Grafana FlowCharting Plugin*

15.4.3 Status panel

The status panel plugin enables users to create centralized, customizable status indicators to monitor the health and performance of systems or services. As shown in *Figure 15.7*, its ability to integrate with data from various sources makes it a powerful tool for visualizing and analyzing the status of critical components in real time:

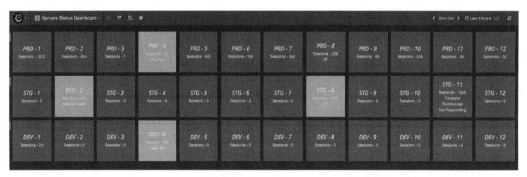

Figure 15.7: *Grafana Status Panel Plugin*

15.4.4 Discrete

The discrete plugin provides a simple and effective way to visualize discrete data in a horizontal graph. It is commonly used to display categorical data like event counts or binary values, and it provides several customization options like color mapping and labels. As shown in *Figure 15.8*, the discrete plugin is a great tool for quickly visualizing data in an easily understandable format:

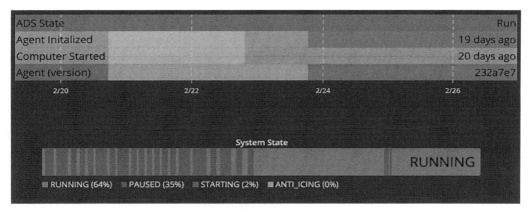

Figure 15.8: Grafana Discrete Plugin

15.4.5 Polystat

As shown in *Figure 15.9*, the polystat plugin enables users to visualize multiple metrics in a single, customizable polygon. With features like color coding and threshold alerts, it is a great tool for monitoring complex data sets and identifying trends or patterns. The polystat plugin is a valuable addition to any data visualization toolkit:

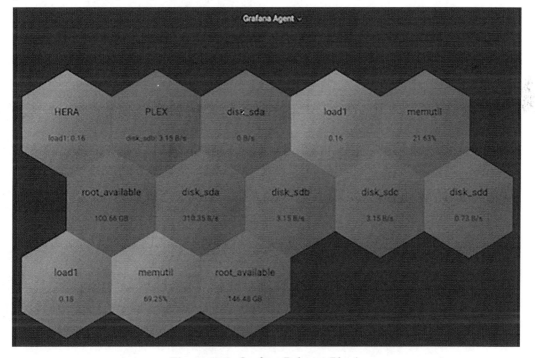

Figure 15.9: Grafana Polystat Plugin

15.5 Building your own plugin

Building your own Grafana plugin allows you to customize the platform and create specific visualizations that meet your unique data monitoring and analytics needs. To get started, you will need a basic understanding of web development technologies like JavaScript, HTML, and CSS. The first step is to decide the type of plugin you want to create: data source, app or panel.

Then, you will need to set up your development environment and install the necessary tools, including the Grafana CLI and Node.js. From there, you can create a new plugin project, add your desired functionality, and test it using the Grafana development server.

To make your plugin available to others, you will need to publish it to the Grafana plugin repository. This involves preparing the plugin for distribution, including packaging it into a ZIP file and creating a metadata file. Once submitted, the plugin will undergo a review process before being made available to the public.

Creating your own Grafana plugin can be a rewarding process, allowing you to tailor the platform to your specific needs and share your creations with others in the Grafana community. With the right tools and a bit of development knowledge, anyone can build their own plugin for this powerful data visualization and monitoring platform. It is advised to work on creating plugins only when you are familiar with the Grafana platform and have in-depth knowledge of all the existing plugins and their capabilities. Your approach should be focused on solving an existing problem or bridging the capability gap with the new plugin development. As shown in *Figure 15.10*, you can learn all about the plugin development from **https://grafana.com/docs/grafana/latest/developers/plugins/**.

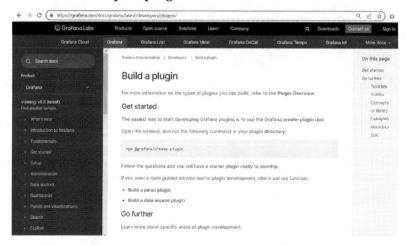

***Figure 15.10:** Grafana Plugin Development*

Conclusion

Grafana plugins are one of the best features in Grafana, enabling innovation and community involvement. Plugins can help you show the data in different ways, which is not possible with pre-existing Grafana features. With the help of the robust Grafana plugin, you can easily design complex dashboards and panels. You can make the most of the Grafana plugin and develop genuinely creative and useful dashboards for end users by leveraging current plugins and being open to new concepts. This chapter covered the significance of Grafana plugins and explained the three major types of plugin categories: Data source plugins, Apps plugins and Panels plugins.

Moving on, we listed the five best Grafana plugins to download and try on your dashboard visualizations: Boom Table, FlowCharting, Status Panel, Discrete and Polystat. Finally, we also looked at the resources that can help you build new plugins once you have mastered Grafana tool. Everyday development of newer plugins and feature enhancement are constantly happening in the Grafana eco-system, so what may seem impossible today may just be a new plugin away. The key to success is to stay updated with the latest plugins, find opportunities to enhance the plugin features and continuously improve the approach to using the tool.

In the next chapter, you will learn about K8S monitoring.

Multiple choice questions

1. What is the purpose of using a Grafana plugin?

    a. To enhance visualization of data on the dashboard

    b. To create customized and interactive dashboards

    c. To restrict access to specific data sources

    d. To increase dashboard security

2. Who can develop Grafana plugins?

    a. Only users with advanced programming skills

    b. Only third-party developers

    c. Users, third-party developers and Grafana labs

    d. Only admin

3. What are some benefits of utilizing Grafana plugins?

   a. Enhanced visualization options

   b. Connecting to new data sources

   c. Custom functionality and data processing

   d. All of the above

Answers

1. a

2. c

3. d

Join our book's Discord space

Join the book's Discord Workspace for Latest updates, Offers, Tech happenings around the world, New Release and Sessions with the Authors:

https://discord.bpbonline.com

CHAPTER 16
Kubernetes Monitoring

Introduction

Monitoring Kubernetes clusters will be explored in detail in this chapter. Kubernetes has revolutionized the way modern operations teams launch and scale applications. Although it has dramatically simplified the use of containers in production, it does not obviate the necessity for a comprehensive monitoring solution that enables you to query the status of your systems. Kubernetes monitoring is required so that you can follow performance metrics, audit changes to deployed environments, and collect logs that assist with debugging application errors. Without a monitoring system, troubleshooting Kubernetes is time-consuming and prone to mistakes, causing problems to worsen since they frequently go undiscovered. We will discuss the fundamentals of monitoring Kubernetes clusters and how to enhance the visibility of your workloads by finding critical opportunities to gather Kubernetes data using Grafana and Prometheus monitoring tools. This will enable earlier error detection in the system's lifespan. Popular monitoring tools for Kubernetes clusters include Prometheus and Grafana.

Structure

This chapter will address the following topics:

- Reasons to monitor Kubernetes
- Setup and access Prometheus and Grafana dashboards
- Monitor Kubernetes resources and workloads
- Alerting for Kubernetes cluster with alert manager

Objectives

This chapter aims to provide a comprehensive guide to the monitoring and alerting of Kubernetes clusters using Grafana, Prometheus, and Alert Manager. It will cover the basic concepts of Kubernetes monitoring and alerting, and the tools and techniques needed to set up a robust monitoring and alerting system.

16.1 Technical requirements

Since Grafana is a web-based application, you'll need to run a few commands to get it up and running. The following are the technical requirements and prerequisites for installing and running Grafana v9.0:

- Knowledge of the command shell
- Homebrew
- Helm
- Docker Desktop
- Minikube

16.2 Reasons to monitor Kubernetes

Monitoring production applications is necessary for error detection, resource optimization, and cost management. Kubernetes is no exception: monitoring is frequently the deciding factor between a successful cluster and one that is underutilized and underperforming:

- **Real-time alerts and early error detection**: Proactively monitoring your Kubernetes clusters enables you to spot faults before they impact users. Log files, traces, and performance measurements give visibility into what is happening in your cluster, alerting you in advance to use spikes and error rate increases. Real-time notifications may notify you as soon as a problem arises, preventing the unpleasant interaction that might arise when users discover a problem first. This reduces service restoration time, protecting your brand's image.

- **Better workload management and optimization**: Thorough monitoring enables better task management and more efficient resource utilization. Monitoring your Kubernetes cluster might indicate excessive resource contention or disparate application pod deployment across nodes. Simple scheduling tweaks, such as setting affinities and anti-affinities, can dramatically improve speed and reliability, but you will miss these chances if you lack knowledge of actual cluster utilization.

- **Easier troubleshooting**: Monitoring is beneficial for diagnosing issues. Collecting logs from your application and Kubernetes components is typically the most effective method for identifying reproduction stages and locating root issues. Without a monitoring system, you would have to guess the likely causes of problems and then test potential solutions through trial and error. This increases the strain on developers, particularly those inexperienced with the technology. Early problem identification reduces downtime and fosters participation from all members of the team.

- **Real-time cost visibility**: The Kubernetes pricing shock is real. Auto-scaling designs allows you to respond to fluctuating demand in real time, but this might result in quickly escalating expenses. Monitoring is required so that you can determine how many nodes, load balancers, and persistent volumes have been deployed to your cloud account. Often, your provider will charge different fees for each of these items.

- **Powerful insights**: Kubernetes monitoring can provide unique insights into infrastructure and application performance that highlight chances to improve your service. Monitoring goes beyond simple performance indicators to disclose how users engage with your application, which might drive future product decisions. Data from components like ingress controllers will disclose the most-requested endpoints and the volume of data moving through your system. This information serves as a starting point for identifying features that require additional development owing to high user engagement or low use resulting from poor discoverability.

16.3 Set up and access Prometheus and Grafana dashboards

Prometheus and Grafana may be deployed into a K8s cluster as a pre-baked Helm package to provide users with very granular and easy-to-read information about the cluster's health. Prometheus operates by scraping time series data from specified endpoints established inside your cluster. This implies that each datapoint it handles is obtained by repeatedly querying a certain endpoint at a user-determined interval. This enables the tracking of several datapoints, such as CPU usage and the amount of time spent processing a particular process, across the lifespan of your cluster, allowing you to detect any changes in the health of your cluster and the software operating within it. In this chapter, we will deploy Prometheus and Grafana on a macOS cluster with Minikube and interact with it, as shown in *Figure 16.1*:

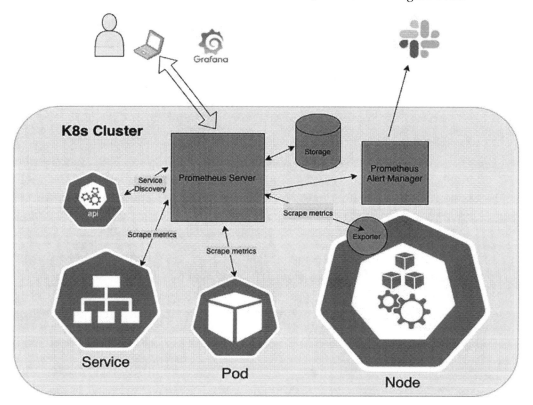

Figure 16.1: Kubernetes Monitoring using Grafana, Prometheus and Alert Manager

The Prometheus server communicates with the K8s API to discover the services or isolated pods whose metrics it must scrape. There is also the idea of node exporter, which functions as a type of sidecar for nodes, third-party software, and bespoke software that gather and transfer metrics from various sources to the Prometheus server by providing a scrapable endpoint. Prometheus may store data locally using a proprietary, extremely efficient on-disk storage solution, or it can be linked with a third-party cloud storage alternative. In addition, Prometheus has an alert manager that delivers user-defined alarms (such as "X" percent of CPU utilization being fulfilled) to platforms like Slack or Pager Duty, allowing support workers to respond to issues immediately. Grafana functions as a UI layer on top of Prometheus, which makes seeing the data being reported far easier and more enjoyable.

16.3.1 Prerequisites for exploring Prometheus on macOS

Use the following combination of commands to create a local, single-node cluster and gain access to a graphical user interface dashboard, as shown in *Figure 16.2*:

```
minikube start
```

```
minikube dashboard
```

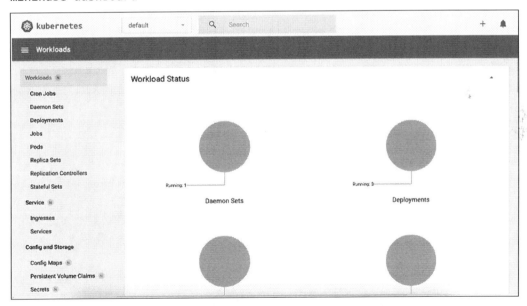

Figure 16.2: *Minikube Dashboard*

With the mentioned components in place, we can proceed with Prometheus and Grafana deployment on our new cluster. To do this, we will use Helm to install a package containing both tools. Nevertheless, we must first install Helm itself, as follows:

```
brew install helm
```

Once Helm has been installed, the following command can be used to add the prometheus-community repository displayed in *Figure 16.3* to our Helm instance:

```
helm repo add prometheus-community https://prometheus-community.github.
io/helm-charts
```

```
helm repo update
```

Figure 16.3: *Kube Prometheus Stack*

Then, we can deploy the application to our local Minikube cluster, as follows:

```
helm upgrade –install kube-stack-prometheus prometheus-community/kube-
prometheus-stack –set Prometheus-node-exporter.hostRootFsMount.enabled-
false
```

```
kubectl get pods -l "release=kube-stack-prometheus"
```

```
kubectl get crds
```

```
kubectl get pods
```

After all the components are up and running, we can obtain our Grafana login credentials using the following command:

```
kubectl get secret my-kube-prometheus-stack-grafana -o jsonpath="{.data.
admin-password}" | base64 –decode; echo
```

16.3.2 Accessing the dashboards

We may proceed to examine the Prometheus and Grafana dashboards now that we have our credentials. Access the Grafana dashboard at **http://127.0.0.1:3000** by port forwarding the Grafana service using the following command, as shown in *Figure 16.4*:

```
kubectl port-forward svc/my-kube-prometheus-stack-grafana 3000:80
```

Figure 16.4: *Grafana Dashboard*

Figure 16.5 illustrates the Grafana dashboards installed as part of the helm repository installation:

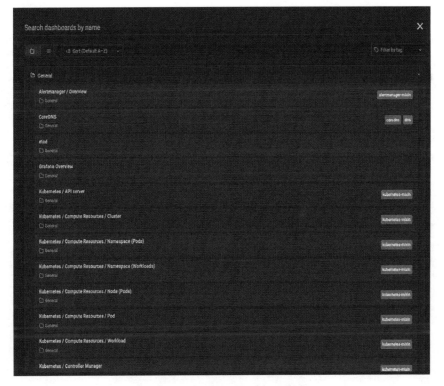

Figure 16.5: *Grafana Dashboards Page*

Execute the following command to access the Prometheus dashboard at `http://127.0.0.1:9090` by port forwarding the Prometheus service, as shown in *Figure 16.6*:

```
kubectl port-forward svc/my-kube-promethues-stack-prometheus 9090:9090
```

Figure 16.6: Prometheus Dashboard

Targets automatically registered in Prometheus as a result of the release are listed in *Figure 16.7*:

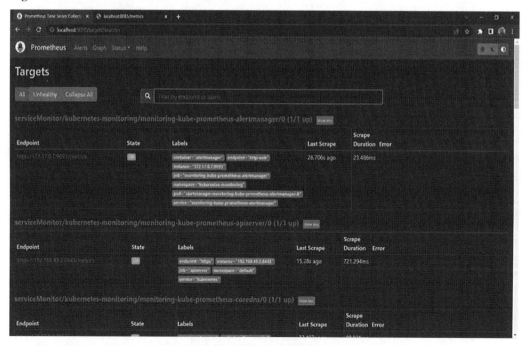

Figure 16.7: Prometheus Target Page

Several Kubernetes internal and monitoring components are established as Prometheus targets on `http://localhost:9000/targets`, as mentioned in the preceding section.

16.3.3 Visualizing Prometheus Data with Grafana

We will be able to enter PromQL searches using the search box in the sidebar of the Prometheus dashboard's Discoveries page, as shown in *Figure 16.8*. Also, you will be able to integrate relevant data into logically ordered dashboards using the **New |** **Dashboard** button on the same sidebar:

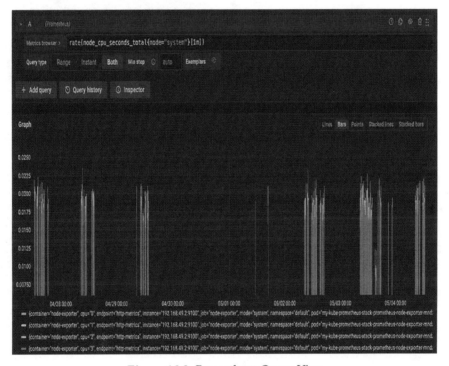

Figure 16.8: Prometheus Query View

16.4 Monitor Kubernetes resources and workloads

This section will provide information on the various Grafana dashboards linked to Kubernetes Monitoring.

16.4.1 Kubernetes cluster level compute resources dashboard

This dashboard in *Figure 16.9* displays the CPU utilization, CPU request commitment, and constraints, along with the memory consumption, memory request commitment, and memory limit commitment. It will assist you in monitoring and managing system resources. The Kubernetes Cluster Level Compute Resources Dashboard is a dashboard that presents data on the compute resources used and available in a Kubernetes cluster:

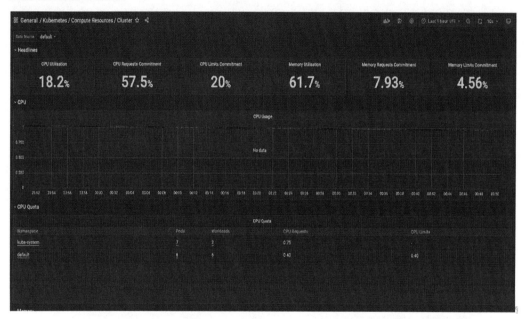

Figure 16.9: Kubernetes Cluster Level Compute Resources Dashboard

16.4.2 Kubernetes node exporter dashboard

Kubernetes Node Exporter Dashboard in Grafana is an exporter dashboard for Kubernetes Nodes. This dashboard provides a host option that displays CPU, Memory, Disk Usage, and Network TX/RX, as show in *Figure 16.10*:

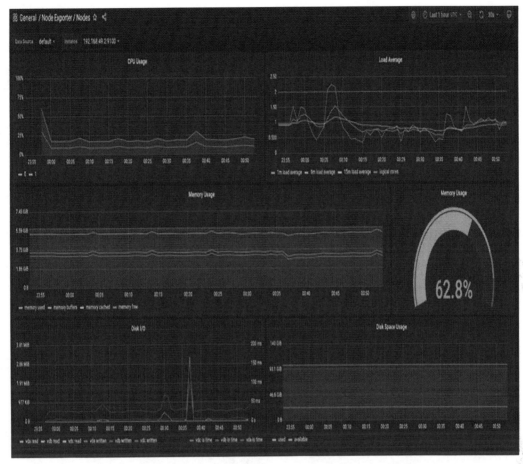

Figure 16.10: *Kubernetes Cluster Level Compute Resources Dashboard*

16.4.3 Kubernetes CoreDNS dashboard

Service Discovery is aided by the Kubernetes CoreDNS dashboard in Grafana, which provides insights into the cluster's health and performance, as shown in *Figure 16.11*:

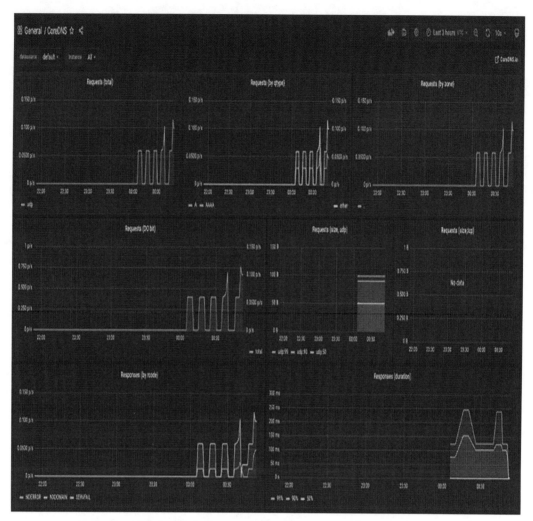

Figure 16.11: Kubernetes CoreDNS Dashboard

16.4.4 Kubernetes namespace level compute resources dashboard

The Kubernetes Namespace Level Compute Resources Dashboard provides users with information on how compute resources may be requested, allocated, and consumed at the namespace level, as shown in *Figure 16.12*:

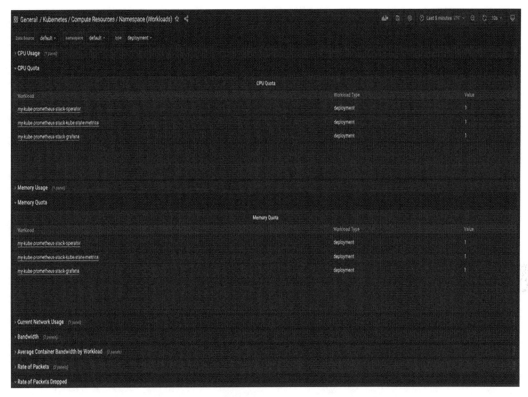

Figure 16.12: *Kubernetes Namespace Level Compute Resources Dashboard*

16.4.5 Kubernetes API server dashboard

Dashboard for Kubernetes API Server is intended for monitoring the Kubernetes API server. It offers information on API server latency, request rates, and response codes. The dashboard also provides warnings and notifications for API server-related issues, as shown in *Figure 16.13*:

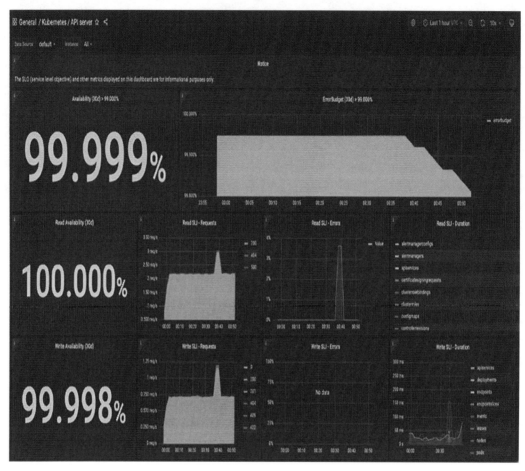

Figure 16.13: Kubernetes API Server Dashboard

16.4.6 Kubernetes node exporter utilization dashboard

Grafana's Kubernetes Node Exporter Usage Dashboard gives a complete view of node metrics, including CPU, memory, disk utilization, and network consumption. This dashboard gives a host option that displays CPU, RAM, Disk Utilization, and Network TX/RX consumption, as shown in *Figure 16.14*:

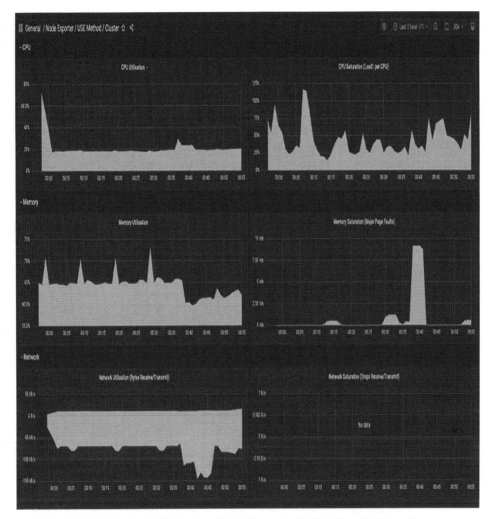

Figure 16.14: *Kubernetes Node Exporter Utilization Dashboard*

16.4.7 Prometheus overview dashboard

Review of Prometheus the dashboard gives a complete view of node metrics, such as CPU, RAM, disk utilization, and network consumption, as can be seen in *Figure 16.15*:

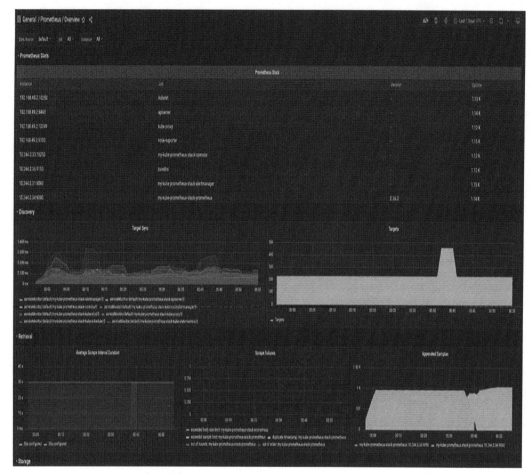

Figure 16.15: Prometheus Overview Dashboard

16.5 Alerting for Kubernetes cluster with alert manager

With **Alert Manager**, a user may configure an alerting system that monitors their Kubernetes cluster and view these alerts in Grafana. The dashboard in *Figure 16.16* provides an overview of **Alert Manager**:

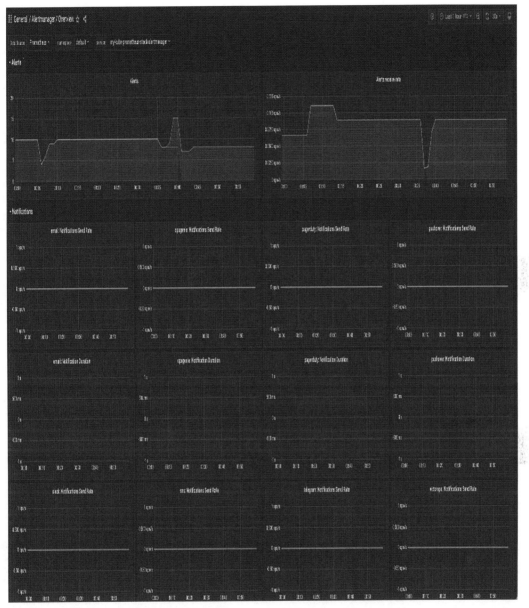

Figure 16.16: *Alert Manager Overview Dashboard*

Alert rules defined in Prometheus for Alert Manager are depicted in *Figure 16.17*:

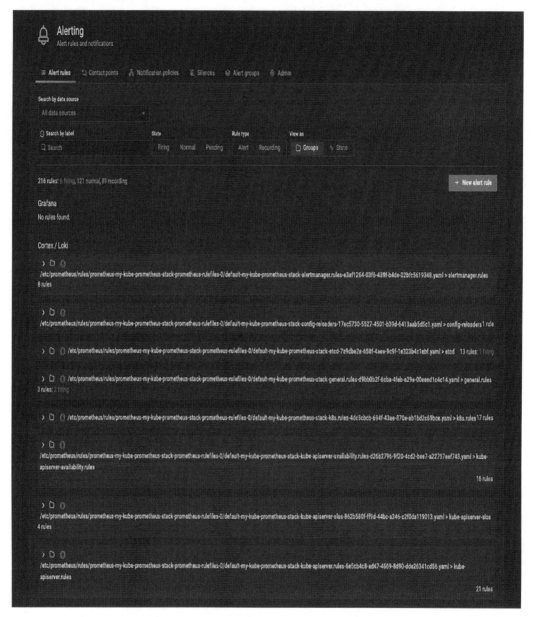

Figure 16.17: *Alert Rules View in Grafana*

Figure 16.18 illustrates the default contact point – Grafana default-email – used to transmit warnings:

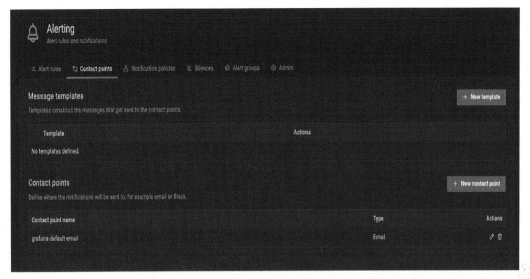

Figure 16.18: Contact Points View in Grafana

Conclusion

In conclusion, this chapter has explored the essential aspects of monitoring and alerting within Kubernetes clusters. We have discussed the reasons why monitoring is crucial, emphasizing the need for a robust system in place. By providing step-by-step instructions, we have guided readers through the setup and access of Prometheus and Grafana dashboards, enabling them to monitor Kubernetes resources and workloads effectively. Additionally, we have shed light on the significance of alerting and introduced Alert Manager as a tool for managing alerts within the cluster. This chapter has successfully achieved its objective of equipping readers with the knowledge and tools necessary to establish a comprehensive monitoring and alerting system for Kubernetes clusters using Grafana, Prometheus, and Alert Manager. In the next chapter, reader will learn about Grafana Cloud.

Multiple choice questions

1. Which of the following checks are supported as part of synthetic monitoring?

    a. Real-time alerts

    b. Better workload management

    c. Easier troubleshooting

    d. All of the above

2. Minikube and Docker Desktop can be used to spin up local K8s cluster in a macOS machine.

   a. True

   b. False

Answers

1. d
2. b

Join our book's Discord space

Join the book's Discord Workspace for Latest updates, Offers, Tech happenings around the world, New Release and Sessions with the Authors:

https://discord.bpbonline.com

CHAPTER 17

Grafana Cloud

Introduction

Grafana Cloud is a cutting-edge open-source platform designed for data visualization and monitoring. Unlike the approach we have seen in the earlier chapters, where Grafana is installed on-premise, Grafana cloud resides and runs directly on the cloud infrastructure. It provides a comprehensive and user-friendly interface that allows users to easily analyze and present data from various sources in a meaningful way. With its advanced features, Grafana cloud empowers users to make informed decisions based on real-time data insights. The platform is designed to be flexible and scalable, making it an ideal solution for organizations of all sizes. Whether it is monitoring real-time metrics, creating interactive dashboards or setting up alerting systems, Grafana cloud has all the solutions covered. With its intuitive interface and powerful capabilities, Grafana cloud is quickly becoming the go-to solution across companies.

Structure

In this chapter, we will cover the following:

- What is Grafana Cloud?
- Grafana Cloud subscription

- Setting up data source
- Monitoring a Windows machine from Grafana Cloud

Objectives

The objective of this chapter is to provide a comprehensive understanding of Grafana cloud, including its features, architecture and use cases. By the end of this chapter, you should have a good understanding of how to subscribe for Grafana cloud and how Grafana cloud can be used to effectively visualize and monitor Windows machine usage statistics.

17.1 Technical requirements

Most of the required installations are already done. In addition to those, you will need a Windows machine with admin privileges for this chapter.

17.2 What is Grafana cloud

Grafana Cloud is a cloud-based solution that runs on the infrastructure provided by Grafana Labs. It eliminates the need for users to manage their own infrastructure, providing a fully managed and highly scalable solution. This is a good option for organizations that don't have the resources to manage their own infrastructure, or for those that want a more streamlined solution. Like Grafana, Grafana cloud also provides a comprehensive set of tools for data visualization and monitoring. But in comparison, Grafana cloud has several additional feature offerings, such as built-in data sources, automatic backups, and 24/7 support. As shown in *Figure 17.1*, Grafana cloud has a simple architecture, where, most of the time, an agent residing in the target machine will collect required data and transfer it to Grafana cloud for processing and visualization. Grafana cloud stands out mainly for the quick deployment model and the comfort it provides user to not maintain any software in local machine.

Some of the major advantages of Grafana Cloud over Grafana are as follows:

- Easier and faster deployment
- Greater scalability
- Enhanced security, managed by experts with regular security updates
- Availability of premium features like alerting, collaboration and data source plugins

- User-friendly way to visualize and monitor data, without the need to manage and maintain the underlying infrastructure

Figure 17.1: *Grafana Cloud Architecture*

17.3 Grafana cloud subscription

Now that we know the Grafana cloud can be one of the best ways to leverage all the capabilities, let us look at how we can get the required cloud subscription and start utilizing it. Grafana has a simple signup process: visit **https://grafana.com/**, as shown in *Figure 17.2*, and **Create a free account**. Email ID is sufficient to create a Grafana cloud account; as of now, Grafana does not even require any credit card or payment information:

Figure 17.2: *Grafana Cloud Signup*

Once you have successfully created your account, upon logging in, you will see the home page, as shown in *Figure 17.3*, with all the current subscription information. Additional options for security, support and billing will be accessible from the left-hand side panel:

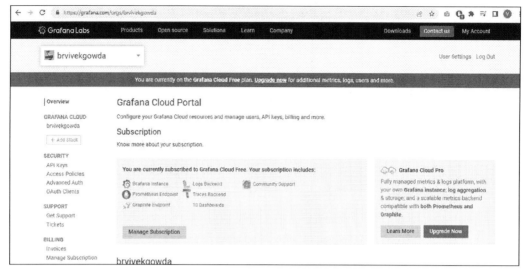

Figure 17.3: *Grafana Cloud Home Page*

With **Cloud Free** subscription, you can do sufficient monitoring and visualization and try most of the available options. Based on the need, you can also opt for **Cloud Pro** or **Custom** subscription, which will unlock even higher capabilities, as shown in *Figure 17.4*:

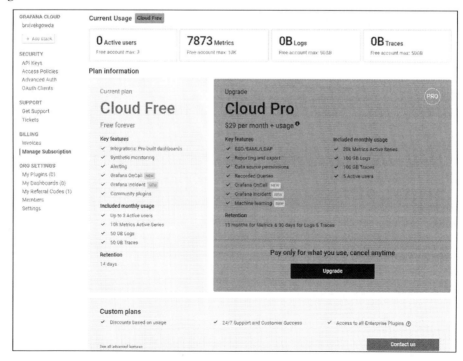

Figure 17.4: *Grafana Cloud Subscription Options*

17.4 Setting up data source

Now that we have Grafana cloud subscription and are familiar with the cloud home page, as a next logical step, we will look at how we can access Grafana and connect to a data source. As shown in *Figure 17.5*, scroll down to the bottom of the home page to see all the existing subscription details. By default, Grafana will have a couple of subscriptions, and Grafana is one of them. Click on **Launch** to see the Grafana cloud instance:

Figure 17.5: Launching Grafana from Grafana Cloud

You will be automatically navigated to the Grafana home page, as shown in *Figure 17.6*. Here, you will see more options on the left side panel as compared to on-premises Grafana. Your current usage can also be tracked from the home page. Click on the + **Connect data** in the top-right to add required data source:

Figure 17.6: Grafana Home Page

A long list of data sources can be accessed from here, as shown in *Figure 17.7*. This emphasizes on one of the biggest advantages of using Grafana cloud. A wide range of data sources can be connected and visualized without actively managing it.

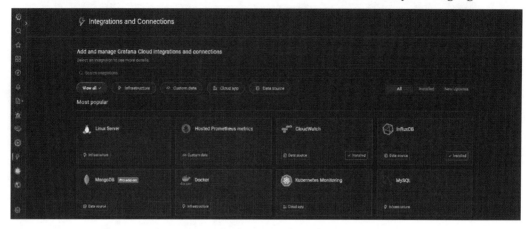

Figure 17.7: Grafana Cloud Data Source List

17.5 Monitoring a Windows machine from Grafana cloud

In this section of the chapter, we will set up a data source and visualize it; you will see how simple the process is in comparison to the on-premises Grafana data source setup. For demonstration purposes, we will capture basic utilization metrics from a Windows machine. We will start by making the necessary installations and visualizing data.

In the data source section, search for **windows**, as shown in *Figure 17.8*. This will display the Windows option; click on it.

Figure 17.8: Adding Windows Data Source

Only Windows will be displayed in the **Choose your OS** section as we have selected **windows installer;** you will get additional options in the dropdown if the data source can run in more than one OS. Click on **Install Integration,** as shown in *Figure 17.9:*

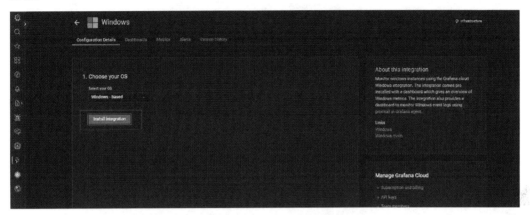

Figure 17.9: *Installing Windows Integration*

As a prerequisite, we need to run a couple of commands as a one-time activity on the target Windows machine so that we can establish connectivity. As shown in *Figure 17.10*, copy and run the two commands one after the other in your Windows machine from the command prompt using admin privileges:

Figure 17.10: *Grafana Agent Installation*

On successful execution, you will see a message as shown in *Figure 17.11*. If you face any issues with the execution, directly download and execute **Grafana Agent Windows Installer**. After completing the mentioned steps, click on **Test Integration,** as shown in *Figure 17.10*, to ensure that you have a successful connection to the target Windows machine:

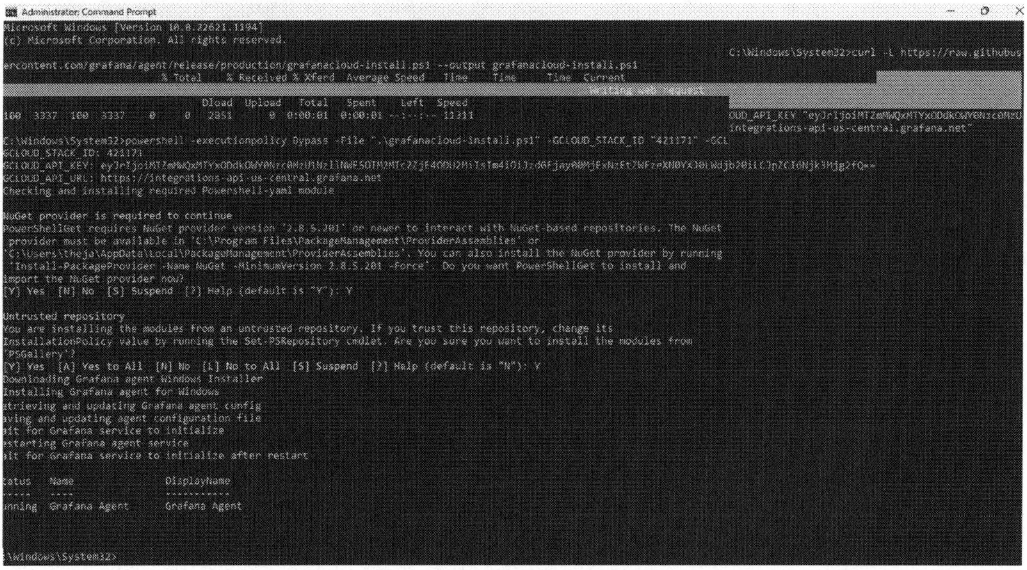

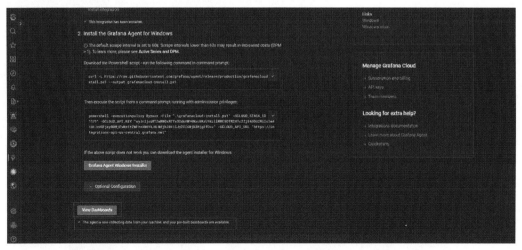

Figure 17.11: Grafana Agent Installation from Command Prompt

You will see a successful connection at the bottom of the page as **The agent is now collecting data from your machine, and your pre-built dashboards are available**. Grafana intelligently pre-builds dashboards for your convenience; click on the **View Dashboards** option, as shown in *Figure 17.12*:

Figure 17.12: Successful Grafana Cloud to Windows Integration

Select the pre-built dashboard **Windows overview**, as shown in the *Figure 17.13*; you have the flexibility to choose any pre-built dashboards or build a new one using the

New option in the top-right of the page as per the requirement:

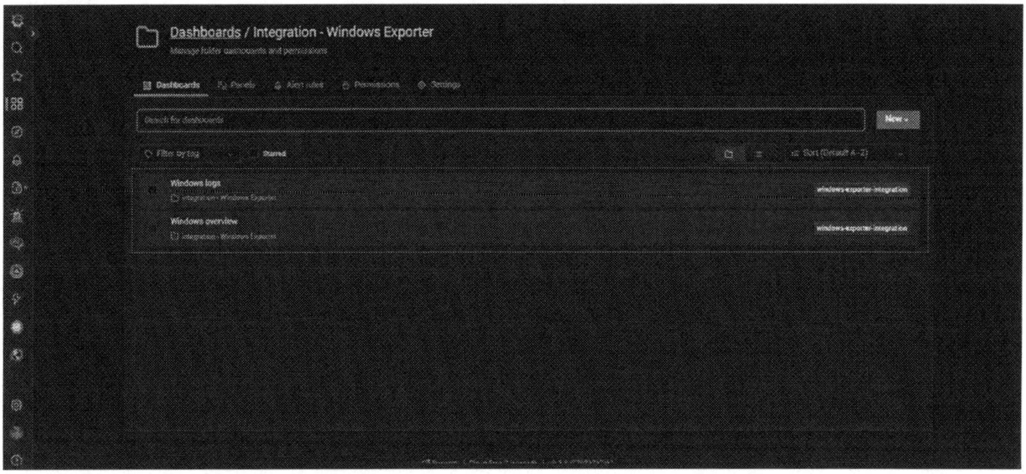

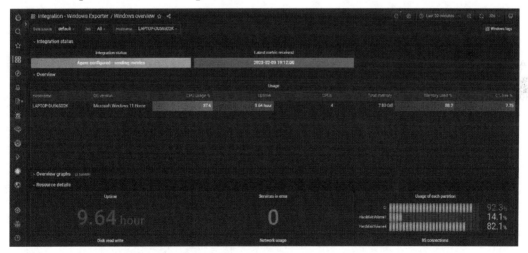

Figure 17.13: Grafana Cloud Pre-Built Dashboards

Now, you are presented with a beautiful dashboard visualization of your Windows server utilization, as shown in *Figure 17.14*, with just a few steps. And within minutes now, we can monitor the target machine seamlessly. You can further customize the dashboard panels or add new panels to make it more suitable for the end users.

Figure 17.14: Grafana Windows Overview Dashboard

Conclusion

As you may have realized, Grafana Cloud is a very powerful option for users and organizations who do not want to spend more time on managing the infrastructure, installations and patches. With many pre-built data source connectivity options, a pre-built dashboard and dedicated support based on the subscription, it is superior compared to the on-premise Grafana. In this chapter, we learnt how we can subscribe to Grafana cloud, how we can connect data sources and finally, what the step-by-step process to install Grafana agent and monitor Windows server metrics is. You are encouraged to explore all the different features and capabilities of the Grafana cloud; an easy starting point will be to add different data sources and collect relevant metrics and visualize using pre-built dashboards.

In the next chapter, we will deep dive into the concept of AIOps monitoring.

Multiple choice questions

1. What is Grafana Cloud?

    a. An open-source platform used for visualizing data

    b. An on-premises platform used for visualizing data

    c. A cloud-based platform used for visualizing data

    d. A platform for data storage

2. What premium features are available in Grafana Cloud?

    a. Alerting and collaboration
    b. Data source plugins

    c. Scalability
    d. All of the above

3. Can Grafana Cloud be used to monitor real-time data from various sources?

    a. Yes
    b. No

Answers

1. c

2. d

3. a

Join our book's Discord space

Join the book's Discord Workspace for Latest updates, Offers, Tech happenings around the world, New Release and Sessions with the Authors:

https://discord.bpbonline.com

CHAPTER 18
AIOps Monitoring

Introduction

This chapter focuses on providing background information on AIOps monitoring, the benefits of implementing it, and the challenges it presents. It also includes information regarding well-known AIOps products that are readily accessible on the market today, and it provides an illustration of how one of the most effective AIOps tools can be linked with Grafana.

Structure

This chapter will address the following topics:

- Benefits and challenges of AIOps monitoring implementation
- Popular AIOps monitoring tools available in market
- Moogsoft AIOps plugin integration with Grafana

Objectives

The objective of this chapter is to provide a comprehensive overview of AIOps monitoring, including its benefits and challenges. The chapter will introduce you to the popular AIOps monitoring tools available in the market and their features, and it will guide you to selecting the right tool for specific monitoring needs. Additionally, it will explore the integration of Moogsoft AIOps plugin with Grafana and demonstrate how it can be used to improve the efficiency of IT operations and automate incident resolution. By the end of this chapter, you will have a good understanding of AIOps monitoring and its applications in improving the efficiency of IT operations.

18.1 Technical requirements

Since Grafana is a web-based application, you'll need to run a few commands to get it up and running. The following are the technical requirements and prerequisites for installing and running Grafana v9.0:

- Knowledge of the command shell
- Install Grafana on the machine of your choice using a terminal application or an SSH
- Java 8 or higher
- Python 3.5 or later
- Git CLI tool
- Docker
- Docker-Compose

Optionally, you will be able to login as an administrator using the command line to set up and run Grafana.

18.2 Pros and cons of AIOps monitoring setup

Artificial Intelligence for IT Operations (AIOps) monitoring systems often integrate **machine learning (ML)** algorithms, **artificial intelligence (AI)** methods, data analytics, and automation to collect and analyze massive volumes of data from diverse sources, such as log files, metrics, and events.

18.2.1 Pros of AIOps monitoring setup

Here are some of the benefits of AIOps monitoring implementation:

- **Faster problem resolution:** AIOps helps identify and resolve issues faster by automating the process of detecting, diagnosing, and resolving IT incidents. This means less downtime and more efficient operations.

- **Increased efficiency**: With AIOps, IT teams can automate routine tasks and free up valuable time to focus on more complex issues. This can lead to increased productivity, reduced costs, and better resource utilization.

- **Improved accuracy:** Machine learning algorithms used in AIOps can analyze large amounts of data and identify patterns that are difficult for humans to detect. This can lead to more accurate predictions and proactive problem resolution.

- **Better visibility**: AIOps can provide a comprehensive view of IT systems, including infrastructure, applications, and services. This can help IT teams understand the root cause of problems and make informed decisions to improve operations.

- **Scalability:** As organizations grow and IT environments become more complex, AIOps can help manage the increased workload and complexity. This can ensure that IT operations remain efficient and effective even as the organization expands.

Overall, AIOps can help IT teams operate more efficiently, reduce downtime, and improve the quality of IT services.

18.2.2 Cons of AIOps monitoring setup

There are also several challenges that organizations may face when implementing AIOps monitoring. Here are some of the common ones:

- **Data integration:** AIOps monitoring requires integrating data from multiple sources, such as logs, metrics, and events. This can be a significant challenge, as these sources often use different formats and structures. Organizations may need to invest in tools and processes to standardize and normalize data from different sources.

- **Data quality:** AIOps monitoring relies on high-quality data to generate accurate insights and predictions. However, data quality issues like incomplete, inaccurate, or inconsistent data can significantly impact the effectiveness of AIOps monitoring. Businesses may need to spend money on data quality technologies and processes to guarantee reliable information.

- **Skill gap**: Implementing AIOps monitoring requires specialized skills in areas like data science, machine learning, and AI. Many organizations may not have the required expertise in-house and may need to hire new talent or invest in training and development programs.

- **Change management:** Implementing AIOps monitoring often requires significant changes to existing IT processes and workflows. Organizations may face resistance to change from employees who are used to working in a particular way. Changes in management strategies like communication, training, and support can help mitigate this challenge.

- **False positives and negatives:** AIOps monitoring can generate many alerts and notifications, and all of them may not be relevant or accurate. Organizations may need to invest in tools and processes to reduce false positives and negatives, such as refining the algorithms used to detect anomalies and events.

- **Cost:** Implementing AIOps monitoring requires significant investment in tools, technologies, and talent. The costs can be high, and organizations may need to carefully evaluate the ROI of implementing AIOps monitoring to ensure that the benefits outweigh the costs.

Overall, organizations must carefully evaluate their needs and capabilities to determine whether implementing AIOps monitoring is the right choice for them, and invest in the necessary tools, processes, and talent to ensure successful implementation.

18.3 Popular AIOps monitoring tools available in market

There are several AIOps monitoring tools available in the market. Here are some of the popular ones:

- **Splunk**: Splunk is a leading platform for AIOps monitoring that helps organizations gain real-time insights into their IT systems by analyzing machine data, logs, and metrics. It uses machine learning algorithms to identify patterns and anomalies that may indicate potential issues.

Figure 18.1: Splunk Logo

- **Dynatrace:** Dynatrace is an AIOps monitoring tool that provides end-to-end visibility into IT systems, from user experience to application performance and infrastructure. It uses AI algorithms to automatically detect anomalies and issues, and provides insights into the root cause of application and infrastructure issues.

Figure 18.2: Dynatrace Logo

- **Moogsoft:** Moogsoft is an AIOps monitoring platform that helps organizations detect and resolve incidents faster by using AI to identify patterns and predict potential problems. It offers real-time collaboration and workflow automation capabilities to help IT teams work together more efficiently.

Figure 18.3: Moogsoft Logo

- **Datadog:** Datadog is an AIOps monitoring and analytics platform that helps organizations monitor and troubleshoot their IT systems. It offers a unified view of logs, metrics, and traces and uses ML algorithms to identify anomalies and correlations.

Figure 18.4: DataDog Logo

- **New Relic**: New Relic is an AIOps monitoring tool that provides full-stack observability across applications, infrastructure, and user experience. It uses AI algorithms to detect and resolve issues faster, and offers real-time collaboration and automation capabilities to help IT teams work together more efficiently.

Figure 18.5: New Relic Logo

- **BMC Helix:** BMC Helix offers an AI-powered IT operations platform that can help IT teams improve their incident management, problem management, and change management processes.

Figure 18.6: BMC Logo

- **AppDynamics:** AppDynamics is a performance monitoring and AIOps platform that leverages machine learning to offer real-time insights into application performance and user experience.

Figure 18.7: AppDynamics Logo

These are just a few examples of the AIOps monitoring tools available in the market. Each tool has its own unique features and capabilities, so it's important to evaluate them based on your specific needs and requirements.

18.4 Moogsoft AIOps Plugin Integration with Grafana

Accessible from inside Moogsoft Enterprise, the software provides robust reporting and dashboard capabilities. Take the following steps to begin using the Moogsoft AIOps App: Only Moogsoft Enterprise versions 8.0.0 and later support this Grafana application.

18.4.1 Plugin installation for Moogsoft AIOps

- Grafana Cloud plugin installation for Moogsoft AIOps

  With the following settings, locate the Moogsoft AIOps application in the plugins list and enable it:

  o **Password:** <graze password>

  o **User:** <graze username>

  o **URL:** <URL for Moogsoft Enterprise>

- Local Grafana installation of the Moogsoft AIOps plugin

  To install and update plugins for local instances, a simple CLI command is utilized. Plugins are not automatically updated; however, you will be notified when updates are available directly inside Grafana. Using the Grafana-cli tool, install Moogsoft AIOps with this command line:

  ```
  grafana-cli plugins install moogsoft-aiops-app
  ```

  The default location for Grafana plugins is /var/lib/grafana/plugins, where the installation will take place.

18.4.2 Enable the Moogsoft AIOps Application:

Following are the steps to enable Moogsoft AIOps application in Grafana:

1. Go to the main menu's **Plugins** section. Click the **Apps** tab under **Plugins** and choose the newly installed program.

2. To enable the app, select the **Settings** tab. Click the **Enable** button after following the application's instructions. The developer's original intention was to make the app and any supplemental UI pages available from the app's main menu.

3. If dashboards are supplied with the program, an attempt will be made to automatically install them. Click the **Dashboards** tab on the app page to examine the dashboards and re-import or remove specific dashboards.

After installing the Moogsoft AIOps application, you can view the default dashboard, as shown in the following figure:

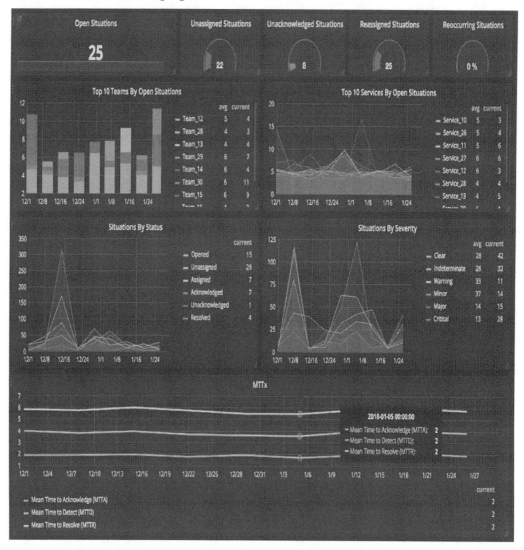

Figure 18.8: Moogsoft AIOps Default Dashboard in Grafana

Conclusion

In conclusion, this chapter has provided a thorough examination of AIOps monitoring, highlighting its benefits and challenges. We have explored the diverse range of popular AIOps monitoring tools available in the market, enabling readers to make informed choices based on their specific monitoring requirements.

Furthermore, we have delved into the integration of the Moogsoft AIOps plugin with Grafana, showcasing its potential to enhance IT operations efficiency and automate incident resolution. Through this chapter, readers have gained a comprehensive understanding of AIOps monitoring and its invaluable applications in optimizing IT operations for improved productivity. Armed with this knowledge, they are well-equipped to leverage AIOps to drive operational excellence. In the next chapter, readers will learn about dashboard setup for performance testing and engineering.

Multiple choice questions

1. AIOps monitoring is supported by which of the following monitoring tools?

    a. Splunk

    b. DataDog

    c. NewRelic

    d. All of the above

2. Which of the following are benefits of AIOps monitoring implementation?

    a. Increased efficiency

    b. Improved accuracy

    c. Scalability

    d. All of the above

3. Which of the following are challenges of AIOps monitoring implementation?

    a. Data integration

    b. Data quality

    c. False positives and negatives

    d. All of the above

Answers

1. d
2. d
3. d

Join our book's Discord space

Join the book's Discord Workspace for Latest updates, Offers, Tech happenings around the world, New Release and Sessions with the Authors:

https://discord.bpbonline.com

CHAPTER 19

Dashboard Setup for Performance Testing and Engineering

Introduction

Grafana has become a widely used tool across various teams within software development, with a significant impact in the area of performance testing and engineering. These teams rely heavily on collecting and analyzing application metrics to gain deeper insights into the behavior of their applications. These insights play a crucial role in making informed decisions about infrastructure, application capacity and the overall business. While other market-leading tools offer features similar to those of Grafana, they often come with a high cost of licensing, which can significantly increase the budget for project delivery. Grafana, on the other hand, is a market disruptor as an open-source tool with free monitoring and visualization capabilities and the option to upgrade for a nominal fee for both individuals and companies. This affordability has led many organizations to switch to Grafana. This chapter will explore how Grafana can help create the best dashboard views for performance testing and engineering teams.

Structure

In this chapter, we will learn about the following:

- What is performance testing and engineering?
- Role of Grafana in performance testing and engineering
- Grafana dashboards for performance analysis

Objectives

This chapter aims to provide a basic introduction to performance testing and engineering concepts, how Grafana is useful for achieving performance-related goals and readily available dashboards that can be leveraged. By the end of this chapter, you should have understand how to utilize Grafana dashboards for performance testing and engineering.

19.1 Technical requirements

The required installations are already done; no additional installation is required for this chapter.

19.2 Performance testing and engineering

Performance testing and engineering is a vital aspect of software development that focuses on evaluating the performance of applications, systems and infrastructure. This process identifies and resolves potential performance issues, ensuring a smooth user experience. Performance testing involves simulating real-world scenarios to assess the performance of an application, including response times, throughput, resource utilization and stability under load. Testing can be done at various stages of the development process, such as unit testing, integration testing and acceptance testing. On the other hand, performance engineering is a comprehensive approach to designing, building and deploying high-performance systems. It encompasses activities like capacity planning, performance tuning and performance monitoring. Performance engineering aims to design systems with performance in mind, rather than trying to improve it after the fact.

Performance testing and engineering teams utilize a range of tools and techniques to collect performance data, including load testing tools, performance monitoring tools and profilers. The data collected is analyzed to identify improvement areas and resolve performance bottlenecks. One of the main challenges in performance testing and engineering is the complexity of modern systems and applications. With the rise of cloud computing and microservices architecture, it can be challenging to identify and isolate performance issues in a complex, distributed system. To overcome this, performance testing and engineering teams often employ advanced performance testing techniques, such as stress testing, scalability testing and chaos engineering, to test the resilience and reliability of systems under real-world conditions.

As shown in *Figure 19.1*, the main focus areas of the performance testing and engineering team are validation, optimization, load handling, resource utilization and user experience:

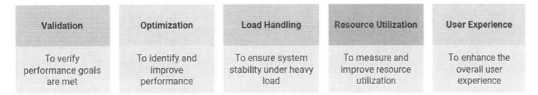

Figure 19.1: *Performance Testing and Engineering Focus Areas*

19.3 Role of Grafana in performance testing and engineering

Performance testing and engineering executes a very high volume of requests to evaluate system stability and is heavily dependent on monitoring and profiling tools. A great monitoring and visualization tool can provide an instant view of application behavior and contribute towards decision making. Most of the important information is usually hidden in plain sight; it is required to have a great monitoring tool that can direct you to the right metrics at the right time. Grafana is a tool that can significantly aid in performance testing and engineering by offering a centralized platform for the visualization, monitoring and analysis of performance metrics.

To list, following are some of the ways in which Grafana can assist:

- **Immediate data representation**: Grafana provides a user-friendly and sophisticated interface for displaying real-time performance data, allowing teams to monitor metrics in real time and quickly identify and solve performance problems before they escalate.

- **Tailored dashboards**: Grafana empowers users to create customized dashboards that can be adapted to meet their organization's specific requirements. This makes it easier for teams to monitor and analyze performance metrics by only viewing data that is relevant to their specific needs.

- **Alerts and notifications**: Grafana has a robust alerting system that can send notifications to relevant team members if performance metrics fall below a set threshold. This helps teams to quickly identify and resolve performance issues, ensuring that their applications maintain high levels of performance and reliability.

- **Integration with other tools**: Grafana has numerous plugins and integrations that make it easy to integrate with other tools and systems that organizations are already using. This streamlines performance testing and engineering processes by bringing together data from multiple sources on one centralized platform.

- **Historical data analysis**: Grafana enables teams to view and examine historical performance data, which is useful for identifying trends and patterns over time. This helps teams better understand their applications' performance and pinpoint areas that need improvement.

- **Performance profiling:** Grafana provides a means of thoroughly profiling performance metrics, enabling teams to delve into specific aspects of performance and determine the root causes of any issues.

- **Collaboration:** With Grafana, multiple team members can access and analyze performance data in real time, creating a collaborative environment that facilitates effective teamwork and informed decision-making.

- **Scalability:** Grafana has been designed to handle a large volume of performance data, making it capable of scaling to meet the demands of even the most complex applications.

- **Intuitive interface:** The user-friendly interface of Grafana is simple to use, even for individuals with limited technical knowledge. This makes it accessible to teams of all skill levels, and it streamlines the performance testing and engineering process.

- **Low cost:** Grafana is an open-source tool available at no cost, making it a cost-effective solution for organizations looking to optimize their performance testing and engineering processes.

19.4 Grafana dashboards for performance analysis

So far, we understood how performance testing and engineering plays a major role in ensuring application stability and how Grafana can complement the entire process. In this section, we will look at some major performance dashboards that are used for performance testing and engineering activities; the focus will be more towards showcasing the dashboard capabilities and visualization patterns. Explaining performance testing tools and executions is beyond the scope of this book; it is assumed that an active performance test will be set up to collect and visualize the metrics. This will allow us to focus on the design and visualization aspects of the performance dashboard, which can greatly help in interpreting and understanding the results of a performance test. Grafana has some pre-built dashboards by the Grafana labs and from the user community, which will provide visualization specific to your need, and of course, you can customize further as you need. You can access the current list of dashboards from **https://grafana.com/grafana/dashboards/**; as shown in *Figure 19.2*, you can use the search bar to find the specific dashboard:

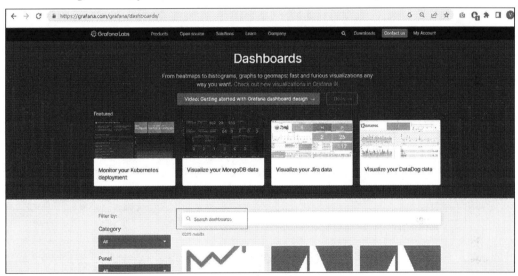

Figure 19.2: Grafana Labs Dashboard

19.4.1 JMeter load test

There are several industry tools available for performance testing. Among them is JMeter, an open-source tool widely used for its capability to load and stress test the web applications. Developed in Java, JMeter allows users to simulate heavy loads on servers, networks and objects to assess their performance under different conditions. Its user-friendly interface, scripting abilities and compatibility with multiple protocols make it a popular choice among developers and testers. Grafana has a pre-built dashboard available for JMeter, as shown in *Figure 19.3*. You can search for 'JMeter Load Test' from the main dashboard page to access this dashboard. Carefully check and implement the prerequisite for dashboard to work seamlessly, and the dashboard can be downloaded from the **Import the dashboard template** section, either by **Copy ID to clipboard** or **Download the JSON**:

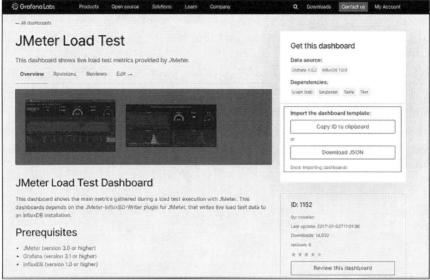

Figure 19.3: JMeter Load Test Dashboard

Once you complete the required setup and plug the required information per your performance test into your dashboard, you can expect to see visualization, as shown in *Figure 19.4*. Remember that these are the sample views provided by the dashboard just for reference; now you can edit the existing panels or add new panels as per user requirements in your own dashboard copy:

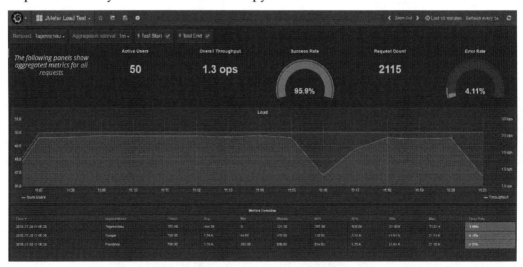

Figure 19.4: JMeter Load Test Dashboard Sample View 1

Additional visualization panels can be seen in the second half of the JMeter load test dashboard, as shown in *Figure 19.5*:

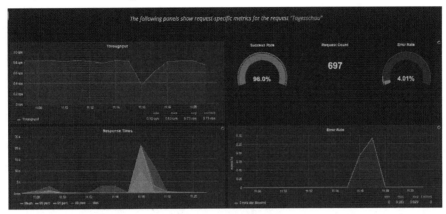

Figure 19.5: *JMeter Load Test Dashboard Sample View 2*

19.4.2 OracleDB monitoring

All applications will have a database component, and Oracle DB is a widely used database. It is a popular and powerful relational database management system used by organizations of all sizes to store and manage their data. It offers a range of features, such as scalability, security and high availability, to ensure efficient data management. With its easy-to-use interface, Oracle Database allows users to easily create, update and manipulate their data. You can search for `OracleDB Monitoring – performance and table space stats` from the main dashboard page to access this dashboard, as shown in *Figure 19.6*:

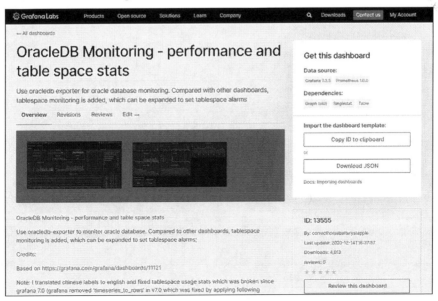

Figure 19.6: *OracleDB Monitoring Dashboard*

Once you complete the required setup and have the database information in your downloaded dashboard, you will see the visualization shown in *Figure 19.7*. These dashboard views are just for reference and for providing a pre-visualization about you can expect before you download. Customize the panels further to suit the requirement as per your project.

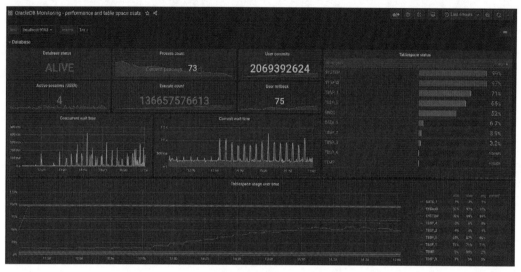

Figure 19.7: *OracleDB Monitoring Dashboard Sample View 1*

Additional visualization panels can be seen in the second half of the OracleDB monitoring dashboard, as shown in *Figure 19.8*:

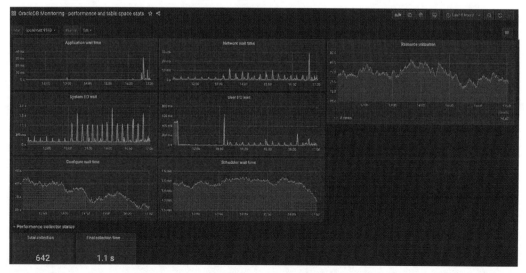

Figure 19.8: OracleDB Monitoring Dashboard Sample View 2

19.4.3 Zabbix for server monitoring

Zabbix is an open-source network monitoring and management software that enables users to monitor and track the performance of their IT infrastructure in real time. It provides a comprehensive set of features like network monitoring, application monitoring, alerting and data visualization; it is a popular tool for IT teams worldwide. Zabbix may have capabilities similar to Grafana, but when it comes to wider aspects like visualization, data analysis, dashboard capabilities and community support, Grafana has an upper hand. Grafana does have a pre-built dashboard available for monitoring server status via Zabbix; search for **Zabbix - Servers Status Table** from the main dashboard page to access this dashboard, as shown in *Figure 19.9*, and download from this page. If you are interested in contributing to the Grafana community and want to be an active part in improving the dashboard, you can do so by providing feedback on your experience.

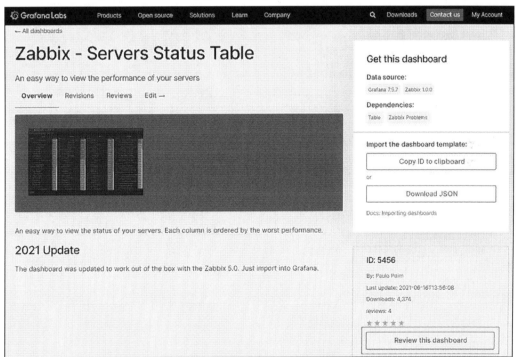

Figure 19.9: Zabbix Monitoring Dashboard

You will have to plug in your relevant host information for the dashboard to start displaying monitoring statistics; on successful setup, you will see a visualization similar to the one shown in *Figure 19.10*. Again, this is just a sample view to give a glimpse of what the dashboard would look like. Based on your requirements, customize the dashboard further to include more relevant visualization, and use this dashboard as a template and build on top of it:

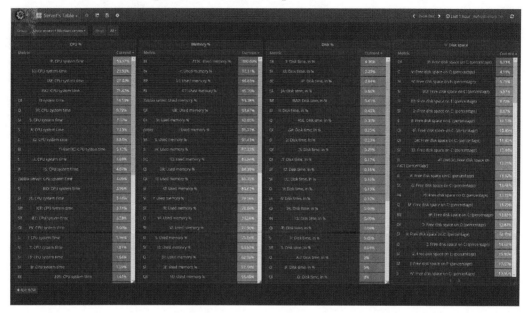

Figure 19.10: Zabbix Monitoring Dashboard Sample View

Conclusion

Performance testing and engineering are crucial steps in the delivery process for any application, especially those with a large customer base and high traffic. The success of a company or product, along with its reputation, revenue and customer satisfaction, depend heavily on the application's overall performance efficiency. Grafana provides essential visualization and real-time monitoring, aiding the development of highly efficient, high-performance applications. Grafana's powerful capabilities empower performance teams to track and analyze performance metrics, identify potential bottlenecks, and optimize application performance. In this chapter, we understood what performance testing and engineering is, and how Grafana plays a role in the success of application performance; finally, we looked into three different dashboard samples: JMeter, OracleDB, and Zabbix. These dashboards are easily downloadable and customizable. You are encouraged to try different dashboard templates, customize them, and also help the community by providing feedback and by publishing your own dashboard version.

In the next chapter, we will look at the best practices you should be following for working in Grafana to get the best outcome.

Multiple choice questions

1. What is Grafana used for in performance testing and engineering?

   a. Data visualization

   b. Code profiling

   c. Monitoring and analysis of performance metrics

2. What advantage(s) does Grafana provide in performance testing and engineering?

   a. Easy-to-use interface

   b. Scalable solution

   c. Limited user profiles

   d. Both A and B

3. What makes Grafana a cost-effective solution for performance testing and engineering?

   a. Paid service

   b. Open-source tool

   c. Integration with other tools

   d. Alerting

Answers

1. c
2. d
3. b

Join our book's Discord space

Join the book's Discord Workspace for Latest updates, Offers, Tech happenings around the world, New Release and Sessions with the Authors:

https://discord.bpbonline.com

## CHAPTER 20

Best Practices of Working with Grafana

Introduction

We have reached the end of this book; now, you have good knowledge on the Grafana tool and its endless capabilities. What next? Well, it is a good time to recap what we have learnt and specifically, inform you of the best practices you can follow when working with Grafana. It may be tempting to start exploring on your own and figuring out how everything works as you go, but knowing the correct methods to use a tool to realize its true potential is strongly advised. To help you in this journey, a consolidated list of best practices suggested by the Grafana labs, the user community and by our own experience is presented in this chapter. In order to make the most of this tool, it's important to follow best practices that ensure a smooth and effective workflow. Following these best practices will ensure that you are aligned with the Grafana framework, reduce unexpected errors, and keep your visualization user friendly and dashboards easy to customize and share. So, take a step back, reflect on what you have learned and start implementing these best practices to make the most of Grafana.

Structure

In this chapter, we will learn the following:

- Significance of using Grafana best practices
- Designing effective dashboards
- Optimizing performance
- Ensuring security
- Collaboration and version control

Objectives

This chapter aims to introduce you to the best practices suggested by the experts, which should be incorporated when you work with Grafana. By this chapter's end, you will understand the most optimal way to design, visualize, optimize, secure and share Grafana dashboards.

20.1 Technical requirements

The required installations are already done; no additional installation is required for this chapter.

20.2 Significance of using Grafana best practices

Utilizing best practices when working with Grafana is crucial in order to avoid common pitfalls that could impede your ability to maximize the potential of the software. Failure to adhere to these practices may result in a loss of time, decreased productivity and inaccurate or incomplete data visualizations. Poor data visualization can lead to ineffective decision-making, inefficient use of resources, or even cause harm to an organization by provoking wrong business decision which is based on data inaccuracy. Some common mistakes that new users make are overloading the system with excessive dashboards or panels, utilizing slow and overly complex queries, or neglecting to back up important data. By avoiding these mistakes and implementing best practices, users can optimize their experience with Grafana and achieve their data visualization goals more efficiently and effectively.

Best practices will definitely help you be a pro and unlock extended tool proficiency. Some of the areas in which you will be benefitted are as follows:

- By following best practices for designing effective dashboards and visualizations, you can ensure that the data you are presenting is accurate, clear, and easily understood by your team.

- By following best practices for optimizing performance, you can ensure that Grafana runs smoothly and efficiently, saving time and improving productivity.

- By following best practices for ensuring security, you can protect sensitive data from unauthorized access or theft, which is essential for many organizations.

- By following best collaboration and version control practices, you can ensure that all team members are on the same page and that changes to Grafana objects are properly tracked and documented.

20.3 Designing effective dashboards

When working with Grafana, designing effective dashboards is a critical step in visualizing data in a meaningful way, as the end user will be relying on the statistics seen in the dashboard view to make decisions. To ensure that the right information is conveyed in a clear and concise manner, it is essential to follow best practices. Here are some of the best practices you should follow:

- **Keep it simple**: When designing a dashboard, it's important to keep things simple and avoid clutter. The more complicated the dashboard view you create, the more difficult it will be to communicate the important details to the dashboard users. Choose a simple and consistent layout, use clear and concise labels, and avoid unnecessary graphics or visual elements that might distract users from the main message. As shown in *Figure 20.1*, sometimes all you need is to communicate a few simple metrics to give a good insight:

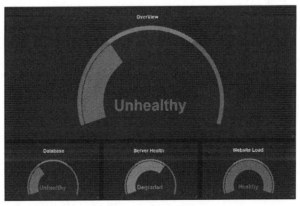

Figure 20.1: *Simple Dashboard Metrics*

- **Use visualization best practices**: When creating charts and visualizations, it's important to follow best practices specific to data visualization. This means choosing appropriate chart types, using colors effectively and labelling data accurately, as shown in *Figure 20.2*. In fact, the Google SRE handbook suggests that when measuring a user-facing system, the four most important metrics to focus on are known as the **Four Golden Signals**. These signals are Latency, Traffic, Errors and Saturation:

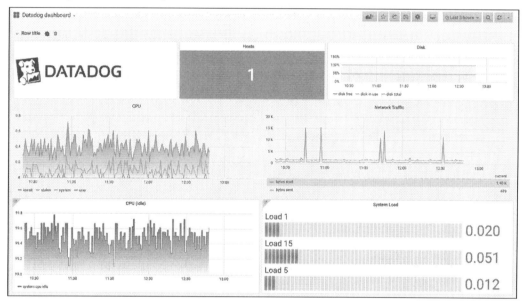

Figure 20.2: Visualization Best Practices

- **Use dashboard templates**: One of the best ways to ensure consistency and efficiency when designing dashboards is to use templates. Templates can save time, give you the required initial direction and ensure that all dashboards follow a consistent design and layout. You can access the latest list of templates from **https://grafana.com/grafana/dashboards/**, as shown in

Figure 20.3:

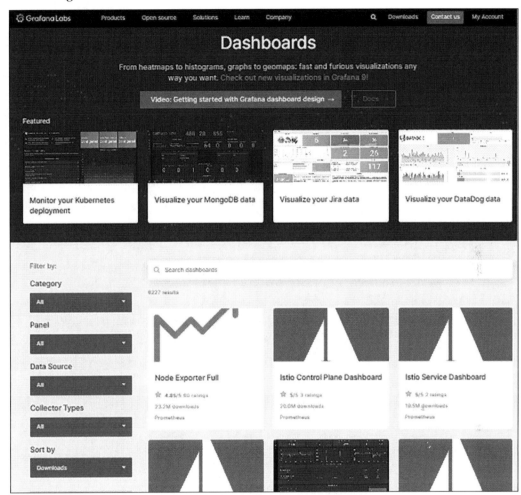

Figure 20.3: *Simple Dashboard Metrics*

- **Focus on user experience**: When designing a dashboard, we must keep the end user in mind. An effective dashboard should be designed to cater to the user's specific needs, preferences and technical abilities. It's important to have active collaboration with the end user during the design process to understand their needs and ensure that the dashboard meets their requirements. This can help create a dashboard that is intuitive and easy to use, leading to better engagement and more efficient decision-making. Be open to feedback and frequently make appropriate changes to the dashboard where required. User feedback can give good insights into how the dashboard is being utilized and help identify improvement areas.

20.4 Optimizing performance

Another important aspect of working with Grafana is optimizing performance to ensure that the tool runs smoothly and efficiently. If the setup is complex, it will add overhead to the tool performance and will result in latency. Here are some best practices for optimizing performance:

- **Choose the right data source**: The choice of data source can significantly impact the performance of Grafana. It is important to choose a data source compatible with Grafana and optimized for performance, and evaluate multiple data sources and their capabilities to find the one best suited for your needs.

  Many data source tools provide comparison details to other major data source tools to showcase the different features and advantages. Let us look at one such example of InfluxDB to gain better insight into the tool; you can take a look at the comparison of InfluxDB v/s other time series databases at **https://www.influxdata.com/products/compare/**. As shown in *Figure 20.4*, this will help you gain a better understanding of the capabilities and make informed decisions:

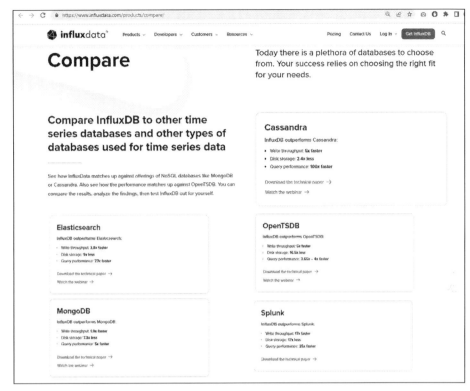

Figure 20.4: InfluxDB v/s Other Time Series DB Comparison

- **Use appropriate querying techniques**: Poorly designed queries can run for a very long time and sometimes cause deadlock issues. To ensure that queries run efficiently, it's important to use appropriate querying techniques. This means limiting the scope of queries, using caching and avoiding unnecessary calculations.

- **Monitor performance**: It's important to regularly monitor the performance of Grafana to identify and address any issues that may arise. This can be done using monitoring tools like prometheus or Grafana's own built-in monitoring tools; self-monitoring is still not a very stable feature, but **Grafana Enterprise Metrics (GEM)** provides a convenient way to monitor the health and stability of the software itself by allowing the direct recording of self-monitoring metrics. These metrics are automatically written to a built-in tenant called **system**, which can be queried using tokens created under the corresponding access policy. This enables easy access to the metrics collected about GEM, providing valuable insights into its performance and overall health. You can visit **https://grafana.com/grafana/plugins/grafana-metrics-enterprise-app/** to explore more on GEM plugin, as shown in *Figure 20.5*:

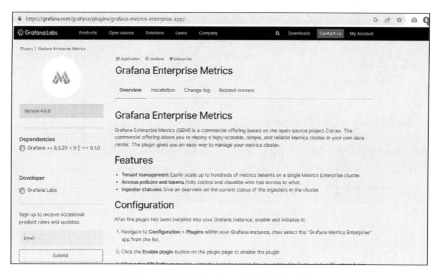

Figure 20.5: Grafana GEM Plug-In

- **Optimize dashboard layout**: The layout of a dashboard can also impact performance. It's important to optimize the dashboard layout to ensure that it loads quickly and runs smoothly like the order of the panels, to show the most important information first, not using too many panels on a single dashboard and avoiding using too many complex visualizations. It will be an ongoing effort, frequently revisiting the dashboard and identifying opportunities to customize it for your current needs.

20.5 Ensuring security

Security is critical when working with Grafana, particularly when dealing with sensitive data. Having a weak security system will only make way for external security breaches. By following the best practices, you will ensure peace of mind knowing that your data is safe and secure in Grafana. Here are some best practices for ensuring security:

- **Use role-based access control**: The **role-based access control (RBAC)** is the best way to ensure that data and feature access is provided to only the relevant users. It's important to set up RBAC properly and ensure that it's regularly audited. Grafana cloud has three basic roles, defined as follows:

  o **Admin**: Has the highest level of access and can perform all tasks

  o **Editor**: Can modify dashboards and data sources

  o **Viewer**: Can only view dashboards

  Each of the roles has specific tasks that are permitted to be performed, as shown in *Figure 20.6*:

	Admin	Editor	Viewer
View API keys	Y	Y	Y
Manage API keys	Y		
View organization billing information	Y	Y	Y
Manage organization billing information	Y		
Manage Grafana Cloud subscription	Y		
View Grafana instance plugins	Y	Y	Y
Manage Grafana instance plugins	Y		
View stacks	Y	Y	Y
Manage stacks	Y	Y	
Manage organization members	Y		
View invoices	Y	Y	Y
Pay invoices	Y		
View Enterprise licenses	Y	Y	Y
View OAuth clients	Y	Y	Y
Manage OAuth clients	Y		
View support tickets	Y	Y	Y
Open support tickets	Y	Y	

Figure 20.6: Grafana cloud basic roles

- **Use secure connections**: When working with sensitive data in Grafana, using secure connections is a critical security measure. This helps prevent external security breaches and protect the integrity of the data. The first step to ensuring secure connections is to use HTTPS for all connections. It is also important to ensure that certificates are properly configured to guarantee the server's authenticity and prevent unauthorized access. This can help mitigate potential security risks and give users peace of mind knowing that their data is being transmitted securely.

- **Limit access to Grafana**: Another key security measure is to limit access to Grafana to only those who require it. This means defining user roles and groups beforehand and ensuring that access is granted only to those needing it. Limiting access can reduce the risk of unauthorized access and security breaches. One way to do this is to use firewalls and other access control measures to restrict access to Grafana. It's important to review and audit access permissions regularly to ensure that access is appropriate and necessary for each user or group.

- **Monitor for security issues**: Regular monitoring for security issues is an essential part of maintaining the security of your Grafana installation. This can be done by setting up alerts for any unusual activity, such as logins from unusual locations or changes to access permissions. Several security monitoring tools can help automate this process and detect any potential security threats. It's important to take immediate action if you see any security concerns, including investigating and addressing the root cause of the issue. By conducting security audits regularly, coupled with penetration testing, is the best way to identify and rectify any vulnerabilities in your Grafana installation before they can be exploited.

20.6 Collaboration and version control

Effective collaboration and maintaining the version changes correctly are important considerations when working with Grafana, particularly when multiple team members are involved. Here are a few best practices for collaboration and version control:

- **Adopt a version control system**: Using a version control system that is well established, such as Git, allows for better collaboration and teamwork when working on dashboards and other Grafana objects. Multiple team members can work on the same dashboard simultaneously, with changes and updates being tracked and merged seamlessly through the version control system. This can save time and prevent conflicts that could arise from manually sharing dashboard files. It also enables easier debugging of issues that may arise when changes are made to the dashboards, by viewing the history of changes made to the dashboard over time.

- **Establish a workflow**: It's important to have a structured workflow to help ensure that the changes are properly reviewed, tested, and approved before implementation. This can prevent errors and ensure that the changes align with the organization's goals and best practices. It's important to establish clear roles and responsibilities for the different steps in the workflow and testing procedures to verify that the changes are working as intended.

- **Use a collaboration tool**: Collaboration tools like Slack or Microsoft Teams can also help in organizing and keeping track of discussions, providing a centralized location for team members to access relevant information. Additionally, it can increase transparency and facilitate effective communication, leading to better decision-making and overall productivity.

- **Document changes**: Documenting changes to Grafana objects is important to maintaining a clear audit trail. It helps keep a record of what changes were made, who made them and why. This information can be valuable in cases where an issue arises, and a review of the changes made is needed. Using commit messages or other documentation tools can help explain the purpose and impact of each change and ensure that everyone involved clearly understands what was done.

Conclusion

We are almost certain that you were unaware of some of the best practices shared in this chapter. We hope this chapter has provided you with a comprehensive understanding of the best practices to follow when working with Grafana. By incorporating these practices into your workflow, you can harness the full potential of this tool and gain confidence in its capabilities. This chapter covered the significance of following Grafana best practices, delving into the best way to design effective dashboards, optimize performance, ensure security, and collaborate effectively while performing version control. It's important to remember these practices, especially during the initial phase of working with Grafana, and to remain open to learning more efficient ways to use the tool. As you continue to learn and enhance your knowledge of Grafana, you may discover new and innovative ways to use it, contributing to building a stronger community. Remember, the key to success is to stay updated with the latest best practices and continuously improve your approach.

You have successfully completed this book! Welcome to the world of Grafana.

Multiple choice questions

1. What is the best practice for securing Grafana?
   a. Use a weak password for user authentication
   b. Share login credentials with team members
   c. Use unencrypted connections to the Grafana server
   d. Set up two-factor authentication
2. What is the best practice for optimizing performance in Grafana?
   a. Use as many dashboards as possible to monitor all your data
   b. Use caching to store frequently used data
   c. Use slow and complex queries to get the most accurate results
   d. Use the same query for multiple panels to avoid duplication
3. What is the best practice for designing effective dashboards in Grafana?

a. Use as many visualizations as possible to show all available data

b. Use bright and clashing colors to make the dashboard visually interesting

c. Use consistent and meaningful labels and legends

d. Use the default dashboard template without customizations

Answers

1. d
2. b
3. c

Join our book's Discord space

Join the book's Discord Workspace for Latest updates, Offers, Tech happenings around the world, New Release and Sessions with the Authors:

https://discord.bpbonline.com

Index

A

advanced queries
  examples 89, 90
  executing 84
  Prometheus, probing 84
aggregations
  applying, to query data 74-78
  threads, detecting with 73
AIOps monitoring 263, 264
  benefits 265
  challenges 265, 266
AIOps monitoring tools
  AppDynamics 268
  BMC Helix 268
  Datadog 267
  Dynatrace 267
  Moogsoft 267
  New Relic 268
  Splunk 266
alert expressions 218
  testing 219
Alerting 27, 28, 147
  Alert Manager 30
  alert rules 28, 29
  contact points 29
  on probes 219
  threshold setup 148

Alert Manager 248
  overview 248
  used, for alerting Kubernetes cluster 248-250
Alerts
  accessing 149, 150
  configuration 149
  notification, setting up 153
  setting up 150-152
  silences 157
  state history and management 155
  state history, viewing 156
  to notification channel 152
  triggers 154, 155
annotations
  creating 167
  deleting 168
  editing 167
  using, in dashboard 166, 167
  viewing/hiding 168
API keys 37
AppDynamics 268
application programming interface (API) 224
app plugins 225
artificial intelligence (AI) methods 264

B

Blackbox Exporter 197, 198
  blackbox.yml file, setting up 200

blackbox.yml file, updating 200, 201
  executing 202-204
  installing 199
BMC Helix 268
boom table plugin 227

C

Cascading Style Sheets (CSS) 222
collaboration and version control
  best practices 294, 295
comma-separated values (CSV) file 27
contact point 29
counter metric 76
Create dropdown menu 19-21
custom plugin
  building 230

D

dashboard, creating 105, 106
  dashboard, saving 115
  data source, selecting 106, 107
  panel link, for external website 111, 112
  panel, saving 115
  panel standard options 109, 110
  query inspector 113, 114
  refresh frequency 117
  threshold 112
  time range 116
  title change 109
  visualization 107, 108
dashboard designing 102
  target audience 102
  TestData DB, installing 103-105
dashboard folder 138
  creating 138, 139
  dashboards, adding 139, 140
  deleting 140, 141
  management best practices 141, 142
dashboards 101
  alerting dashboard 9
  annotations, using 166, 167

application performance 9
  deleting 144
  endpoint dashboard 9
  hierarchy 162
  infrastructure dashboard 9
  linking 161, 162
  links 163-165
  List panel 144
  marking, as favorites 142
  organizing 135
  Panel links 162, 163
  starring 142
  synthetic dashboard 9
  tagging 143
  tags, adding 143
  templating, with variables 160, 161
Dashboards dropdown 23, 24
dashboard settings 18
dashboards, exporting 168, 171
  direct link, sharing 169
  link, sharing 169
  snapshot, publishing 170
dashboards, naming 136
  best practices 137, 138
  renaming 136, 137
database 3
Datadog 267
data series
  generating, in Query tab 47, 48
data source plugins 223, 224
Data Sources 30, 31
  users 32, 33
data storage 4, 5
data visualization 4, 5
  tools 5
Debian Linux
  Grafana installation 10
discrete plugin 228
display aggregation 80
Docker
  Prometheus, installing from 62-65

URL 12
Dynatrace 267

E

effective dashboards
  dashboard templates, using 288
  designing 287
  user experience 289
  visualization best practices, using 288
Explore feature 26
  inspector 27
  logs 27
  Query Management 26
  tracing 27

F

flow-charting plugin 227
folder creation 22
Free Forever Cloud accounts
  restrictions 8

G

gauge 76
Gauge panel 126, 127
  value options 128
Gauge panel plugin 226
Google OAuth2 authentication
  configuring, in Grafana 193, 194
  testing, in Grafana 194
Grafana 1, 6
  dashboard, creating 9
  dashboards 9
  features 6, 7
  for Debian Linux 10
  for Linux 10
  for Mac 11
  for Mac, using command line 11
  for Mac, using Homebrew 11
  for RedHat Linux 10, 11
  for Windows 11
  hardware recommendations 3

  in Docker container 12
  installation 10
  managed Grafana, on cloud 12
  monitoring 9
  plugins page 8
  server connection 12, 13
  supported databases, for
      configuration storage 3
  supported web browsers 3
  supporting operating systems 3
  versions 7
Grafana best practices
  collaboration and version control 294
  effective dashboards, designing 287, 288
  performance optimization 290-292
  security 292-294
  significance 286, 287
Grafana Cloud 253, 254
  advantages 254
  data source, setting up 257, 258
  subscription 255, 256
  Windows machine, monitoring 258-260
Grafana dashboards, for performance
      analysis 276, 277
  JMeter load test 277-279
  OracleDB monitoring 279, 280
Grafana Enterprise Metrics (GEM) 291
Grafana Interface
  home dashboard 16, 17
Grafana organization
  editors and viewers 190
  Grafana admin 190
  organization administrator 190
  teams, establishing 190, 191
  users, managing 190
Grafana plugins 221-223
  apps plugins 225
  best plugins 227
  boom table plugin 227
  custom plugin, building 230
  data source plugins 223, 224
  discrete plugin 228

flow-charting plugin 227
Panel plugins 226
polystat plugin 229
status panel plugin 228
graph editing, in Panel tab
axis 53
data links 55
display styles 53
legend 52
panel options 51
standard options 54
thresholds 56
tooltip 51, 52
value mappings 56
Graph Panel 43
creating 46, 47
simple Data Source, creating 45, 46
user interface 44
Graph panel plugin 226

H

home dashboard, Grafana 16, 17
alerting 27, 28
API keys 37
Browse tab 24
Dashboards dropdown 23
data sources 30, 31
dropdown menu 19-21
Explore feature 26
folder option 22
importing 22
left sidebar 19
library panel 26
manage tab 24
organization preferences 34-36
Orgs tab 39
Playlists tab 24, 25
Plugins 34
Server Admin 38
settings 18
Settings 39

sidebar menu 17, 18
Snapshots tab 25
Stats tab 40
Teams tab 33
user preferences 36
Users tab 38, 39
view modes 18
Hypertext Markup Language (HTML) 222

I

import dashboards 22
information-heavy Grafana dashboard 117
graphs placement 118, 119
multiple panels 117

J

JavaScript 222
JMeter load test 277-279

K

key permissions concepts
admin role 189
dashboard-level permissions 189
data source-level permissions 189
editor role 189
folder-level permissions 189
inheritance 189
organizations 188
panel-level permissions 189
permissions 189
roles 188
teams 189
viewer role 189
Kubernetes cluster
alerting, with Alert Manager 248
Kubernetes monitoring 233
Grafana dashboards, using 236
Kubernetes API server dashboard 245, 246
Kubernetes cluster level compute
resources dashboard 242

Kubernetes CoreDNS dashboard 243

Kubernetes namespace level compute resources dashboard 244, 245

Kubernetes node exporter dashboard 242, 243

Kubernetes node exporter utilization dashboard 246

Prometheus and Grafana dashboards, accessing 238-241

Prometheus data, visualizing with Grafana 241

Prometheus overview dashboard 247

Prometheus, using 236

purpose 234, 235

resources and workloads, monitoring 241

L

left sidebar 19

library panel 26

Linux
  Grafana installation 10

List panel 144

Loki 173, 174
  adding, as data source 181, 182
  architecture 174
  config files, setting up 176
  executing locally 180, 181
  installing 175, 176
  logs, visualizing in Grafana 183, 184
  log visualization 181
  .yaml files, updating 176, 179

M

Mac
  Grafana installation 11

machine learning (ML) algorithms 264

monitoring, with Alert tab 57
  alert rule 57
  conditions 57
  data loss 58
  error handling 58

  notifications 58

Moogsoft 267

Moogsoft AIOps Plugin
  enabling 269, 270
  installing 269
  integration, with Grafana 269

N

New Relic 268

O

Open-Source Software (OSS) 28

OracleDB monitoring 279, 280

organization preferences 34
  tiers 35, 36

Orgs tab 39

P

Panel plugins 226

Panel tab
  graph, editing 51

performance testing and engineering 273-275
  Grafana dashboards, using 276, 277
  Grafana, using 275, 276

Playlists tab 24, 25

plugins 34

polystat plugin 229

private probes 214

Prometheus
  executing 202-204
  Explorer tool, using for investigation 67-69
  exploring 66
  Grafana metrics, configuring 69, 70
  prerequisites, for macOS 237, 238

Prometheus data source
  configuring 65, 66
  limitations 78
  metrics query, typing 71, 72
  process metrics, querying for 72, 73
  querying 70, 71

Prometheus, probing
  $__rate_interval variable, using 87
  annotations 88
  Dashboards' query editor 84, 85
  interval and range variables, using 87
  Query Editor, in Explore 86
  query variable 86, 87
  templating 86
  variables, using in queries 88
Prometheus server
  installing 62
  installing, from Docker 62-65
PromQL 70, 75
Promtail
  config files, setting up 176
  executing locally 180, 181
  installing 175, 176
  .yaml files, updating 176, 179
public probes 214

Q

query 48
Query tab
  data series, generating 47, 48
  features 48-50

R

recording rules 218
RedHat Linux
  Grafana installation 10, 11
role-based access control (RBAC) 292

S

sample queries
  examples 88, 89
security best practices 292, 293
series aggregations
  querying 78, 79
server admin 38
Server Admin
  Settings 39

sidebar menu 17, 18
Snapshots tab 25
Splunk 266
Stat panel 122-124
  stat styles 125, 126
  value options 124
Stats tab 40
status panel plugin 228
synthetic monitoring 211, 212
  best practices 217
  check, configuring 214
  DNS check 213
  home page 213
  HTTP and HTTPS check 213
  HTTP check creation 215-217
  initialization 214
  Ping check 213
  TCP check 214
  Traceroute check 214

T

Table panel 130, 131
  settings 132
teams
  establishing, in Grafana 190, 191
Teams tab 33
TestData DB
  installing 103
time aggregations
  querying 79, 80
time series databases 31
time series data display 91, 92
  aggregating time series option 92, 93
  data, collecting 94
  monitoring 93
  Time Series Database 93, 94
Time series graph panel 44, 45
Transaction-Specific Databases (TSDBs) 93
trends
  detecting, with aggregations 73

U

user preferences 36
users and organizations
  administering 191-193
Users tab 38, 39

V

vertical axes
  baselines, aligning 99
  contrast, increasing between series 98
  correlation, finding 97
  dual axis graph, setting up 96, 97
  dual axis graphs, risks 98
  log scale 95
  resource utilization 97, 98
  right Y-axis 95
  setting 95
view modes 18

W

website monitoring dashboard 4
websites performance monitoring 204
  prerequisites 204
  visualization, in Grafana 205-207
Windows
  Grafana installation 11
Windows machine
  monitoring, from Grafana cloud 258-261
World Map panel 129, 130
  data sources format 130
Worldmap panel plugin 226

Z

Zabbix
  for server monitoring 281, 282

Made in the USA
Las Vegas, NV
05 December 2023

82007710R00184